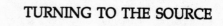

TURNING TO THE SOURCE

TURNING TO THE SOURCE

AN EASTERN VIEW OF WESTERN MIND
USING INSIGHT MEDITATION AND
PSYCHOTHERAPY FOR
PERSONAL GROWTH, HEALTH & WHOLENESS

DHIRAVAMSA

BLUE DOLPHIN PUBLISHING, INC.
1990

Also by Dhiravamsa

•

THE MIDDLE PATH OF LIFE
THE REAL WAY TO AWAKENING
A NEW APPROACH TO BUDDHISM
THE DYNAMIC WAY OF MEDITATION
THE WAY OF NON-ATTACHMENT

First edition, October 1990

Published by
Blue Dolphin Publishing, Inc.
P.O. Box 1908, Nevada City, CA 95959

ISBN 0-931892-20-1

Library of Congress Cataloging-in-Publication Data

Dhiravamsa.
    Turning to the source: an Eastern view of Western mind /
Dhiravamsa. — 1st ed.
        p.   cm.
    ISBN 0-931892-20-1 : $19.95

    1. Buddhism—Psychology.   2. Psychotherapy—Religious
aspects—Buddhism.   3. Spiritual life (Buddhism) I. Title.
BQ4570.P76D49 1990
                                                        90-47087
                                                        CIP

Illustrations: Hana Berkow and Jino

Printed in the United States of America
Blue Dolphin Press, Inc., Grass Valley, California

Dedication

THIS BOOK IS DEDICATED to my **Most Venerable Master, Phra Dhammadhiraraj Mahamuni** (*Nyanasiddhi Mahathera*), Tripitakacarya and the Principal Vipassana Master of Thailand, who has passed on to me the Dharma teachings and the Essence of Vipassana Practice as well as wholeheartedly supported me in the capacity of teaching this unique meditation in the Western Hemisphere.

Acknowledgements

MY HEARTFELT THANKS go to Rikke Goldhersh, Alan Towbin, Sonja Zarek, and Ingrid Fabianson for their invaluable help in editing and transcribing the text. My deepest appreciation, beyond words, goes to Sonja, who has done a wonderful job with many chapters in this work.

Many other friends, whose names are not mentioned here, have been of great assistance to me in typing and correcting my English. I acknowledge them all with my warm heart.

I most deeply appreciate Paul Clemens of Blue Dolphin for his enthusiasm in arranging this book for publication by his own company. Without his loving assistance, and the generous support of Frank and Linda Cassirer, the book might not have been reproduced to serve the benefit of the readers.

In addition, I would also like to thank my many friends and students who have encouraged me to share this book with the world even though it is rather radical and transcultural in its approach to spiritual development.

San Juan Island, Washington
Summer 1990

V.R.Dh.

Table of Contents

Introduction

A S I HAVE BEEN HIT again and again by *insight* into the fundamental, basic condition of human problems, both psychological and emotional, I wanted to write a book in order to share my discoveries with the world as a small but beautiful contribution. For this reason, this book has been written; and it is the first book ever actually written by me. My previous books are products of my talks. They were transcribed and edited with my final editing, of course. My way of writing this present book, *Turning to the Source*, is very meditative, which gives me tremendous joy and peace. I just sit down in front of my typewriter and wait there on attention until words and ideas flow through me. When nothing comes up, I simply have a good sitting and then get on with other things that require my attention.

Thinking about the title of the book, *Turning to the Source*, I would like to share with you, the reader, some meanings that are relevant to me. First, it means "returning to the Origin"; that is, the *Oneness* of Being, the indivisible and non-dualistic wholeness in which all are one and one is all. This is the transpersonal realm of consciousness where all the illusions, including the illusive notion of self as a separate being, cannot reach. In this connection, I would like to make it clear that Oneness or Wholeness is not an idea or a belief, but a level of Consciousness that is a living reality. It is an actual experience. In experiencing this Oneness/Wholeness consciousness, there is no problem to be conceived of, for everything is just what it is—there is nobody there to make a problem out of anything. But at the level of so-called self-consciousness where duality and dichotomy exist, we always find someone there trying to create a problem in life, out of ignorance, attachment, and deeply rooted patterns of conditioning, including fears.

The psychological needs for self-defense and self-protection arise in this level of consciousness of having a separate self. As our logic goes, when "self" is created, "other" or "not-self"—as an opposite—comes into being and existing. It then becomes inevitable that there must be a boundary between them. Hence, conflict arises as a result of dualism. Take another example: divine love and human love. These two forms of love as opposite polarities divide us—humans—into the religious and the secular, the spiritual and the materialistic. Most of us are unable to integrate these concepts. Instead, we cling to the idea or the word so tightly that we become deeply divided and, therefore, perpetuate the conflict between human love and divine love. One is better or purer than the other. Here the gap gets wider, and it's all in our computer mind. Beyond this, love is just love, or love *is*; the concept of "divine" or "human" doesn't make any difference to love. For love does not discriminate; it only unites and unifies everything. There is no higher or lower, better or worse for the truth of love. If we transcend the concept and experience love within our hearts as well as in the energy field of love in the entire universe, there is no idea about divine or human love, but just love as pure energy of oneness, connectedness, and wholeness. For this reason, returning to the source or origin helps us solve all the problems simply because there is no problem to be found in the first place. It is just our own creation. When we quit creating it, it simply disappears.

Secondly, *Turning to the Source* implies and indicates that there is a source within us as well as outside of us where we get knowledge, information, help, and the answer, and from where energy springs. This kind of source may be called "resource" as we recognize the fact that our human nature is resourceful. We always find the way out of our stuckness, or out of anything that challenges us at the time. We just have to turn to the source and listen to it with an open mind and heart, and also have *trust* in the source, allowing it to work through and for us without interference on our part. For example, in terms of bodywork, when a spontaneous movement occurs, and a sudden sound, or a certain sensation is felt, either in the physical body or in the psyche, just be open to it with simple, clear awareness and let it come into full experience. In this way, the inner source can work more effectively so that the block will be removed and transformation will take place. Therefore, we move on, as we are the source of our own journey through our psycho-physical systems and beyond. In our everyday living, we do things and perform our functions or duties by using our own source and are not under the influence or authority of anybody else. This means that all our actions are carried out with authenticity and autonomy. There is no dictating voice behind our actions. Our own source moves us and provides us with energy and everything required for the work at hand. For that matter, we say with confidence that we are guided and taken care of by whatever name we want to call it, for the unnameable has many names, as Alan Watts put it. The Dharma, God, Tao, and the One Being are among those unnameable names that we are familiar with in our cultures. When we live and act out of our own source, we are in harmony with the universe so that things go well and our lives flow beautifully like the dance of the Tao (the Way, the Upstream, the Supreme Consciousness, etc.). The phrase, "our own source," used here does not refer to a personal possession. In actual fact, it is universal. Every individual has access to this source because it is also located within each of us. At the same time it is out there in the universe available for all of us at any moment. Just keep your eyes open for seeing, your ears for hearing, your mind for understanding, and your heart for receiving and emanating. The source is infinite, boundless, and endless.

Thirdly, *Turning to the Source* is an instruction for solving problems or for overcoming conflicts as they occur in the process of our living and interacting with other people. We must go to the root causes, the original conditions, the source of conflicts, problems and challenging situations that are facing us: our relationships, our family, our community or group, our society, and our world in which we live. When the cause is dealt with wisely and intelligently, the solution is found. On the contrary, by attempting to keep the surface in control while suppressing the causes and by merely removing the symptoms without touching the root, nothing is solved, nothing is healed and nothing is cured. Worse still, sooner or later, the covered-up things will burst out and erupt with greater destruction like a dead volcano with its potential disruption. So, all our psychological difficulties, emotional problems, social and political conflicts must be attended to by penetrating the source and removing the root causes to enable us to achieve the real solution, the cure. Bear in mind that whenever something happens that requires our attention, the first thing to do is *turn to the source* as the primary awareness before taking action or non-action.

This book, *Turning to the Source*, points out clearly how separation from our Origin of Wholeness/Oneness causes so many psychological and emotional problems in life. Living our lives under the energy system of a separate self brings about tremendous challenges, including the fundamental illusion as to self and other, distorted perception, and conception of reality. We then lose sight of our *real beingness*, getting confused and muddled up with what is illusive or unreal and what is real. As a result, most of us end up taking the unreal as real, and the real as unreal. For example, the primary illusion of a separate self is taken into our belief system as a solid reality, while the void, the absence of such a separate self, is considered a sheer illusion. So, the truth is distorted and turned upside down—we are left in the darkness of ignorance, while still imagining that we live in the light of clarity. The loss of reality is not even conceived of in our conscious process. Consequently, we follow extreme practices in life. Some of us maintain that only the spiritual matter is real and the psychological and physical world is unreal; some others hold the view that only the physical/psychological world is real and the spiritual realm of existence is unreal. This is the basic game of illusion that ignorance is playing on us. But upon returning to the source of Wholeness/Oneness, the ultimate consciousness of love and wisdom, all our problems disappear just like smoke vanishing into the sky. In the experience of supreme consciousness, no one exists to create a problem, while in the experience of ordinary consciousness there is always somebody sitting there creating problems out of anything that arises. And all the problems stem from the original wound of our separation from Wholeness/Oneness. Believe it or not, we all try to heal this deep, deep wound in many different ways and by various means so that we can return to our complete union with the Void, the Tao, the Dharma, or God, while still living in harmony with the illusion of a separate self. Once the world of illusion is seen and recognized as an illusion, instead of becoming illusive about the illusion, we manage to draw strength out of such an illusive matter and integrate it into our daily living.

As the author, I have endeavored to throw some light on the issue of Consciousness, the most comprehensive and confusing subject in our time. In the chapter on Consciousness, you will see how it can be both the source of energy, knowledge, information, understanding, development, and evolution, as well as the manifestations of that source. As a matter of fact, we are the source and its manifestations for the simple reason that we are nothing but Consciousness with all its contents both conscious and unconscious. Our daily manifestation as well as the evolution process of all humankind is truly the manifestation of Consciousness in which myths and archetypes are included. All the fairy tales and folktales of different cultures are the symbolic contents of human consciousness manifested in such a form and source of information. In that chapter I shared some of Buddhist mythology and tales as parts of consciousness commonly experienced in that tradition, which is in essence universal to all other traditions as well. With such a basic understanding of consciousness, we are able to have a glimpse of universal human unity. We are all one as the matter of consciousness and different only in the symbolic manifestations in terms of concepts and words (or languages). Transcending all the symbols, myths, cultures, and organized religions, there is no difference between us humans. We are always one, and our experience of unity consciousness, or loving oneness, confirms that fact.

Finally, I would like to clarify the last chapter, "Oriental Meditation and Western Psychotherapy." It is included in this present work because East and West actually have just *one quest*, and that is *total freedom*, in which we find our wholeness, health (the dynamic balance of all levels of our realities), our enlightened state of being, and integrated way of living. Love, light, harmony, beauty, and truth become relevant to us as the living reality, resulting from our achievement of total freedom. Although East and West have different approaches (meditation and psychotherapy) to the same goal, they are not in conflict with one another, unless a lack of knowledge, arrogance, or prejudice within some of us creates conflicting attitudes. In the essence of both principle and practice as shown and shared in that chapter, you will, I hope, see the truth of the matter and feel the joy for bringing together the two approaches for dealing holistically with human development and growth in all directions. I see that Vipassana or Insight meditation is the most practical method that can be applied to every form of therapeutic technique and healing art that we can know of both here in the West and surely in the East.

Psychotherapy emphasizes the "grounding" to life, job, relationship, marriage, partnership, etc. Psychotherapy and Oriental meditation both emphasize "letting go" of that which is unhealthy, binding, negative, destructive, and obstructive to growth and development. Certainly, being inwardly grounded to oneself is the primary requirement for Oriental meditation, and without it there will be no development and maturation into the spiritual realm of life. Just looking at these two essences, we see Western psychotherapy and Oriental meditation moving along together and walking arm in arm with no actual conflict whatsoever. As we know, to become a healthy and whole person, we must free both body and mind of all the blocks, attachments, fears, and compulsive patterns of conditioning that imprison us. With the removal of all those hindrances, the doors are wide open to the free flow of creative energy both within each individual and out there in the universe, so that each one of us can become an unimpeded channel for the energy flow as well as for the connection of all energy fields. When we have completed the integration process in which our inward and outward journeys merge and form a large, free way of life, we can become both personal and transpersonal at the same time without feeling limited or restricted. This is the free flow of life between the personal and the transpersonal as a flesh-and-blood human being walking on earth and living in this ever-changing world.

By bringing together Western psychotherapy and Oriental meditation, we actually stop dividing the world into East and West in our Consciousness. If we insist, as some of us do, on keeping meditation separated from therapy, or therapy from meditation, for the purpose of maintaining their purity (which is only an *idea* and not an actuality) or of retaining a tradition, we are not treading the middle path, the way of dynamic balance. Instead we are conforming to an extreme practice of life filled with self-deception. Purity doesn't exist in the form but in the formless; and there is no form that is pure anyway. So, on letting go of the very *idea* of purity, one finds an open space within for the integration, the bringing together, of all approaches to health and wholeness. East and West are one in our *consciousness*. They become two only within the *concept* of directions as our discriminating, conceptualizing minds invent it. Let us transcend concepts while still using them and move forward toward the *Void*, the *fertile One*, without *dwelling on It*.

Pearls Beach, Australia   *Dhiravamsa*
1985

CHAPTER ONE

Oneness and Separation

IN SOLVING THE PROBLEMS OF LIVING we are taught to go to the root. The real cause of the problem can then be dealt with directly. Otherwise, we only eliminate the symptoms and believe all is well. Having left the root untouched, the rotten material sends out its poisons again and we get hit even harder. Most of us seek remedies that are provided by our social institutions or belief systems. We rarely look for something new to cure our illness, whether physical, emotional, mental, or spiritual. This is because our minds are trained to *dwell* on the concepts of security and safety. What we are most familiar with carries the most weight and dominates our decisions on all matters of life. Such a petty, dwelling mind finds it difficult to explore beyond its familiar territory. Unfamiliarity begets fear and fear pours its passion into doubt and uncertainty. As a result, we either get caught in confusion or draw back to stay with our familiarity. This familiar world illusively gives us a false sense of security. This is our basic problem in existing and conducting our lives.

If we allow ourselves to make some inquiries, we will look more deeply into the real issue of life and our true nature. By doing this we will come to some understanding of what is the basic or fundamental cause of human problems. We will come to understand how conflicts exist on many different levels of our experiences: personal, interpersonal, communal, national, and international. Wouldn't you think that when we have wandered so far away from our Origin, our intrinsic nature, we would naturally feel homesick? That is to say, we don't feel at home either with ourselves or with anyone else. This is the beginning of our longing for home-returning, for being re-united with our Origin—the source within,

Oneness or Universal Unity in which there is complete harmony, full being, and totally integrated health.

In actual fact, there is no conflict whatsoever when we feel totally connected with everyone and everything around us. In this state of connectedness, we feel healthy, spacious, expandingly flowing, full of joy, love, and beauty. More than that, we have clarity of consciousness and understanding, and we are surrounded by illuminating light. Personal self is transcended. We become completely boundless and universally united without any trace of psychological self. Our functional self goes on, not as a solid reality, but as a flexible, dynamic process of becoming, founded on universal unity.

Self-Image: The Identity of Separation

What is it then that prevents us from being whole and feeling connected all the time? The answer is *separation*. When concepts and notions develop in our lives through our perceptions of the world, both inner and outer, we collect names, labels, and ideas. These enable us to communicate our experiences, feelings, and thoughts. In this process of conceptualizing and communicating, we become the owners of what we express. This strengthens the sense of "I," "mine," and "me," which leads on to building a solid reality, self-image, or identity. We create something we can hold on to in order to believe that we are somebody or something in our existence. This ownership of, and act of identifying with, our bodies, feelings, perceptions, thoughts, ideas, and consciousness process creates a separateness between us. We identify as an individual and function as a unit of personality. We thereby develop our own worldview of people or objects. Life experiences, as well as the games we play with others, deepen our patterns of conditioning. Our self-image as a separate individual gets stronger and becomes more solid. We feel the need to protect ourselves, to maintain our created individualities; we fear our intrinsically universal and whole being. To feel secure and safe, we build walls around us and put ourselves into psychological boxes. We, then, exist within our own boundaries; we limit our space. As we exercise the right to our own territory, we expend tremendous energy on maintaining and defending it. From this point on, all kinds of emotions and thoughts are invested in the objects and ideas we possess or relate to. This emotional investment or psychological conditioning brings about passions and desires for having more and becoming more. Hence, the wheel of life is set in motion and is tremendously hard to reverse. As a rule, the more we get, the more we want; the more we want, the more separate we become and the less integrated we are. Therefore, we sink deeper and deeper into the mud of separation and loneliness. This is certainly the danger in our human situation.

Let us go into this matter of self-image or identity a bit more deeply. Being humans and living in the world, we do, to some extent, need some identifications for functioning. This kind of identification, if we understand its scope and purposes, as well as know how to use it, does not cause any trouble, for we do not take it seriously. We use it as a tool for getting things done in our daily living. We are able to remain disidentified. There is nothing to lose if the identifications get hit and hurt. We still recognize our being and have a space in which to exist without restriction. In other words, we are not what we become and what we become is not what we are. In the ultimate sense, body, feelings, perceptions, ideas, and thoughts are just a group of energies put together in a certain pattern. They are not us and we are not them. Within this structure we operate our lives using them with caring and understanding as a vehicle for purification and liberation. Certainly, our total freedom lies within our full understanding of these aggregates of existence without any emotional investments in or attachments to them. They do not become burdens to us; we no longer have to carry their weight. As life goes on, they flow along with us and we float along with their currents. This is the state of dynamic harmony we can maintain while using some identifications for functioning effectively in the world. We are neither this nor that; we are a dynamic process. We are existing and living. We, the process, are both predictable and unpredictable!

We can, however, get into trouble in our relating to our self-image when our relationship to it becomes distorted. This means we believe our own self-image. We believe we are what we become. The pretend self-image becomes so real to us that we lose connection with our being. We cannot connect ourselves with our Origin. We are totally caught in the patterns of conditioning. We regard the unreal as real and the real as unreal. This is the state of total separation in which all kinds of distortions and confusions prevail. In terms of perceptions, we perceive the impermanent as permanent, the unsatisfactory as satisfactory, the no-self as self. In analogy, it is said that in the moonlight we see the rope as a snake. This distortion of perception leads us to the distortion of thoughts and opinions. We think and feel according to how we perceive. This creates a cycle where distorted thinking and feeling condition our perceptions and ideas. We are driven into a state of having no choice but to grope for the right action in a wilderness of distortions.

We can see the reasons we are asleep in our ordinary state of consciousness. Realizing this, we quest for awakening from our psychological sleep and from our ignorance. Before realization dawns on us, we are at the mercy of the destructive forces we create through believing in our self-image and the images we create and project onto others. Looking into our life situations, we see how much energy we consume and expend on trying to protect and defend false self-images. Very rarely do we examine and learn to understand, in depth, the truth or falseness of what is perceived or experienced by us. For example, we all fall into the psychological cycle of feeling criticized or emotionally attacked by someone. When someone gets angry at us and yells every nasty word at us that he/she can find in his/her vocabulary, what do we do? Are those words heavily loaded with emotional impact for us? Do we identify with them? Or, are we able to give our attention to what is going on without reacting emotionally? With self-image or a sense of being somebody or something, we automatically react with our emotional conditioning and with our rationalizations. We express ourselves by fighting out the event emotionally, verbally, or even physically so that our ego-self can feel good and have a sense of survival. Or, if we feel a sense of desperation and helplessness, we may play a "poor me" game, wanting sympathy and mercy. All these reactions come into being because our self-image feels crushed or threatened. The ego feels that it must fight or die. It fears not having control over life situations and of being taken advantage of. Rather than experiencing this fear, we jump into emotional depression. Very few of us know the path between these two extreme habits. Being caught in self-image, there is no space for the middle path. We cannot look straight ahead; we either turn to the left or to the right. As soon as we stop defending our self-image, we feel a wide opening and perceive the expansion of space. Then, our eyes, both inner and outer, naturally focus themselves on what lies in front of us and all around us. Left and right restrictions have no place in such a spacious and non-limiting state of being.

To illustrate, here is a story about the King who had three sons. Two of the sons were said to be very intelligent. The youngest son was considered to be stupid and was called Dumpling. As the King grew older, he became more and more worried about his sons. He constantly churned inside, worrying about which son would succeed him as King. One day he called his sons to him and told them that they were to enact a ritual that would earn one of them the right to inherit the throne. They were each to attempt to bring home the most beautiful carpet in the land. The King and his three sons went out into the courtyard where the King threw three feathers into the air. Each son was to follow the direction of one of the feathers. One feather flew to the East, another to the West, the third one barely flew straight ahead before it fell straight down. As was the custom, the oldest son had first choice. He chose to go to the East. The second son chose the West. Dumpling was left with no choice but to follow the third feather. The two older brothers laughed and said that stupid Dumpling wouldn't find anything! Seeing them laugh at him and take off on their way, Dumpling felt sad and wished for the opportunity to travel far and wide in search of the beautiful carpet.

Having put his disappointment behind him, he walked straight over to where the feather lay. Then and there he found a trap door. When he opened it there was a stairway leading down into the ground. Traveling down this stairway, he arrived at the cottage of Mother Toad and her twelve little daughters. They were singing a beautiful song with tremendous joy in their hearts. Dumpling rapped gently on the door. Mother Toad answered it and invited him in. After welcoming him with a warm reception, she asked what he wanted of them. He replied, "I need a beautiful carpet to bring to my father so that I may become King." Mother Toad immediately sent one of her daughters to fetch a box and handed it to the Prince. Dumpling opened the box and beheld the most beautiful carpet he had ever seen. He thanked them heartily and returned home to present his father with this gift. It was the most beautiful carpet in the land. The other two brothers came home disappointed and dismayed. The oldest brother had found only rags. The second brother had found nothing at all. According to the rules of the ritual, Dumpling was the winner and was to become King.

The two older brothers could not believe that the throne would go to the simple Dumpling. They wanted one of them, who was more clever, to rule. They requested their father to create another competition and the King agreed. This time the winner would be the one who found the most beautiful ring. Again the feathers were thrown and again they fell in the very same pattern. Mother Toad gave Dumpling a very beautiful ring to take back to his father. The older brothers returned with nothing but rusty old nails. They were exhausted from their wasted journeys. The King declared Dumpling the winner again. He was to succeed as King.

With feelings of pain, disappointment, and envy, the two older brothers asked the King to give them a third competition. This time the sons were to bring the most beautiful wife they could find. The three feathers were thrown and again they fell into the same pattern. Each brother followed his same path. By now Dumpling knew his way well and asked Mother Toad for her most beautiful daughter. She gave him a carrot carriage in which was seated her youngest and most beautiful daughter. She told the Prince to carry the carriage through the water of the pond. As soon as he did this the little toad turned into a most beautiful, alluring young woman. Then and there Dumpling married her and brought her home to meet his father. The older brother brought home a wife with no teeth and the second brother brought home a wife who had no hair. Once again, Dumpling won the competition with no trouble.

Driven by desperation, the two older brothers asked for a final competition to which the King readily agreed. This time the two older sons, thinking themselves clever, proposed the competition. A hoop was to be hung in the middle of a room. Whichever of their wives could jump through the hoop would win the kingdom for her husband. They believed that their wives were stronger and healthier than Dumpling's wife. She was slim and graceful. The oldest son's wife went first; she fell and broke both of her legs. The second son's wife jumped and also broke both of her legs. At last, it was Dumpling's wife's turn. She jumped through the hoop as if she were a puff of cotton flying through the air. The two older brothers were exhausted and bewildered. Dumpling became the King and ruled the Kingdom in peace with profound and great wisdom.

Learning to Trust the Inner Voice of the Middle Path

Now, by this story we can see that the journey into the treasure of life is neither right nor left but lies straight ahead, in *front* of us and *within* our human reach. When rising above our imitation and conformity, we place trust in our intuition and follow our natural flow, our inner guide or *still voice*. The right or wrong way is no longer an issue in our healing and questing journey. Sense of direction comes to us when we are inwardly calm and clear, without any emotional turbulence. This clarity and sense of balance open the doors to right action and creativity. As in the story, after having overcome his emotional concern, Dumpling had no hesitation. He walked directly ahead and gave his attention to his surroundings. With attentive awareness and clearness of action, he found the trap door, *a hidden place*, which led him to discover what he was looking for. The symbolism of looking to the right or to the left (East and West) implies that we are under the influence of fears, the fear of doing something wrong, the fear of not getting approval, and the fear of rejection. We wrap ourselves up in the principles, ideas, ideologies, dogmas, rules, and assumptions symbolized by the dichotomy of right and left, East and West. The two older brothers in the story show us that following the "right" path with the expectation of accomplishing the goal is just as fruitless as following any less "right" path. They travel far away and move farther and farther from themselves—deeper separation. The youngest brother moves closer and closer to himself—Loving Oneness—by beginning *where he is* and expanding his consciousness to *see* what is all around him.

When we focus attention on the whole front of ourselves with our eyes closed and let energy flow into just looking without concentrating on anything at all, a sense of closeness and intimacy with the *total self* (a unified whole) comes over us. We feel realistically solid, centered, unified, and grounded. As a result, more space opens up for us and we expand into infinity. The grip of territoriality loosens and eventually fades away, leaving us with a tremendous sense of spaciousness and unification of being. The notions of opposites, right/wrong, true/false, good/bad, do not matter for us anymore. Even the concept of middle path disappears altogether. It is like a Zen saying: being with the Self without knowing (conceptualizing) the Self is truly our liberation!

Having arrived at this point, I would like to clarify further my position regarding the right and the left. In the process of working on ourselves, it is inevitable that we bounce back and forth between the two extremes of right and left. Without considerable experiences of those two ways, the middle path, the dynamic balance of the practice of life, will not be found. People, like Gotama the Buddha, had to go through the same process of self-indulgence in sense-pleasures and self-mortification before realizing where the middle path really lies. What we must do is look, listen, and learn when exposing ourselves to any paths. We keep our minds and hearts open to any experiences that will come to us through any adventures we happen to undertake. Awareness of what is going on and attention to what we are doing at any single moment is the golden key for unlocking the locked, uncovering the covered, and simplifying the complicated.

The right has its element deeply rooted in history and is rigid and inflexible. The left is anti-right and looks for an ideal alternative that would totally deny the right. This reaction is seen not only in political and social matters, but also in the so-called spiritual movement. While building their own identity and territory, they divide the world. Some of them have fallen into the illusion and have strong ambition for changing the whole world to believe as they do. Rather than contributing to the world what they know and who they are, they retreat into a small world, dividing and separating themselves. They move away from Oneness of Being. Through sharing our knowledge, insightful experiences, and integrated beingness with the world, we may act locally while thinking globally. We do not feel small and separated; we feel one with all others living on this planet and other planets.

It becomes clear to us that a feeling of disconnection and separation together with an act of misidentifying deprives us of being universally unified and one with others in existence. Each time we experience our actual separation from the beloved ones (parents, lover, partner, intimate friend), the wound of *primal* separation gets deepened and we suffer almost unbearably. We are usually caught in the world of illusion, thinking that being a separate individual is the only reality. With this illusive conviction holding such a firm grip on the individual self, we channel all our energies into feeding, maintaining, and developing this notion of a separate reality. As the need for security and safety becomes greater and greater because of separateness, we build walls around us and place security guards at every checkpoint. We can become totally numb to the feeling of *loving* oneness. When worst comes to worst, we are even terrified of the idea of human unity. The very idea of unifying ourselves with the rest of the universe can cause our ego-self to reel from the fear of death. In hiding ourselves in this well-protected, boundary-laden system of body and ego, we are similar to turtles living in their shells. Most activities carried out in life stem from this false core of personality systems, or energy patterns of sub-personalities. We live our lives, compulsively running off a set of patterns of conditioning. We act, behave, and conduct our lives from the idea center of "me." Everything we do is done for the "me." This is supported and strongly encouraged by our society and the world in which we live. And, as we are, so is the world. It is our own reflection: the *shadow* of our individual, separate self longing to return home. We each are, and the world is, longing—consciously or unconsciously—to regain oneness of being.

"Sleeping with Tradition": Obstacles on the Path

On our way home we meet with the many obstacles we have created during the period of separation when we have been cut off from the larger stream of life. We have to work through and live through the pain of loneliness, isolation, alienation, and abandonment, as well as the agony of feeling forsaken and deserted. We struggle with our resistance to letting go of our predicaments and with our resistance to opening ourselves to the new freedom. We fear the changes that come with embracing the *new* completely. The *old*, the familiar, has tied us firmly to the *image* of who we were supposed to be or should be. This image has tremendous power over us and tries to fasten us to our identity. We cling deeply. The most frightening time is when we are getting close to the point when big changes are going to take place, when we will lose all control over our familiar self. We fear we may not be able to get hold of our minds at all. What appears to us during such a transition period is a feeling of emptiness and uncertainty. We have to face this with naked reality. We are tortured with fears of not having anything solid to hold on to. We fall into a critical situation of not being able to enter the new fully. We choose the more comfortable feeling and go on sleeping in the patterns of our conditioned existence. Whatever we do now or plan to do in the future is heavily conditioned by our experiences and the way in which we used to carry out our activities in the past. We handle our emotional/psychological difficulties in exactly the same way we did before. This means we are fixated with our modes of behavior and our reactions to life situations, and are still unmistakenly predictable. We have no choice but to react in the way we are preprogrammed to do. There is no freedom for being spontaneous or for taking immediate action without any hesitation. This indicates that we have psychologically and unconsciously appointed a judge or judges (super-ego, top-dog, protector/controller) with ultimate authority to look over our shoulders and tell us what to do and how to be. If we happen to do what we think we shouldn't, feelings of guilt overwhelm us. We may even fear punishment from these judges or fear going to hell.

It has by now become clear just how much power we give away to our false selves (over-identified selves and/or disowned selves), and how heavy are our debts that make us feel morally obligated. We feel we must pay them off even though it may take us a lifetime. This is what the Buddha called "sleeping with tradition." In our own terms, we may label it *psychological sleep*. As we observe ourselves, we see that our everyday lives are conducted under the influence of our ordinary consciousness, which is psychologically asleep. I use the term "sleep" to mean a deep clinging to familiarity both at conscious and unconscious levels. Our actions, reactions, behavior patterns, habitual routines, and ways of relating are in conformity with the *norm* designated for us by our culture, religion, society, and

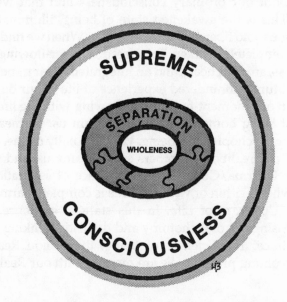

Our True Origin is **wholeness**. In the process of growing up to become individual persons, we **separate** ourselves from the wholeness by forming an *ego state* in which many sub-personalities or compulsive patterns of conditioning come together. Consequently, we each have a personality and a sense of separate self and create an endless divided world. Hence, we experience feelings of loneliness, strangeness, and alienation. In short, we experience pain, anxiety, fear, and insecurity in the course of our existence. Nevertheless, when the primary **wound of separateness** is healed through the development of *consciousness process*, we reach **supreme consciousness**, which is our intrinsic, true nature, the Oneness of being. Here suffering ends, and we open to the full unfolding of liberated joy, total freedom, love, and the complete union of opposites

significant others. These are our own internalized authorities. We hardly find a moment to act cleanly and clearly without any biases or conformity of any sort. We are slaves to our own creations! Those of us who do not realize this common truth go on sleeping and often think we are free. This only deepens our psychological sleep and perpetuates our slavery and imprisonment within our minds.

For those of us beginning to look within ourselves to investigate the human condition, there arises a precise, clear *insight* into the truth about our ordinary consciousness and that which lies beyond it. This is the awakened state of being, illuminated with pure, luminous, and liberated consciousness. When we find our true nature, we completely awaken. Total freedom, ever-flowing insightful awareness, an open heart, and an integrated, clear mind become an actual, natural, unhindered experience of life in our day-to-day living and in our moment-to-moment flowing with the life stream. A feeling of being home at last arises within us, permeating the whole of our psychophysical being. We feel totally connected with all levels of our reality, with others surrounding us, and with the universe or Dharma/God. There is no trace of separation to be found anywhere within or without. This is complete harmony, our Origin, the Upstream of Life. In this state of existence, all our problems arising out of dichotomy and dualistic thinking dissolve without a trace. The Oneness of Being, the I-Thou Reality, the Dharma-Becoming prevails. We are merged with our Real Nature, our Be-ing.

CHAPTER TWO

Illusion Versus Reality

MAYA (ILLUSION) IS A VERY IMPORTANT CONCEPT in many traditions. "The Turtle's mustache," "the Hare's horns," and "the rope and the snake" are often-used metaphors in Oriental philosophy. In the Buddhist teaching the story is about a man entering the forest and becoming lost. After struggling for a long time, trying to find his way out, he sees a very beautiful road. He is very excited upon seeing this road and begins to follow it, hoping it will lead him to his home. However, he finds himself in a devil's town instead because the devil has made the road to deceive him! This story is meant to illustrate the fact that as we all experience the world of illusion, it is very exciting and highly stimulating. It is also very dangerous. Without illusion we would feel our lives to be very boring. But when we get lost in the world of maya and lose contact with what is truly real, we encounter many difficulties in our existence. The observable fact is that a turtle has no mustache, a hare has no horns, and a rope is not a snake. When there is no clear seeing, when there is only groping in the dark, our perceptions and ideas about things become easily distorted. We take the appearance and form as the truth without penetrating into the depths. We believe to be true that which we perceive and think, and, with such beliefs we jump to conclusions and remain with them in our mental stagnation.

The Indian story goes like this: There was a young man searching long and hard for the secret of maya (illusion). While walking through the desert one day, he was feeling extremely exhausted. All at once he met up with an old man who asked him his reason for wandering in such a barren place in the boiling hot sun. The young man told him that he was trying to find the secret of maya. Upon

13

hearing this, the old man said, "Bring me a glass of water." In response to this the young man went out in search of water. After a long journey he saw a cottage in the distance. He hurriedly walked toward the cottage with delight as it had been a very dry journey. When he opened the door of the cottage, he found an old couple sitting in their living room drinking tea. As he was a curious young fellow, he began looking around the room. To his great surprise, he saw a beautiful young woman in the kitchen. His eyes lingered, looking into hers as some very deep feelings arose in the both of them. The old couple, who were also very observant, saw this profound contact between the two young people and arranged a wedding between the two of them. They then invited the young couple to live with them in their house. Now they were a complete family.

Not long after this, the old couple died. The young woman and her new husband inherited the house and the land it sat on. When the young woman gave birth to a child, the couple was very happy. A year later the young woman gave birth to another child, which made the family even happier. Soon after the third child was born, the young man had an interesting idea and decided to build a boat for his family's recreation. Just after he had finished the boat, it began to rain. It rained and it poured day after day, week after week, and month after month. It seemed as if the rain would never stop, and the desert turned into a sea. The young family could no longer live in the cottage so the husband put his family in the boat. He thought surely they could escape drowning in this way. Unfortunately, the water moved so swiftly and so powerfully that the boat was wrecked. As the man was trying to rescue his wife, the strong current swept his oldest child away from his right hand. While he was attempting to save that child, he lost his second child, whom he had held in his left hand. His third child dropped from his shoulder while he was making an effort to catch the second child. He thought to himself that he had lost everything that he had created. Deep grief entered his heart and he wept and wept with a more painful sorrow than he had ever experienced before. When he opened his eyes from his grief, the rain had stopped and the sea had disappeared from his sight completely. Then, everything became the desert again. Then and there, the same old gentleman he had met before stood in front of him asking, "Where is the glass of water?"

Understanding the Secrets of Maya

What powerful fantasies most young people have about their futures! Most of us do fantasize our success and happiness at a certain time in our lives. Those of us who try to meditate will be acquainted with similar fantasies and daydreams. In one sitting one meditator might have done a lot of work on the house or garden, while another might have entertained fantasies of a beautiful lover. Someone else might imagine food and wine. The world of illusion is right next door to our phenomenal world. Perhaps above these two worlds we will discover the zero, yet fertile, point with all its stillness and eternal movement of ongoing rhythmic dance. It is usually unknown to our dualistic mind. In the story, the old gentleman always appeared when the young man had reached the critical moment, the moment when confusion, uncertainty, deep pain, and suffering overtook him. Then he dove into the depths within and realized what he was doing to himself. At that particular moment of realizing the truth, he woke up and returned to his basic question of water, *the water of life* and how to find it.

As the story implies, the secret of maya can be found only through the full experience of illusion. Any experience born of impeccable awareness is truly a learning experience for us. We are to live life to its fullest so that we can learn about pleasure, joy, freedom, ecstasy, bliss, and so on, for the positive side; while on the negative side, we discover pain, suffering, entrapment, grief, despair, and so forth. We must bear in mind that in the good experience there is a "black dot" that indicates the ability to change to the opposite; similarly the "white dot" is inherent in the bad experience. With such insightful knowledge, we are free to experience both the pleasant and the unpleasant in life. So, our capacity to let go of that which is unhealthy and destructive to our well-being develops and bears fruit more and more. We then find it easier not to victimize ourselves and not to submerge ourselves in negativity, pain, and suffering. Instead, we remain equable and balanced amid the stormy situations that come into our experience from time to time in this constantly changing world. We are able to flow and bend with changing circumstances, as well as to dance with different rhythms of life. We are, therefore, able to maintain high energy and flow freely and smoothly in higher consciousness.

The secret of maya needs to be understood thoroughly to enable us to live in the world of illusion without falling victim to it. When we know maya very well, we will gain a great deal of benefit from living with it. It is fun to use this world of maya for excitement and amusement so that we don't feel a lack of entertainment in living. We can nurture ourselves in liberated joy, unconditional love, and freedom for being. In any case, maya helps keep us fully aware of all our movements and activities of everyday life. Bear in mind that maya is an inevitable and inseparable part of life. It is absolutely essential for us to understand all of its manifestations, tricks, and secrets. We do this by being aware of our daydreams, fantasies, and unrealities as we experience them, so that the structure of maya will be deeply penetrated and revealed to us precisely. There is no need to be afraid of maya since it is nothing but an object for our mindful awareness and a tool for our lives. In other words, it gives us strength and ripens our maturity.

This is like the Buddha's story of a person being chased by four poisonous snakes. At first, he tries to run away, then he realizes that there is no escape. He finds himself standing in front of a wide stretch of water where there is neither bridge nor boat; he thinks that the only thing for him to do is to make a raft for crossing over to the other shore. He uses his hands, gathering leaves and branches and putting them together in the form of a raft. He crosses over to freedom and happiness in the ever-new land. This land refers to a delightful stretch of level ground that symbolizes the plane of our enlightened consciousness, where maya cannot reach. This is our true security and our greatest refuge. It is within us and can be found in this life on earth.

A yogini who attended a retreat with me in 1979 said that after three painful and suffering hours of tremendous releasing of her bodily and psychological blocks, she saw her own illusive games and came to reality. She wrote,

I opened my eyes expecting to see all those supportive people around me and no one was there but me. I wondered how long I had been there by myself. At first I felt perturbed that these people had gone off and left me (they just left the meeting room when the session was over). I may have needed them to assist me as I was going through this traumatic experience! And then, it dawned on me that all my fears about cracking-up, freaking-out or losing my marbles, were all my mind games, the *fantasies* I created. I wondered at the reason for my being so afraid and then it occurred to me that I had been programmed to believe that I couldn't take care of myself. I had learned that I was very weak and in order to survive I would need to rely on others to hold me up. I also realized that this belief meant I had no self-confidence, which of course kept my self-esteem low. Also, needing others was a way I learned to get attention and love. So, great! I could give and receive love without all the games of helplessness and be open to change without so much fear!

Later, she had a talk with me in which I instructed her to just trust her own inner guide that knows exactly when to let go of whatever is ready to flow and change. She also understood what I meant when I said, "Follow your breath." She later wrote,

I had been so busy trying to keep everything under control, including my breath, that it was no wonder that I was being shaken loose like ripe apples off a tree. I was attempting to stop the flow of change. When I saw Dhiravamsa again that evening, I was just happy to see him; I didn't feel the same clinging attachment for his protection of my survival. Just lots of love. I was awakened in the wee hours of the morning by a tremendous blast of energy moving in my belly. I kept getting the message, "Get up and go to the meditation room." I thought, "Oh, no, it's too cold, I think I'll just go back to sleep." The waves of energy became stronger and I realized there was no way I would be allowed to lie there peacefully. I had no choice. I got dressed and practically ran to the meditation room. I sat on my pillow, but not for long. I suddenly felt the need to release a burst of rage that blasted through me like a volcano. I turned and hit some pillows that were behind me. It felt as though a tidal wave had rushed through me, and when I was finished, I felt totally at peace. I sat quietly experiencing the sounds and sensations of a very strong river surging through me. At one point, I thought to myself, "Oh, this must be enlightenment." And then the song, "You've only just begun" chimed in my head. I laughed at my mind trapping me again in the ego trip of, *now* I've reached my goal.

Later on this same yogini had shared with me her clear insights into her own situations and that of others in contact with her. She then reported,

> As my meditation progressed, the more I released, the lighter I felt. Each day I looked forward to sitting as I felt increased vitality, unlimited energy and more open and loving to everyone around me. I began to see that if there was someone who I felt negative toward, that I was projecting something onto them that I wasn't willing to accept in myself or that they were pushing buttons related to my unfinished unpleasant experiences that I had carried with me from the past. So, I understood how each person who crosses my path is a teacher for me. If we feel closed toward them for some reason, then it is important to be aware that it is not them that is making us feel negativity but some unfinished experience from the past that is interfering with a clear perception of them. Throughout the last week at the retreat, we would meet as a group and it was an opportunity for each of us to clear projections with each other. I was amazed at how sensitive I was to picking up when someone was feeling negative toward me, and when I would ask what was going on with them, they would let me know what they were feeling. This type of meditative practice (Insight Meditation) also brought an understanding of how each of us humans all share on a deep level all the same fears, feelings, and concerns, and that some of us are better at hiding these deep places than others. Some of us even excel at hiding these feelings from ourselves. The first few days of not talking to each other did not take away from really knowing each other at all. When we meditated together, I experienced knowing each one at his or her deepest core as each of us opened our sounds and movements to each other. There was no room for hiding, just openness and sharing; it was validating and supportive for me to open and share all those parts of myself that I had believed were not acceptable.

Living in the world of illusion without awareness really blinds our consciousness, making us believe that it is the truth. A person with this conviction feels unreal if he/she acts differently from the dictates of illusion. For example, some individuals believe that they don't have the right to go and see their teacher or leader during a retreat or workshop if a schedule for private talks or interviews is not posted, although they feel a great need for having such a session. This is the influence of the illusive state; it says either permission must be given, or you can't ask for anything. Such a compulsive pattern of conditioning comes from the upbringing, the family rule. When a child is prohibited by a parent and told this should be done and that should not be done, then many stupid rules are laid down. This is due to parents' preferences or ignorance or rigid attitudes toward life and the world. Such children will have to conduct their lives according to the dictates of illusion. They see all illusion as reality in the course of living; they must release this illusive energy that intrudes from their childhood experiences.

Coming out of illusion is like emerging from the clouds and seeing clear, blue skies for the first time. Before this, you can't believe that such a sky could exist. When the real appears, the unreal just disappears instantly, like the appearing of the light dispersing the darkness simultaneously. But, while being influenced by and dictated to by illusion, anything different from what you know and are familiar with is not right and unreal to your perception, feeling, and thought.

Now you see how important it is for all of us, particularly parents, not to imprint any false pictures on children's minds. They will carry these illusive things with them probably for the rest of their lives unless they are able to wake up and merge with reality through their self work. All of us who have power over others, whether it is power of love and respect or of authoritarianism, need to be more careful about what we say and how we conduct our transactions. There are many suggestible and malleable people on this planet. We can all help one another if each of us applies constant awareness in living and interacting with our fellow-beings. With constant awareness we know where we come from and what we do, so that we can act with clarity, love, and unitary consciousness. We, also, are able to sense other beings and their modes of relating, or what it is that directs their course of action at the moment. Awareness is self-protection, as well as caring lovingly and intelligently for others. With it we create a world of harmony, understanding, and clear, open, honest communication.

Being under the dictate of emotion, the imbalanced state of feeling, we are in the active hand of illusion; our thoughts, ideas, and perceptions become distorted. As soon as the emotion dissipates through the full experiencing of it, we see reality as it truly is. This is like the moon being free from the clouds and then shining beautifully in the clear sky. In this connection perhaps another report from a Yogi will throw some light. He wrote,

My grief had been mindless—no thought or words occurred to me—but after several hours a set of ideas emerged from the pain. The belief arose spontaneously that I must be from another planet and had found myself here among earthlings. These were creatures without feeling as I knew it, creatures who could drop atomic bombs on children and their families and exterminate Jewish babies in ovens. That was why I felt so cut off from all those others—we were factually alien to each other. This complex of ideas seemed to have a calming effect and my pain was reduced to blubbering. I went to breakfast at that point, wondering if it would be safe to eat earth food. I served myself and sat alone at a table away from others, unable to bear their proximity. I tried to eat, blubbering and occasionally spilling food from mouth to bowl.

After breakfast I met Dhiravamsa on my way to the sink and he asked how it was going. "Terrible," I said. "Let it be," he replied. It seemed the only thing anyone could have said that wouldn't make it worse. I met a friend on the way to the sink and embraced her saying, cryptically, "Susan, you and I are from the same planet." As the day wore on my grief and delusion subsided, and I was reminded of Vonnegut's *Slaughterhouse Five*. The hero believes himself to be transported to a planet called Tralfamador whose inhabitants are very interested in human beings; he goes there, or is drawn there, following each of a series of confrontations with meaningless mass death and destruction. I knew that even as I became calmer and felt more opened up, there was more grief to be faced. After such intense emotional experiences, I find myself super-sensitive to others, able to sense things about them and to understand them with little or no conversation.

Anima/Animus: "Invisible Partners" on the Road to Transformation

At this level of our mental/psychological reality, we, male or female, are under the influences of destructive and constructive forces, the dark and light sides of our existence. It is very essential that we commit ourselves, or surrender totally, to direct experiences of whatever presents itself to us at the moment. By living through any experiences with full attention, we always come out on the other side or reach the farther shore so that growth takes place and a transformation in consciousness occurs. We move through both sides of life in our journey of discovery. In this enduring journey we discover many different conflicting parts of ourselves, including what Carl Jung calls anima and animus. The feminine principle or yin form of energy in a male is called "anima," and the masculine principle or yang form of energy in a female is "animus." On observing our life experiences in everyday living, we see clearly how men are directed by their master of moods and how women are directed by their master of opinions. When driven by anima or animus, we are completely identified in the world of maya. We conduct our lives habitually and automatically in conformity with what is familiar to us. We each conform to the roles imposed on us by our culture and society. Unless we are aware of what is happening, we will go on victimizing ourselves and others throughout our lives. But, with choiceless awareness of our human situation, both inner and outer, we can turn an ugly frog into a prince and an ugly witch into a beautiful princess. It is up to us, for transformation is in our hands.

Let me elaborate on the notions of anima and animus as "invisible partners," as John A. Sanford calls them. When a man is moody and unable to express his feelings or when he cannot accept the dark, negative side of a woman he is attempting to relate to, he is under the influence of his anima. He is confused and troubled. When a man falls in love, he may experience this woman as the most beautiful, the most wonderful woman in the world. Then later, as he begins to see the reality of this woman and realizes she is human, with a dark side as well, he is disappointed and angry and feels betrayed. It is important for him to see his folly and own his projections. This is the world of maya. We don't have to think of anima as a destructive force hiding to get us. It can and should be used as a source of personal growth and integration. The anima represents the male's moods, dreams, imagination, visions, and fantasies in the sensual world. In the world of spirituality, the anima can assist men in their quest for full being, wholeness, complete integration, and dynamic balance with the universe.

The anima within actually knows where the water of life (enlightenment) is and understands perfectly well how to get men committed to such a goal. This is the guide all men must follow when the intellectual, thinking mind cannot solve the problem of disintegration and dichotomy. Men must sink deep down into their inner world, exploring the unconscious and bringing up the unaware into awareness so as to enable them to see all the hidden contents of the unconscious level of existence.

Through this discovery and experiential, insightful, direct contact with inner reality, men unite their conscious and unconscious. They eliminate division and separation, embracing oneness and totally unifying consciousness, eternally embracing the flowing, boundless, non-territorial Stream of Life. At this point, the heart is fully open and flows freely without any impediment whatsoever. Within such a heart there is no discrimination or distinction. The love is for all and remains in the all-oneness-consciousness.

Now, let us look into the animus or yang energy in women. The animus is the female's master of opinions. This aspect is swift to voice views and opinions on any matter, and a female possessed by identification with it deprives herself of feelings and her intuitive side. This misidentification can lead women to identify also with the social roles entailing power, to the extent that they deny the softer, receptive side. We have been talking of animus in a negative way; however, the animus can be very helpful to those females who need to develop their masculine principle. It is possible for a woman to lack connection with her animus and appear very weak and fragile socially. This woman will be submissive, lack self-assertion, and be easily dominated. She is in need of looking within and finding what she truly wants; she must find direction from within.

As for spiritual development, the traditional Western woman does need help from the animus to encourage her to merge her energies and allow the spiritual energy its full expression. This can be quite frightening if her consciousness is not firmly focused. In the Buddha's terminology, there must be a balance between *samadhi* (one-pointedness) and energy (creative power) for reaching out and expanding. The rhythm of contraction and expansion must be in proper proportion and in complete harmony. When this process works in rhythm, the flow of life moves harmoniously and in complete balance with the whole universe. This is purity of being.

In meditation practice women learn to develop a concentrated mind and focused awareness so that their intuitive faculty will merge with this new power and therefore help them penetrate more profoundly into any intellectual and spiritual matters. With faith in their hearts, they are willing to trust themselves as well as their potentiality for becoming fully enlightened. Inwardly, they feel equal to men in having the same capacity to become anything that they want to be. In this way, they can rise above the roles and just be human beings who have a certain form of energy for living and functioning in the world. Then they are able to cultivate the faculties of faith and wisdom to equal degrees. When wisdom and faith are in balance, there is no blind belief; there is no dry intellectual knowledge.

These women become firm and clear in their movements on earth. There is a complete balance of energy with a non-distracted, non-disturbed state of mind. There is balance between active and passive. To achieve this level of development, insightful *awareness* is the key. One sees clearly and precisely what is going on inwardly and outwardly. Such impeccable, all-seeing awareness helps us check ourselves at every point of contact in every situation and at every level of existence. So, we are able to know through our direct contact if we are in harmony or disharmony.

With such immediate and direct knowing we are not delayed in taking the right or essential action. With fully developed spirit, people are able to overcome fears and insecurities. They become their own persons and assert their own power so that their anima and animus, yin and yang, can be fully integrated and function in perfect harmony both within themselves and in their relationships with the rest of the world.

In speaking of relationships, we must examine our motives for entering into them. Are we expecting only happiness, peace, ecstasy, and pleasure? Or, are we clear that a relationship is not a hiding place from loneliness, but a growth process in which we will inevitably meet with sorrow and joy, dark and light sides of life experiences? This union between people serves as a learning situation where we can purify our destructive parts and unify our male and female forms of energy to the point of balance and eventually marry the two forms together within. In turn this inner union will lay a firm foundation for our relationships with external partners. Those of us who are not willing to face ourselves in the difficult situations and circumstances arising from our relationships will continue living in the world of maya and deepen the games of illusion.

Here, it becomes clear to us that a meditative way of living and leading our lives is absolutely essential. With Insight Meditation, Vipassana, we will constantly throw light into different areas of darkness, catching the sight of maya in the distance so that its games can be cancelled by our powerful attention. By so doing we are enlightening ourselves in every moment of living. All misidentifications and all separateness are utterly destroyed without any ashes left behind. This is the true healing and wholeness that we are all seeking to fulfill in this life on earth. We heal the wounds of separation and lift the curtains of ignorance. With such healing and enlightened wisdom, we return to our home of wholeness and universal unity.

Overcoming the Illusion of Self-Image

Now I want to explore with you another form of maya that most of us get caught in, most of the time without even recognizing that we are in it. This is self-image, the "something solid" that we create to identify with and grasp firmly with all our emotions. We define ourselves and put ourselves into a box that we carry with us every moment of everyday life. This is the reason we find it difficult to get along with certain people: our image of us and their image of us clash, or our image of them may be different from their own self-image.

We also tend to project aspects of our personality that do not fit into our box onto others. Getting involved with the games and busying ourselves with the roles, *we become our images* and dwell on who we believe we are. We are unable to be real and true to who we really are. As a result we accumulate resentments toward ourselves and others.

For most of us it is impossible to distinguish between real self and self-image. We end up identifying ourselves with our self-images and do so with such a strong grip and such strong conviction that the misidentity is the only reality there is for us. This is the subtle world of maya. As far as I can see, the maya of self-image creates more delusion in our lives and our relationships than any other aspect of maya.

Instead of relating being to being, we relate as one self-image to another without ever actually coming into contact with the real person. After the game is over we feel empty and lonely. Then we busy ourselves building borders and boundaries to protect and defend; we feel that we must protect our self-image from attack by every other self-image.

Every self-image of ego is out to gain its own satisfaction and furtherment and will use and attack any other self-image that gets in its way. We spend so much time and energy in these pursuits that we become drained, exhausted, and misdirected. We gradually lose our vitality to such an extent that we arrive at the point of not even having a concrete or evident reason for living. Furthermore, when living under the illusion of self-image, we think that we need to feed ourselves on constant excitement and stimulation; otherwise we become bored and discontent. Consequently, we are in a constant state of demanding of ourselves, creating unnecessary pressures and burning ourselves up in a whirlwind of ideas, dreams, fantasies, beliefs, and dogmatic assertions. By the time we realize what we are doing, we have already gone so far that it is quite difficult to turn around. Here again, time and energy are required for making our way back to our Origin.

What can we do with our self-image? The answer is, just *die* to it! We can learn to do this in formal sitting meditation and in everyday living. First of all, we must observe our self-image very closely and precisely so that we can see clearly what kind of image we become at each moment. Recognizing our self-images will help us accept ourselves for who we are. This is complicated by the makeup of self-image; it is not just one image for each of us. We each identify with a myriad of self-images, and we each have an infinite number of sub-personalities. When any of these sub-personalities or self-images is foremost in our minds, that is who we "are" at that moment. When two or more of these vie for expression, we say we are in conflict within. We feel pain, anger, resentment, and even hatred when we are only in *conflict within;* imagine how these feelings are magnified when we begin looking directly at the ego with its many facets and games!

As each self-image is seen and the energy keeping it alive begins to dissipate, the ego tells us that we are dying. Our images, during this process of releasing their energies through the flame of our attention, get weaker and weaker and eventually disappear altogether, leaving us with a clearness for being. As we experience more and more spaciousness, the images become less and less powerful. Because of our seeing with great clarity and profound wisdom that we are not our self-images, but a spaciousness, we will disidentify with our ego-self and become transpersonal to recognize our supreme Identity. This is the way of rising above the false self or mistaken identity, transforming the self-image, merging with the Real Beingness and fusing into the whole.

In the meantime, when we observe ourselves identifying with self-image, we allow it to react with all its feelings, thoughts, ideas, and compulsive patterns so that it will be revealed in its totality and manifested on its fullest scale. In such a situation we need to remain fully aware of what is going on, watching and experiencing with full attention everything that is happening. In this way we can watch part of ourselves identifying with the images and yet not be totally fooled. There is a distance or space created by focused awareness. Within this space insightful experiences take place, creating more light for us and expelling the darkness.

We are, therefore, in a position to understand what to do and how to proceed with our lives. Personal power is regained and compulsive conditioning becomes dissipated and powerless. When more space is experienced, we lead our lives with the clear light of wisdom while objectively observing ourselves and our powerful reactions. In this way, the reactive patterns will lose their grip on us, become powerless, and finally drop away completely. Then our natural flow unfolds, giving us freedom of movement in action and providing us with more and more space for living.

Another question arises. How can the integration of being and becoming take place? The answer is, by simply *letting go* of the image without turning away from it. When the self-image no longer occupies our central space of being, but functions as a moving symbol in the process of becoming or playing certain roles, then it can be used simply as a tool with which to perform our duties and functions.

Underlying the use of this tool is a delightful stretch of level ground, providing us with firmness, grounding, centeredness, and unification of being in an ever-flowing, natural course of life. With the act of letting go we emerge into spaciousness, breaking down the boundaries as well as becoming expansive and unlimited. When we do not turn away from our self-image, there is love, unconditional acceptance, and letting be. We have complete, spontaneous control over our self-image. Just like a herdsman riding on the back of his ox after having caught and tamed it, we return home with unutterable joy and freedom. This is total integration between self-image and the *Self*. The self-image and the Self are no longer an issue; both of them, as concepts and notions, have been transmuted totally. What remains is the natural flow of life as it really is.

Ignorance: The Root Cause of Pain and Suffering

Let us look into the main factor that is operating in the world of maya. It is *ignorance,* the root cause of pain and suffering, that blinds our consciousness, distorts our perceptions and feelings, as well as perverts our thoughts and views. As a result, we mistake reality and unreality; we confuse the superficial with essence. We sink more deeply into maya like an elephant in the mire.

I would like us to understand accurately what is meant by this term "ignorance." It is not just the lack of knowledge or information; it is also absence of insightful awareness. Sometimes we may possess a great deal of knowledge and have a lot of information about things, but when facing the dark force of ignorance, our theoretical knowledge becomes useless, or even worse, a block to the natural flow of insight. It can lead us to the wrong end. The actual fact is that when there is an absence of awareness, we do not look; we stop paying attention. Without looking there is no seeing, and at that moment suffering arises, submerging us into the wilderness of maya. We accumulate karma. It is hard to give up our own suffering because we are so familiar and so acquainted with it. We believe whole-heartedly that we are the suffering. This becomes a game of holding on to negativity for identity and survival.

It is not easy to give up the thing that we identify as ourselves, for it means we will lose all our self-concept and self-definition, including our character structure and habitual patterns of behavior. Being ignorant and fearful, we are not only unwilling to give up our egos, but we also cling relentlessly to our projected future. We hold on to our ideas and beliefs so tightly that we are even blind to the illuminating light of oneness and unlimited unity. We don't know what to do if we do not have this game to play. More than that, we imagine that living without this game will be empty, terrifying, and frightening. Very few of us will say, "If there is nothing there, I can enjoy emptiness itself." Or, "I can just stay in the empty space and see what will happen." To some of us who are courageous enough to think such thoughts, the petty mind might say, "Oh, no—it's no fun. Just dwelling in emptiness has no excitement. I do not want to do that. Perhaps to experience emptiness occasionally for just a short period of time might be tolerable. But, I must have something to play with. Without a toy my whole life will be meaningless and dead."

So, ignorance is seen as a kind of obsession, the domination of our thoughts or feelings by a persistent idea, image, desire. Sometimes, we are obsessed by the idea of or desire for pleasure, thinking that pleasure is essentially an ultimate goal of life. When pleasure becomes something obsessively needed for self-gratification, we seek it compulsively with an unbearable yearning. As a result, if we do not have it, we feel terribly uncomfortable and very unhappy; we may even become neurotic about our sensual pleasures.

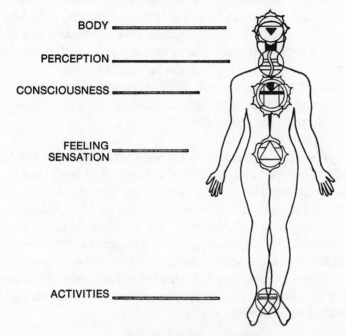

BODY

PERCEPTION

CONSCIOUSNESS

FEELING
SENSATION

ACTIVITIES

Five Aggregates of Existence

According to Buddhist teaching, we human beings are a combination of *body* (form) and *energy systems pertaining to the body, feeling* (including sensations), *perception* (the factor that creates images through sense-perception and ideation), *activities* (*sankkhara*—conditioning processes and energy patterns such as anger, aggression, jealousy, and so forth), and *consciousness* (awareness and experience through six senses: *eyes, ears, nose, tongue, body touch, and mind or inner sense*).

In this figure, the positions of aggregates are shown according to meridian points of energy in the Tantric System. The body or form corresponds to the head with white color; perception corresponds to the throat with red color; consciousness corresponds to the heart with blue color; feeling and sensation correspond to the stomach (navel, to be exact) with yellow color; and activities correspond to the feet with green color. Also, corresponding to those five aggregates are the syllables of OM AH HUM SVA HA, which are used as mantras in Tantric Meditation; and which, when grouped together, result in a notion of self, individual, being, etc., as well as in ATTACHMENT. On the other hand, when these aggregates are separated out, then such a concept of self, or of ego as a unified whole, disappears altogether. This is *shunyata*, a Fertile Void, according to the Buddha's Complete Insight into the Ultimate Truth. Finally, at the Awareness level there is always NON-ATTACHMENT operating with Love and Freedom.

New sensations and constant stimulation become a way of life. Under such influence, we are totally intoxicated and obsessed by the passion of ignorance. This dominating power blinds our consciousness and blocks our flow of awareness so much that we do not see any danger or destructiveness in seeking pleasure with obsessive thought and persistence. This obsession of ignorance is constantly seeping into us, moving underneath every action, feeling, emotion, thought, or perception.

In the presence of this ignorance we unintentionally create pain and suffering for ourselves and for others. All of our behavior is under the complete control of obsessive ignorance. We display stubbornness in pursuing our goal without ever looking, listening, thinking, or seeing in a different way. We blot out all other possibilities of directing the course of life; we open only to the narrow, superficial channel of passionate ignorance, the invisible movement of dark force. Ignorance is always looking for a chance to step in and condition the activities of our lives, compelling us to think, feel, perceive, and act in its direction.

We must begin now to establish impeccable awareness in every moment of living. This is the only answer for curing our illnesses caused by the obsession of such passionate ignorance, the iron bar locking the gate to self-discovery and realization of truth. In practical matters of life, we can understand how the absence of awareness brings about disaster. As a friend of mine was relating to me, she went hiking in the Scottish Highlands one day alone. At the start of the hike she was very aware of her walking, her climbing, and the steepness of the mountain. When she was fully aware of her every movement, everything went fine. But, on the way down, at a certain point, her awareness slipped. At that moment, she fell and broke her leg.

Surrendering with Awareness: Allowing Playful Insight to Dissolve the Power of Ignorance

With the coming in of ignorance and the going out of awareness, we are groping in the dark. Even though trying to act appropriately, under the powerful force of ignorance there is no choice open to us except to follow the destiny determined by the dark force. Because the movement of such a dark force is invisible, it is hard for us to resist falling victim to it. It can hit us at any moment. This is the reason we need to be alert and vigilant at all times.

Awareness is the friend of wisdom. Ignorance, its opposite, is the friend of attachment, conditioning, craving, and becoming. The elements of deception, delusion, and unconsciousness are very deep within our psychophysical processes. We can be easily deceived and deluded by our definitions and ideas and even by our incomplete insight. We take flashes of insight as complete within themselves. We deceive ourselves when we get excited with trivial or untrue realization. It is very much like the story of the blind men touching different parts of an elephant; every blind man touches a particular part. One touches the legs, another the tail, and yet another the tusk and so forth. They all talk about the elephant in different ways according to where they touch it. The one touching the tail says, "An elephant is something very long with a bushy end." The one touching the legs remarks, "Oh, the elephant is like a pair of boots, a really big pair!" But none of them knows exactly how the elephant looks because none has experienced the whole. Worse than that, the elephant is indeed like the things that they have touched. So, the truth is distorted.

We see that it is essential for us to be in a constant state of observing ourselves. We know we deceive ourselves by building up images about ourselves and living according to a certain definition. "I am so-and-so; everybody else is so-and-so." These definitions are very powerful in our lives. Sometimes when people have this strong sense of self-definition and live up to it, they become very narrow and shallow. They block out other possibilities for themselves and do not see beyond their definitions. But, in fact, there are many other human resources apart from our self-definitions. We are able to allow them to emerge whenever we need to make use of them.

We must allow ourselves to be vulnerable, to be totally in any situation we participate in, throwing ourselves into anything that we are exposed to and then seeing what we can do and what will happen. In this way we find our hidden capacities and discover hidden tendencies within us. In other words, we are shining light into various dark places, places we haven't seen before. With the light of wisdom we see things as they truly are. Awareness helps us to move on. With open awareness we can throw ourselves into anything without hesitation, without desire for anything in return, just for the experience and learning. This is the way of playing the game *totally*. We are part of the game; yet, we know all the rules of the game. Then we see what actually happens in that game. Because we see it clearly and completely, we know for sure if the game is essential for us or not. At this point, the willingness to give up the game will come to us naturally, without having to make rules to use in letting go. When the willingness to give up anything actualizes itself, we no longer desire to live by rules.

Karma is so deep within us that we cannot give up our games or transcend them right away. Sometimes we cannot avoid repeating games even if we don't want to play again. In a way, we like our games because we know them well and can play them well. We don't need to acquire any new techniques. We think, "I will do something new. Oh . . . what should I do now? . . . I don't know anything about this." So we have to spend time learning about this new thing. Or, we say, "No, I don't want to spend all of my time learning about this new thing." Maybe we learn the new thing in order to add to our capacity in playing the old games. We might like that if we still want to maintain our games. So, the sleeping dog is strong and powerful; it's biting us most of the time. The only way to be safe and free from this dog of ignorance is to be fully vigilant and totally aware at every moment.

We can see ignorance in the sense of outflowing energy. It flows out constantly with its invisible movement. The energies of ignoring and inattention flow out with other passionate energies from within us—flowing out with our feelings, flowing out with our thoughts, flowing out with our ideas, and flowing out with our physical, verbal, and mental expressions. So, it is both flowing within us and flowing out with all our manifestations. It has enough energy to cover the whole field of our existence. It is very hard for us to prevent the passion of ignorance from flowing out because it is flooding us when we don't even see it. It is only through clear and dustless awareness that we see what flows out with our feeling. Is the feeling a reactive one or is it stemming from the depth of our beingness? What I call reactive feeling refers to such judgments as pleasant or unpleasant, good or bad, agreeable or disagreeable. It is reactive because it is caused by a perception in which specific ideas are involved. We react to an experience with ideas, thoughts, or attitudes fixed in our minds. The other form of feeling comes with the clarity of knowing or sensing. That is the reason that in certain traditions they say, "I feel," instead of "I think." "I feel this is right." Or, "I feel right." We can also show the difference like this: the feeling that comes from the ego level of our existence is a reactive feeling. The one that stems from our non-ego level of reality is an intrinsically pure feeling.

Yet, sometimes, when we feel right about a thing, it is still a reactive feeling. Or, we may feel that a pure feeling is not right because it is disagreeable. So, we must watch very carefully to see whether it is a reactive response or a real bubbling up from deep within us. We give our attention to this. If we feel right about something, we can explore that feeling by experiencing it fully with our impeccable awareness. Then we see what happens. By restricting ourselves, we make room for ignorance to operate. For it is still hiding and flowing out unnoticed. On the other hand, by allowing ourselves to move into different spaces, we are able to see, with profound wisdom, how ignorance actually operates in our lives. Such seeing itself is a creative action for eliminating and dispersing the passion of ignorance. The moment the seeing has gone, ignorance flows in to fill the space. We cannot get rid of ignorance no matter how hard we try. The only thing we can do is to allow the light of clarity, the immeasurable light of wisdom, to shine in the present with all its brightness and unlimited power. In this way, the energy of ignorance can be utterly dispelled.

It is not a matter of trying to fight with ignorance; we are not attempting to eliminate it. Energy cannot be eliminated: it can only be transmuted, transformed. Let us transform it into this positive, realistic way of being, *awareness*, letting the light of insightful wisdom shine in every moment of living. So now, we know for sure what to do in regard to the outflow of ignorance. When we are totally aware of our feelings, our emotions, our thoughts, and everything that comes from within, we can see without distortion what is actually happening. That is the light of clarity; it can flow constantly with awareness.

If, for example, we feel sad, we can be aware of that sad feeling and see the connection between the sadness and something else. It may be in the mind, something we remember or some current situation. We look at our feeling, see it for what it is and experience it fully. We can, then, understand how this sad feeling arises and how it affects our psycho-physical systems. By doing this, our sadness is dealt with and can be transmuted. If there is anything the emotional body is wanting to do, like crying, tears might come. This is okay. Crying is natural. Or, there may be only sadness and a melting away of the sadness after a while. But, if there is something in the mind to feed that sadness, then it stays longer. If we are in a very clear space, without reaction, focusing attention on whatever arises, then sadness can fade away. We feel good and clear when no reaction takes place; there is just experiencing and a kind of space for being. This entails the absence of ignorance. If there is some reaction, we simply observe it without identifying with it. In this way we create a clear space for ourselves.

Reactions come from ideas we hold in our minds. A Chinese story illustrates this. Once upon a time, a Chinese Master was performing a funeral service for his dead Master. Then and there in front of thousands of people he burst out crying unexpectedly. This was a big surprise and created a furor. All the closest disciples rushed to the platform, chiding their Master, saying, "Oh, no, Master! You must not cry, you are an enlightened being. It's not right for you to cry. It's a public disgrace!" "I am not crying. The body is discharging," responded the Master. So the body was crying, and the Chinese Master saw clearly where the crying came from. He was totally free, witnessing the bodily discharge.

We tend to judge actions and appearances without penetrating into the depths. So, we inevitably make mistakes. We interpret actions and appearances, so they seem wrong to us. Our conceptual knowledge and perception cannot comprehend that which it has yet to examine or learn. The state of mind and inner being of a person who is clearly aware is beyond our ordinary comprehension. Reactions are possible and in fact must occur as long as we occupy human bodies; yet, this can occur without identification. Also, when we live together, our energy interacts with the energy of the other people to whom we are close. We can also dispel this energy when it is triggered in our bodies. I had an experience like the Chinese Master when my mother died. I felt as if my left arm disappeared. My left hand was completely gone. Only eight months after this I received news of my father's death while traveling with my teacher in London in 1964. I felt as if my right arm and hand were gone. I had no arms! At the moment of experiencing this my body broke out crying, weeping and weeping and weeping almost all night. I was amazed at witnessing this event. I was alone in my room, crying and weeping for the final loss of my hands as well as for my brother and sisters who had lost their parents and did not have an elder brother to comfort and take care of them. In our Thai tradition, it is the big brother who will replace the father and mother when they die, in providing emotional security and in distributing wealth. The villagers do not write wills. When the crying stopped, I felt totally clean and clear in my whole system. There was no sadness to be found for my loss or for my brother's and sisters' situations. The crying and weeping are natural ways of expressing certain energy patterns in the emotional field.

By reacting to actions we suppose to be committed out of ignorance, by condemning ourselves or others, we are accumulating karma and feeding our own ignorance. So, be aware of this dark force that comes from anywhere at any moment. It's our work to spot ignorance at the moment it appears, thereby feeding wisdom so that it grows. As a matter of fact, it grows all the time provided that we make constant effort to remain aware or to wake up from our ordinary consciousness, our psychological sleep. Sometimes we may say, "Oh, I lost my insight. I came back to my old pattern." Even so, just notice that. Pay attention to how you return to your old pattern and how you lose your insight. By so doing, our wisdom keeps growing and insight keeps returning. For, it is never lost completely. We are not in touch with our wisdom for a time, but it will be available some other time when we are fully in the present and inwardly quiet. Just keep flowing with awareness and with life. For with constant awareness, you never lack insight; it always flows along. The point being that we must not forget awareness; we always remember to be aware and to bring awareness into every movement of our lives.

Sometimes people say that they do not have much fun if they must be constantly aware. In fact, we have great fun with awareness. In the full state of awareness, we accept everything and everybody unconditionally; we do not even conceptualize. Love flows, and our joy, our pleasure, our fun is enormous and complete. There is nothing interfering with our experience. There is no thought, no inner dialogue, in the back of our minds. We enjoy ourselves fully. We know everything that is going on and allow ourselves to go into action and experience completely, without holding back. In this way, we cannot avoid having fun, *great* fun in life. With the natural flow of awareness, we are not only free of the power of ignorance, but also feel the spirit of playfulness in conducting our lives. Because we are playful in working as well as in living, we do not put ourselves into stress or create any tensions. We can always relax and have fun with life to its fullest. We are able to nurture ourselves and be nourished by our work or whatever we do. So this spirit of playfulness leads us on to wellness, which is the next subject of our discussion.

CHAPTER THREE

Toward Wellness

WE ALL APPRECIATE WELLNESS and a healthy state of existence, but not all of us follow the way to health and wellness. Generally, when people are ill, they go to doctors for medicine. Sometimes the medicine helps to eliminate the symptoms of the ailment but, at other times, the illness persists or even gets worse due to a life-style or way of living that is unhealthy or destructive to psychological, emotional, or physical well-being. Nevertheless, those of us who are dominated by sickness keep taking pills either for physical wellness or for emotional and psychological health; this enables us to continue functioning. After recovering from their illnesses, such persons give no thought to developing a healthy life-style. Those of us living in this way go on leading the same kind of life-style that is opposed to wellness and, when we become ill again, we return to doctors for pills. Thus the cycle goes on and on.

The fact remains that millions of people are sick even though thousands of doctors are trained to fight illness and disease. To me, it seems that most of us are unaware of the difference between dealing with the symptoms of illness and actually moving along the path of wellness. Trying to cure illness without giving attention to establishing and maintaining wellness is like building sand castles; there can be no permanence. Many of us want wellness but are unwilling to change our way of living to get it. We believe that sickness results from some physical disorder or infection and that Western medicine is the answer for getting well. This belief system keeps most of us at the edge of illness and never allows us to achieve wellness.

What is Wellness?

True wellness is the integration of all levels of our being including the psychological, emotional, physical, and spiritual levels. Gotama, the Buddha, declared, "Wellness is the greatest gain in life." According to him, the fully enlightened state of being is wellness, an everlasting wellness in which no illness can be found.

Wellness, therefore, is not confined to a temporary relief of physical or emotional disorder. It refers to our true freedom for being and enjoying life with no restriction. With wellness we are in harmony within ourselves and with all others. Both self and otherness become one. There is a complete balance of all levels of our reality. Shifts in consciousness are naturally experienced in day-to-day living. Liberated joy, awakening to the ever-flowing larger stream of life, becomes a natural unfolding in every moment of living.

For this reason, as healthy people, we do not allow stress, a predominant psychological disturbance, to enter our hearts and minds. We are able to manage stressful situations effectively so that wellness will not be lost. Instead, we rise above any unhealthy state of existence, maintaining equilibrium and balance.

With wellness consciousness, it is natural for a healthy person to welcome any pressures life brings. These can come from our own personality patterns or from the external world. We possess the ability to adapt ourselves well to any changing conditions of life and the world. This is because we live our lives with an open heart and mind and are guided by an immediate, clear insight into the nature of reality. We can understand quickly what is actually happening. With such insightful awareness and clear consciousness, creative action is always taken, and we are able to maintain health and wellness more easily. As long as there is caring and love for well-being, there arises the natural flow of creative energy used for looking and paying attention to all levels of our realities; we do not neglect any aspect of our existence. Consequently, we become radiant and vibrantly alive both internally and externally with no limitation.

The Nature of Focus: An Essential Aspect of Living

When we exist at the level of disintegration, we tend to do one thing and neglect the other. We become unaware of integrated health and wholeness of being. As a result, many of us experience the frustration of a divided and compartmentalized life in which we lack the capacity to reconcile inner development with the outer world. There is a gap between the way of wellness and our usual life-styles. It is really frustrating when we are unable to integrate our experiences of higher energies into everyday living.

So far as I see it, this happens because of two predominant factors: either too much or too little *focusing*. For those of us whose minds are overly focused on success and achievement in whatever we do—whether in our material lives or in our spiritual fulfillment—there can be a lack of awareness, a lack of consciousness in living. We live our lives without ever being aware of our bodies and numerous voices within—we aren't grounded. We are unable to see the beauty around us, the clear blue sky, the beauty of an old person, the beauty of a child. Those of us in this state are in a limbo created out of our own ignorance. As a result of perverted emotions, the body becomes contracted with many holding points blocking the natural flow of energy. At the same time, the mind becomes increasingly frantic and easily upset when things go wrong or "feel" out of control. Stress and strain exist at the physical and emotional levels and develop into diseases and psychological breakdowns because they go unresolved. When life is in high speed and there is no slowing down for self-observation, we become like the schizophrenic, splitting ourselves into non-communicating segments.

In such a state of existence there can be no letting go, no being playful with life. This is the process through which we forget our experiencing of high energy from spiritual retreat or self-work. There is no connection between the high self and the middle self as spoken of in the Kahunas culture. The middle self, the intellect, or the acquisitive mind, who runs the show, will often seek greedily for acquiring and owning things such as wealth, position, status, or prestige. It never has enough, always thinking that something is lacking. The more the middle self attempts to accomplish its goals, the farther away from the high self it gets. Survival and a false sense of security (money, possessions) become a central issue of living. It cannot align itself with the high self and remains an obstacle in the integration process.

By constantly giving our attention and applying simple, clear awareness to what we are doing and how we are conducting our lives, we will be able to get in touch with our low self, our heart, and our feelings. Then it will be possible to make a direct link with our high self, awakening nature or pure consciousness, so that all our experiences can be integrated. Personality and beingness will be brought together in harmony through embracing ourselves lovingly. At this point we will transcend the categories (in the sense of not taking them seriously) and function from the all-integrated wholeness or Universal Unity of diversities in which no conflict or contradiction can be found.

Now let us view the second predominant factor for the inability to succeed in integrating higher energies or peak experiences into everyday life—the *lack* of clear direction. After such wonderful encounters with the ever-flowing stream of life in which vibrations are fast and energies high, we enter the world, where there exists a great deal of temptation and distraction. These mundane things, including jobs, family, and relationships, challenge us at almost every moment. We are brought back to what is familiar, so to speak. For those of us who do not have a clear direction in life, fears, confusions, and turbulent feelings arise. We can easily lose the heightened state of consciousness and drop out of our high and powerful energy field. In some cases, more pain and suffering result from this letdown. We experience even more difficulty reconciling our inner and outer conflicts and are driven by confusion and uncertainty. We are unable to embrace the daily routines of life and are also unable to return to the high level of spiritual accomplishment we had achieved. All sorts of negative reactions may dominate the course of our lives. The fact is that when we do not have a clear focus in our lives, we are separated from our spirit, and we lack the inner strength and creative power for living and directing the course of our actions.

Focus, therefore, is an essential aspect of living; it gives us clear awareness of what we are doing as well as insight into our direction for the future. Let me make it clear that this matter of focus that I have been stating is not a rigid, fixed point or purpose. It is a clear, lively, unified state of being and becoming in our everyday living. In other words, having a focus means that we know exactly what we want and how we feel so that there is a great clarity and trusting willingness to embrace all parts of life within us fully. When we lack focus, we space out, become scattered, have no clear inward direction, and walk aimlessly in life. More than that, we are often confused because of not knowing what we really want and how we actually feel about things and ourselves.

Searching for the Water of Life

To illustrate how we generally handle our sicknesses and how we can reconcile our inner and outer worlds, I want to share this fairy tale with you.

Once upon a time, there lived an old, sick King who had three sons. There was no remedy for his illness to be found in all his kingdom. Many remedies had been tried, and all the doctors in his kingdom had been called in to attend him. But, instead of getting better, he got worse and worse until there was no hope for him to live. Everybody gave up hope for the King's survival, and his three sons were grieving deeply. One day while the sons were out in the courtyard, crying, weeping, and berating themselves, an old gentleman appeared before them and inquired as to the cause of their grief. In response, they told him that their father was dying and that there was no remedy. To their pleasant surprise, the old man said that he knew of one that had not been tried, but it was very hard to find. That remedy was the water of life. After having spoken, he disappeared.

The brothers were very happy about this information and had renewed hope. One at a time they went to their father and asked permission to go searching. The oldest brother asked first. But, when he was unable to tell the King where it was that he was to look, the King felt that the venture was too uncertain. He did not want his son to go; he felt that he would surely lose him; he preferred for his son to stay by his side while he died. But, because his son insisted so persistently, he at last gave his reluctant permission. The son thought to himself that if he succeeded in obtaining this remedy for curing his father's illness, he would surely become his father's favorite and be the one to succeed him to the throne. The oldest son set out on his horse riding in a great hurry, although he still did not know where he was going. He had no idea of where to find the sacred water. After a long while, he came across a dwarf who stopped him and asked what made him hurry so. The Prince barely took the time to look at the little fellow and said haughtily, "Oh, you little shrimp!" At that the Prince took off riding again. He had so angered the dwarf that he wished the Prince an evil wish. The Prince was sent in the wrong direction by this wish and fell into a ravine. The more he tried to get out, the narrower the space became. He became so wedged in that he could go neither forward nor backward; nor could he dismount his horse. He was wedged between two mountainsides.

Impatiently, the King and the other two Princes awaited news of the older brother. When no word of him came, the second brother approached his father and asked to be allowed to seek his lost brother and the water of life. The King was reluctant to let yet another son venture from home, but he finally relented. The middle Prince set out on his journey in exactly the same manner as his brother had done. He also met the dwarf who flagged him down and asked him the same question. The second Prince also insulted the dwarf and hurried on his way. The dwarf wished the same wish for the middle Prince and he, too, found himself lodged in the ravine.

Now, the youngest Prince was the most pure of heart, the most innocent of greed, and he thought of no gain except to find the water of life to cure his ailing father. When the only remaining Prince asked his father to let him go, the King said, "You are the only Prince left! Who will look after the Kingdom when I die? You must stay here!" It took a long, long time for the King to give his consent even though the young Prince insisted vigorously. At last the King gave his consent and the youngest brother set out in the same direction as his older brothers. He, too, met up with the dwarf, as he is always in that spot available for lending a helping hand. The dwarf stopped the Prince with the same question he had asked the older Princes. "Why are you in such a great hurry?" The Prince stopped his horse completely and told the dwarf the whole story of his father's illness and his brothers' disappearances. He told the dwarf of the water of life and it being his father's only chance to live. He explained how he must hurry to find it. Then the dwarf said, "You are a good person; you aren't haughty as are your two egotistical brothers. Do you know where the water of life is to be found?" "No," answered the Prince. The dwarf was so pleased with this youngest Prince, who was so pure of heart, that he said, "I will tell you how to find this remedy and how to obtain it. It is in the courtyard of an enchanted castle. In order to get into that castle you must strike the gate with a wand and you must have two loaves of bread to feed the hungry lions inside the gate." The dwarf gave the young Prince a wand and two loaves of bread and said, "Now, you must remember to obtain the water of life and leave the castle before the clock strikes twelve." The Prince was very happy and hopeful; he thanked the dwarf and left for his adventure with the enchanted castle.

When he arrived at the castle, everything was just as the dwarf had depicted. There the iron gate stood towering before him. Remembering the dwarf's instructions, he struck the gate three times. He was amazed to see it swing open before him. Immediately, two fierce lions lunged for the Prince, but he gave them the loaves of bread. With the lions distracted the Prince slipped into the courtyard. When he entered the castle, he found himself in a great hall. It was beautifully painted with frescos on the walls and ceilings. He spent much time enchanted by the beautiful paintings, looking at every detail and brush stroke. There were many young noblemen there enchanted by some unknown force. They were as if frozen in place, like statues. He noticed beautiful rings on the fingers of the frozen noblemen and a sword and a loaf of bread. Coming to from his trance of awe, he took the rings, bread, and sword. He felt that he might need them on his quest. He now moved into the next room where he met a beautiful Princess. He was surprised to hear her speak. She said, "You are the only one who has gotten this far! You are the only one who can save me! Please save me! You must!" "Who

are you and how can I save you? I am here for the water of life," said
the Prince. She then told him that she was the princess of the castle
and he could save her by promising to marry her within a year. If
he would promise, then her whole castle would be free of the evil
enchantment and her whole Kingdom would be his. He agreed that
he would marry her with the condition that he had to get the water
of life to his father first. The Princess told the Prince that the water
of life flowed from the fountain in the courtyard and that a glass
was there awaiting him. Upon hearing this he hurriedly promised
to marry her within the year and dashed off. However, when he
entered the third room there was a clean, soft, freshly made bed. It
looked so inviting after his long, hard journey that he lay down and
fell asleep. He sank deep, deep into a peaceful and blissful state of
the inner life. When he finally awakened himself, it was only fifteen
minutes until twelve! He swooped up his treasures and ran for the
courtyard where he scooped up the glass of the water of life and
sprang through the closing iron gate just in time! The gate closed so
fast that it scraped some skin from his heel, but he was all right. His
horse was waiting there for him, and together they rode off with the
Prince intending to thank the dwarf once again.

As the Prince approached the dwarf, he received a warm
welcome. "I see you are safe and have gained a sword and a loaf of
bread. Do you know the importance of those two things?" asked the
dwarf. "No, I have no idea. I just brought them with me on intuition," said the Prince. The dwarf, who seemingly knew all, said,
"With the sword you can help countries at war to obtain peace. With
the loaf of broad, you can help starving kingdoms to regain wealth
and prosperity. You can enable every single person to have enough
to eat. Both the bread and the sword will always return to you, and
you will never have to suffer deprivation."

The Prince was very happy at hearing this news, but was
worried about his two brothers. He asked the dwarf if he knew of
their fate. The dwarf told the Prince of his two brothers' behavior
and their whereabouts. He also warned the Prince, "You must be
very aware and carefully alert about your brothers because they
have bad hearts. Are you sure you still want to take them back home
with you?" The Prince said he did indeed need to take his brothers
home with him but that he would watch them carefully. The dwarf

then released the two evil Princes. When the three brothers were reunited, the youngest recounted for them his whole adventure with the enchanted castle, the water of life, and his promise to marry the princess. The two older brothers became very jealous of the younger one and felt even more insecure. They felt that he would surely inherit the kingdom and they would get nothing.

While journeying home the three brothers crossed three kingdoms that were at war and in the midst of famine. The youngest Prince went to the rulers of these kingdoms respectively and presented them with the sword and the loaf of bread. All three became prosperous and peaceful. The rulers of these kingdoms were very happy with what the prince had done. They each said they would present the prince with a gift after giving much thought as to what the best gift would be. The Prince said he needed no gift; he was pleased to see people happy and healthy.

After journeying through the three kingdoms, the three brothers had to travel by ship across an ocean. On board ship, the two older brothers whispered between themselves and plotted against the younger brother. One wanted to kill him and take the water of life. The other wanted to take the water and frame the younger brother. They vowed to carry out one of these plans, whichever happened to be easier. The younger brother was so innocent that he never suspected his brothers or suspected any danger. He completely forgot the warning of the dwarf. Being very weary, he fell fast asleep. His two brothers took the water of life from his glass and replaced it with plain sea water. The younger Prince never noticed the change in the water and so took it directly to his father upon arriving home. The King was skeptical and hesitated to drink the water. However, he did take one little sip from the glass. The King became violently ill almost immediately and the two older brothers began accusing the younger one of attempting to kill the King. They said he desired to become King and so had given their father sea water to kill him. They said that they had gotten the real water of life and being so ill, the poor old King believed the two evil brothers. He did not trust them completely and did not want to drink the water of life they presented to him. Feeling that he had little to lose at this point, the King finally did drink the water. Immediately his health began to improve and it got better and better. Eventually, the

King regained his strength and his health. He felt better than he ever had in his life. He was totally cured of any illness.

The older brothers mocked the younger one's stupidity and told him with great mirth their plot and deeds. They felt quite secure in their positions with their father. They threatened to kill the younger Prince if he so much as uttered a word to anyone. The King decided that he must punish his youngest, evil son who had tried so mercilessly to kill him. He decreed that the youngest Prince should be killed. His advisors said that the Prince should die by the arrow of the hunter because that was his favorite pastime. The hunter was to take him to the forest and kill him while on a hunting trip. But the hunter had no heart for his task. He had no enjoyment in his hunting that day; he felt very sad. He did not have it in his heart to take the Prince's life. The Prince noticed the demeanor of the hunter and asked what was the matter with him. The hunter felt that he must tell the prince the whole truth. Upon hearing the story the Prince said, "Okay, let me live. Return home and inform my father that you have done your job. I will dwell in the forest and bother no one." The faithful hunter took the Prince's words and returned home to the King. The Prince went deep, deep into the forest and stayed there alone meditating until he recalled his promise to the Princess. He began to make his way to the enchanted castle and his bride.

Meanwhile, the two evil princes also remembered their younger brother's promise to the Princess and believed him to be dead. Realizing that the year was almost up, they each planned to fool the Princess and marry her themselves. The Princess was at the same time preparing for the wedding. She ordered a golden road laid from the castle's gate to the main road to welcome her Prince. She then instructed the gatekeepers to be wary of evil strangers who might pose as her intended. She said, "If anyone rides either to the right side or to the left side of the road, he is an impostor. Do not let him in! The one rider coming up the middle of the road is my fiancé." The oldest brother arrived first and, believing in traditional manners, he rode on the right side of the road. When he arrived at the gate, he was exposed as an impostor and forced to leave the kingdom forever. Shortly after, the middle brother came up to the golden road. He felt himself to be a clever fellow and decided to ride on the left side of the road to show his ingenuity and cleverness. The gatekeepers told him they knew him to be an impostor and sent him on his way.

In the meantime, the King received a gift meant for his youngest son. It was from all three Kings of the Kingdoms that the boy had saved. It was a royally appointed wagon filled with precious stones and gems. The King was told of his son's wonderful deeds for the three kingdoms. Upon hearing these tales, the King felt he had perhaps been misled and had misjudged his youngest son. The King's guilt feelings led to anger against his two oldest sons. So he called them to him and demanded the truth about the water of life. Out of fear for their lives and feeling secure that their younger brother was dead, the two evil brothers told their father the truth. The King was miserable thinking that he had ordered the execution of his only son worthy of ruling the Kingdom. Seeing the King in this state of mourning, the hunter felt that he must tell the King that he did not kill the young Prince. He did this without fear for his own life because he loved the young Prince so much and wanted him to have his rightful throne. When listening to the hunter's confession, the stone fell from the King's heart. The King sent messengers throughout the Kingdom looking for his son. He wanted him to come home again. He sent out an apology for what he had done out of ignorance and anger.

The Prince was in the process of hurrying to marry the Princess. He rode down the middle of the golden road with no thought of any kind. Upon seeing the Prince's lack of hesitation and his middle path, the gatekeepers opened the gate to the Prince and bowed to him. The Princess came running out to greet the Prince with all her heart. There was a marvelous celebration and great rejoicing. When word came that the Prince's father had apologized and knew the truth, the newly married couple decided to visit the old King. The younger Prince had intended to ask the King not to punish his two brothers, but to try to teach them right. However, when the Prince arrived, his two brothers had already gone to sea. They were never heard from again. The Prince and Princess lived in a state of bliss and in total freedom throughout their lives.

From this tale we learn that the remedy was sought initially only within traditional medicine. The characters did not believe they could find a cure at all and became despondent. This was a limitation of their belief system. They were not inclined to try or even think of anything new. This is typical of our society as well. We respond to our illness by seeking the remedies approved by the establishment and society at large. The sick King in the story found it very difficult to swallow even one tiny sip of the water of life even though it was the only thing that could save him. The old self (the heavily conditioned mind) does not easily trust the new or unfamiliar. The new threatens the old conditioning that the old self is based on. Self-preservation of ego takes hold and we invest all our energies in holding onto the familiar. The old self is utterly terrified of the destruction of itself and all that it has built. From the Buddhist point of view, we say that ignorance and clinging tie the self to its patterns of conditioning for the sole purpose of submerging itself in the pleasure/pain principle until enlightened wisdom awakens it. Otherwise, the old self will carry on living under influences like fear and attachment to the familiar. It will be willing to die rather than embrace the new fully.

Looking more closely into our human situation, we find that in order for us to get well, two major factors are essential. One is the recognition on our part that we are ill; the other is the willingness on our part to get well. Without these two factors there can be no getting well. Those of us who are ill and are unwilling to be cured totally will remain ill. Ego feels real when it perpetuates the conditions of illness or an unhealthy state of being. Those of us who cling to negativity find it strange or unreal to feel good. It is more comfortable to go on sleeping with the familiar. Waking up to the truth, particularly the whole truth, is frightening and painful. The revelation of truth regarding the matter concerned (in this case ill health) will tell us all the information we need about the causes and conditions giving rise to our illness or unhealthy state of existence. We find out that certain parts of the physical body or certain organs do not function correctly because of the food we eat and the way we eat it. This includes certain drinks and other chemicals taken into our bodies. Furthermore, our life-styles and jobs or the way we live our lives might not be conducive to health and wellness. But, instead of changing, we create rushing pressures and dissociation of mind and intellect, body and heart. Physical exercises for fitness, health, relaxation, free-flowing energies, and vitality are essential for staying healthy and enjoying the wellness of living. Meditation, self-work, and spiritual growth become inevitable factors for relieving illness and promoting health on all levels such as physical, mental, emotional, psychological, and spiritual. We must look into many different things concerning life and the state of our health. We can break free of sickness and ill health. We might feel that it is too much, too burdensome, or too painful to undergo treating and training ourselves in accordance with the way of wellness. For these reasons, most of us prefer to just deal with the symptoms of our sickness without bothering to go to the roots. As a result more people get sick; this is actually the reason for decay and death in our human society. Unless we see this soon and put our energies together to integrate our way of living with the way of wellness, we will meet with the disaster of all human health.

Decay and Death: Seeds of Renewal

As far as insightful wisdom can tell us, decay and death are not as bad as we generally think they are, but in fact, they become the conditions of growth and renewal. Decay and death point to the deterioration and destruction of the old, paving the path for the new to emerge. As in the story, the sick, old king did not really want to get cured of his illness. He would rather die in place of risking his sons in search for the new, unknown remedy, which no one had ever heard of before. His linear thought kept him in the darkness of decay and death on one hand, while on the other hand, such a way of thinking challenged his intuitive thought, the new element in his consciousness represented by the old gentleman who brought in the unexpected news of one more remedy, never thought of before. Such a remedy is, of course, hard to find! Nevertheless, we encounter the growth and renewal of our consciousness in this fashion. It is natural for us as humans to respond to the situation of decay and death by looking into how these two factors threaten our survival. By doing this, we find the way to let go of the old and take up the new. That was the reason the sick king finally gave his consent to his son's request for setting off to fetch the water of life, after having had a great struggle with his linear thinking for a long time. In that process of seeking the unknown, we see that some parts of the old self personified by the king's two elder sons still cling to their old-fashioned way of doing things for a specific reason, that is, to get love and the throne in return for their accomplishment of finding the new remedy. But, of course, that did not work out because the old was not quite ready to let go of the resistance to change or open up to the information coming from the still voice within. For this reason, the two elder brothers put down the dwarf, mocked him, and rode away without even caring to answer his simple question. This is a typical behavior pattern of the old self who makes judgements based on considering appearance without looking into that which is under the skin. So, the essence is left out; and the still voice is considered irrational and not worth listening to. Unlike his two false brothers, the youngest prince, who was innocent in heart, represents the ever-new element in our consciousness (which is unconscious to us most of the time). When encountering the dwarf in the middle of the road, he stopped his horse, got off, and had a dialogue with him. This is the journey with an open heart and a pure, innocent mind, so that all the information needed for crossing the border of the known and for unlocking the gate to the unknown is given. As shown in the tale, the dwarf had provided the youngest prince with all the things he needed to enter the enchanted castle to get the water of life. Hence, the decay of the sick, old king paved the way for the emergence of the ever-youthful prince who made a successful trip to the courtyard of an enchanted castle where the water of life was. Also, it was he who did all the integration work, bringing back home with him his two older brothers, after having completed his forward journey. He was bringing together the old and the new. The old selves were still dangerous. Remember how the dwarf had warned him about his two false brothers who had little black hearts. The prince was prepared to keep his watchful eyes on them, at the same time embracing them with his warm arms and loving heart. In that journey back home he had to pay some prices, but he finally succeeded in integrating all parts into wholeness. Thus, our growth, development, evolution, renewal, transformation, and integration processes go on until we reach the ultimate state of being, Supreme Consciousness.

The Way of Wellness

Now, let us look into the four main categories that form the way of wellness. They are: *balanced diet, healthy life-style, extended family and philosophy of life,* and *meditation and bodywork.* As we all obviously know, food is an essential requirement for our existence; without it our physical bodies would be unable to continue functioning. More than this, however, the food we ingest can either contribute to balance and good health, or it can be a poison contributing to imbalance, disease, and emotional instability. The right kind of food, a proper diet, can serve as nourishment for the growth and development of a healthy body/clear mind and as curative fuel for healing and re-establishing the dynamic balance in life.

Balanced Diet

Having arrived at this point, the question arises as to what we mean by a balanced diet. What practical, concrete steps can we take in this direction? Some of us are quite familiar with the Oriental principle of yin and yang (or the "Unique Principle" as the founder of the macrobiotic diet, George Ohsawa, called it). This principle pertains to all aspects of existence such as plants, animals, humans, and non-human things such as rocks. Yin is the name given to receptive energy and yang is the name given to creative/assertive energy. Yin is the in-flowing force while yang is the out-flowing force. The balance of these two energy systems brings about harmony and the middle path of life so that there are no swings, either very high or very low, extremely right or extremely left. There can be for us, in this balanced state, a *dynamic balanced living* in the intrinsically unique and naturally flowing life force. In consuming food, it is absolutely important for us to have both essential elements, yin and yang, in the proper proportions. In all cases we must avoid taking into our bodies either the extreme yin food or the extreme yang food because these two extremes cannot balance each other out. We would cause a wide swing from one extreme polarity to the other, while rushing past the middle space. Our rhythm of natural contraction and expansion in our psychophysical systems becomes disturbed, and we lose our inner harmony. Then these "out-of-whack" energies bounce around spastically until they explode into damaged health at any or all levels. This is the reason Gotama, the Buddha, made it clear in his first sermon to the five ascetics that any extreme practice or practices must be absolutely avoided.

In food, yin exists in vegetables that grow vertically on or above the ground; yang vegetables grow downward as roots penetrating into the earth. Whole grains such as brown rice and cereal grains are balanced in yin and yang. Certain beans like *aduki* and bean products such as *tempeh*, miso, tamari/shoyu, seasalt, and all kinds of meat, fish, and seafood are yang foods. Cooking oils, tomatoes, and potatoes are yin. In order to create balance the recommendations are to eat daily in the following proportions (refer to chart also): 50–60 percent grains, 20–40 percent land vegetables, 5–10 percent beans/bean products and sea vegetables (seaweeds of various kinds), 5 percent fish/seafood, and 5 percent miso soup. Fruits like apple, cherry, apricot, plum, strawberry, and pear may be eaten occasionally, especially in summer, the yang season. Dairy products such as milk, cream, cheese, and butter, as well as sugar, drugs, caffeine, and stimulants of all kinds are to be avoided. Pure wine or beer may be taken in small quantity on occasion. If we eat macrobiotically, we will remain in good health and feel in harmony with nature and balanced in the atmosphere of life.

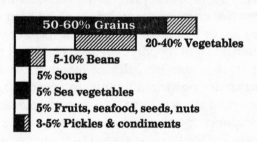

The way in which our food is prepared, the emotion it is permeated with, and our attitude during consumption are as important as what we eat. We need to consume with appreciation and *chew* the food really well until it becomes liquid in our mouths. Likewise, we must prepare the food with love in our hearts and do it consciously. Listen to your body while eating to see if the food is agreeable and contributing to well-being. We have had our eating habits since childhood and will not be able to change them instantly. But, with perseverance and consistency we can make this change. We must no longer see eating as a form of entertainment, but rather as a form of Awareness Meditation. Further information on the macrobiotic diet can be found in texts and cookbooks in many bookstores and East/West centers around the world.

Healthy Life-style

For us to achieve wellness and a lively, harmonious life, we must live a life-style that is healthy and in harmony with the way of wellness. We cannot just pray for our health and well-being while living destructively and without clarity of consciousness. For example, some people are always on the *go*, living their lives under influences of the *pusher* inside themselves, who has all the agendas for them to fill the days, the weeks, the months, and perhaps the year as well. These people always feel that they have lots and lots to do and that there is no time for playing and taking pleasure in life. They are, in fact, *workaholic* and frequently neglect their inner selves to the point of collapse. Another extreme is a *new age* personality, who doesn't care much about anything in this world. They are just waiting for the universe to unfold. These people are not dynamically balanced because of a heavy identification with just one energy system of the new age sub-personality, psychologically speaking. But living in a holistic consciousness with impeccable awareness in every moment is the key for opening the doors to *creative wellness* at all levels. We must live a life of integration and non-injury using *awareness, intelligence, and wisdom*. We must live the movement of unity, the union of opposites within all walks of life. We must celebrate the Oneness of World Community in which there is no division/separation to be found.

Extended Family and Philosophy of Life

The extended family life-style embraces all of us who are willing to develop our inner selves and our material resources to share. Such an extended family provides us with space for creative living and balanced focus on the inner and the outer. This can have an abundantly positive effect on each of us individually and on the universal family as a whole. We must all create an atmosphere for practicing cooperation and unity in daily living. The philosophy of life of such an extended family can be based on insightful knowledge, clear seeing arising from within, and awareness of the phenomenal and practical world. A complete understanding of the pleasure/ pain principle together with knowledge of the causes and conditions giving rise to pain and suffering, pleasure and joy will be the basis of such a family. We need to realize that pleasure/pain and sorrow/joy are mere transient life experiences and can come to an end in terms of our clinging to them because they are not permanent and can be transformed in the course of evolution as we go on developing and enlarging our awareness. For that matter, we are able to make a choice if we wish, either to transcend them or live with them in a loving and liberated relationship in which clear, direct communication is applied. Knowing this clearly and thoroughly, we can live our lives with total freedom, with no dependencies or attachments whatsoever.

Meditation and Bodywork

By meditation I mean the constant application of mindful awareness of whatever arises at the moment. This is a way of providing hospitality for meditative energy, inner power, and non-verbal, non-judgmental awareness to work through our body/mind processes. With meditation we learn to be focused, attentively and alively awake and able to be constantly observing without judging or interfering. At the same time, we can extend and expand into contact with our complexes or unconscious selves as well as with different energy fields and levels of consciousness. In the meditating process, transcendence of conditioning patterns and movement toward high energy centers and full beingness take place simultaneously. For this reason, meditation is the means whereby we dig into ourselves, separating out various energy patterns, deconditioning and liberating our consciousness and our psychological/bodily processes so that we can open our hearts and awaken to the whole of life, seeing things as they truly are. Through the practice of Insight meditation (Vipassana) it is possible for such changes and transformations to take place.

As for bodywork, I mean exercises and movement that lead to the increase of body awareness, unlocking repressed and blocked energies, clearing and cleaning energy channels, and increasingly receiving creative energy both from inside and outside. In this way, the body/mind processes can be completely liberated in their natural unfolding. This is total wellness.

These four categories of the transcendental philosophy of life can be applied to the solution of any problem or conflict faced by an individual, group, community, or society. This is the process: First, identify the problem. Second, discover the cause. Third, see precisely where it will end. Fourth, find the effective means to bring it to an end. This is the middle path by which the dynamic balance of living is found.

CHAPTER FOUR

Love and Unity

Love: The Essential Link to Unity Consciousness

WE EMERGE FROM OUR ONENESS, our intrinsic, real nature with its luminosity, aliveness, unification, connectedness, and universality into a separate, individual self, existing within specific boundaries, limited by time. If we are unable to feel love or a sense of confluence, oneness with other beings, then we will be bound by the sense of isolation tainted by fear of loneliness. As children we are able to survive this cold, harsh "separateness" enforced on us by our society that formulates our ego structure *if* we are able to obtain affection. Whenever we, as children, feel threatened, we run to our "significant others" for warmth and loving feelings. This contact reassures us and enables us to reconnect ourselves from within with the origin of our being. This inner connectedness gives us the sense of safety that we need for our growth and maturation. When I say we "as children," I don't mean just during childhood. We remain children on the emotional level throughout our lifetimes. And we each need affection and reassurance from ourselves primarily. If we have a "significant other" in our adulthood to add more positive fuel to our fire, we are just that much better off! Our growing and maturing need never and should never cease as long as we are in embodied form. With love and safety we are willing to explore ourselves in any new environment in which we find ourselves. A child growing up without sufficient love and affection never learns what it feels like to receive or to expect to receive comfort and aid. These children tend to withdraw from contact with other human beings to varying degrees and are very hesitant to explore "the world." This behavior will continue into adulthood, and these people tend to spend their lives under the shadow of semi-conscious feelings of having been cheated and of being unworthy of even the very most "basic" love. These people may live their lives through the veil of resentment and/or the fear of rejection. Those of us with this problem will always feel insecure or not okay and will, to varying degrees, be unable to develop close, trusting relationships. Lack of love erases the unifying consciousness.

So, we can see clearly that it is the feeling of love that links us, as human beings, with our origin of oneness. Without it, we get lost in the jungles of a separate self; that is maya. The longer and deeper we stay in this realm of separate self, the more frightened and alienated we feel. Consequently, we build walls around ourselves emotionally, thereby imprisoning ourselves and destroying our true freedom. We try to convince ourselves that the world is "out there," unsafe, and full of harm and danger. When there is no love, there is no link; all people and all things are separated and divided. With such a built-in belief system, we inevitably live in confined spaces, boxed in emotionally. But inwardly we are all crying, craving for love and unity. We remain in a constant state of hunger for returning "home" to oneness and unified being. Some of us have conscious awareness of this hunger and some of us don't. However, the silent, still voice is always there, waiting for all of us to hear it. But we must listen! Many, many voices of communication pass by our awareness without our ever noticing because we lack deep, silent, attentive listening.

Learning to Live with Illusion in Full Recognition of Its True Character: Obstacles That Hinder the Natural Flow of Love

There are observable reasons for our being ignorant of our true nature, oneness of being. One reason is the necessity for human evolution and transformation. We cannot remain children or live in the form of apes or lower species. We must evolve and grow into full humanness through the use of our human faculties. We are fully equipped with six senses, five physical for communication with the external world and one mental sense for getting in touch with the internal world of ideas, thoughts, dreams, fantasies, and visions. Our mind acts as an architect, thinking things out and planning them so that we gain all the experiences we need for growth into a fully developed person.

Ego: The Illusion of a Separate Self

In order to live a life in this world, we need to have a unit of organization (or disorganization) called ego, or the "functioning self." Without this, we cannot carry out worldly functions. We move into a more exciting and complicated world or level of consciousness, with the emergence of ego-consciousness. We separate ourselves from others and come to feel separate, adopting a sense of separate self to the point of being unique and autonomous persons having our own lives and managing our own worlds. This strong sense of individuality draws a clear and definite line between oneself and others so that the need for self-defense and self-protection becomes more and more evident and absolutely necessary. Being busy and fully occupied with this new business of a separate self, we lose sight of our real nature. At first, we feel extraordinarily excited and extremely fascinated by our new existence, which gives us a false sense of freedom. This is because it is so different from our previous state of semi-self-consciousness. Once again we are caught in the realm of self-deception, sinking down ever more deeply into the world of maya. But the pain and suffering experienced through identification with this ego structure will wake us up so that we may move on to higher and freer levels of evolution until we can transcend the ego level completely. From then on we are able to find our way home to be reunited with the Dharma, the Tao, the Unborn, and the Unconditioned where love and wisdom flow together powerfully and eternally. As far as I can see, with the full experience of love through the opening of the heart energy center, we naturally rise above and go beyond our ego-self. This means that the compulsive patterns of conditioning are utterly destroyed with no ashes left behind. Instead, there arises and comes into being a total freedom and genuine strength, flowing with love and insightful wisdom as if a vast stream of consciousness were tapped. Yet, this organizing unit of personality can still be used as a tool for functioning in the world. (The ego, as a tool, will need some integration; we will discuss this in a later chapter.)

I want to explore with you, the reader, the obstacles that hinder the natural flow of love and prevent us from achieving a unity of consciousness among all human beings. In addition to the sense of a separate self, the main hindrance to love and unity, we find many others.

Negative Feeling

Negative feeling is one of these obstacles. This category includes anger, hatred, envy, jealousy, and fear.

Anger and Hatred. It is probably obvious to all of us that the degree to which we feel anger with someone or something is the same degree to which we do not feel love and do feel disconnected. At that moment, we are completely cut off from everything except the anger that permeates our bodies and minds. This is a kind of hell for us. We feel even worse when we are unable to express our anger; we then become tortured and burn painfully inside. Unexpressed anger turns into resentment and buries itself as deposits of conditioning in holding points in our bodies. The longer and the deeper it is buried, the more explosive power it accumulates. Because we carry around our resentment and rage without being aware of them, we are their victim. Hatred and irritation destroy the sense of connectedness and increase self-consciousness. It strengthens the belief of "I am me" to the point of acting and reacting merely from the false center of "me" and "mine." Then our perception of reality becomes distorted; we feel anger or hatred toward the person rather than an action or expression by the person. This hate leads to destructiveness toward ourselves, others, or both. *This is the root of evil.* Being under the influence of hateful consciousness, there is no contact with love. As such a person, riddled with hatred, we are argumentative, aggressive, and constantly moving against someone or something believed to be in conflict with us. We may begin to feel more and more isolated and separated, surrounded by enemies. There is no friend except those who help us strengthen our position of hateful consciousness. In this context we can say that the more we assert ourselves, the more separate we become. Yet, self-assertion is often emphasized, without qualification, in psychological circles. We need to understand this concept clearly so that we do not become a victim of ego in this way, too. The true meaning of self-assertion is not to be rude and aggressive but to exercise one's own strength in becoming one's own person. We do this by discerning and stating how we really feel and what we want. This can be done in a gentle and loving way.

There is one more aspect of hatred that I would like to mention here. That is, we need to be specific rather than general in stating what we dislike. This way we can increase our own awareness of ourselves and help the other person pinpoint the exact problem. Using language that is as exact as possible is like providing a much needed mirror for ourselves and for the other person. Words can be used as a medium for revealing patterns of conditioning and allow for a direct experience of what we are talking about. Observing how we talk and what kind of language we employ in a conversation of our ideas and feelings can be a meditative (and/or therapeutic) practice. This observation can be accomplished through the use of Vipassana (Insightful Awareness meditation), which emphasizes *clear seeing*. With this practice we can deal with any feelings, thoughts, patterns, dreams, or fantasies that arise in our minds at the very moment they arise. Through this clear seeing we transcend and move past. We may experience discomfort while the "problem" is still hanging around, but, with our "watchful eye," we can maintain our awareness and remain free of any danger and harm. Safety actually lies in constant attention in which clarity and wakefulness prevail. Staying at this level of consciousness, we can never fall psychologically asleep again and can remain fully in charge of egos and our situations. We can do this while remaining fully in contact, fully "responsible." This is really a very exciting time!

"Hatred can never be overcome by hatred, only by love," said Gotama, the Buddha. A hating feeling cannot be transmuted or dissipated by re-enforcing it or by resisting it. We must allow it to burn out naturally. We neither fuel the fire nor try to smother it. When we happen to feel hate, we merely witness the full experience of it through impeccable, simple awareness. Then love, the energy of warmth, openness, and nurturing, flows in to fill the space left by the disintegrated anger, and love expands throughout our bodies and minds.

Envy and Jealousy. Let us look into two more negative feelings that obstruct the flow of love—envy and jealousy. Envy, here, refers to the desire for some advantage seemingly possessed by someone else and is connected with the destructive force of ill will. Jealousy refers to resentful feelings arising from a lack of self-sufficiency. It is connected with suspicion, rivalry, and unfaithfulness. We have already seen the envious actions taken by the two older brothers in the fairy tale in the last chapter. Out of envy they took the water of life from their younger brother. This is how ill will operates with envy; love cannot be felt. As for jealousy, we can see it operate when our love partner has an affair with someone else. We may feel inadequate or believe our "rival" is more attractive or a better lover. Jealousy is experienced because of the idea of ownership or possessiveness. Underlying jealousy is attachment, not love.

With love in our hearts, personal or universal, we will not experience jealousy, resentment, or fear, for, in love, we always care and understand; we can let go of the unpleasant or what is in conflict with our ideas of how things ought to be. We rise above all kinds of "shouldisms" and judgmental attitudes. Love brings unity, connectedness, and true forgiveness for ourselves and others. This is clean and free living and giving. Each of us can grow and become a whole person transforming and reaching beyond personal self, melting into oneness with and through others. Without a deep, close relationship permeated with love, harmony between yin and yang is more difficult to achieve as is union of the anima and animus within each of us. We provide a mirror for each other so that we can see our own reflections and projections; we help provide each other with opportunities for growth and maturation. In this type of close, personal relationship we have to deal with each other's ever-changing emotions. A life of commitment causes us to work on transcending our ego-identification even more rigorously. Pleasant as well as unpleasant life experiences become virtually unavoidable. Sometimes, after the "honeymoon" is over, the unpleasant and painful experiences exceed the pleasant and loving ones. This is when we are more susceptible to emotional hurt and psychological "all or nothing" decision making than at any other time in life. In many cases, the pain and suffering are more than our coping tools can handle, and we may well close ourselves off from any close relationships in the future. We, at this point, are afraid we couldn't handle

even one more iota of pain. Anything in life, especially love relationships, can send us reeling backwards, causing us to choose to
regress. When this occurs, we encounter in ourselves a great deal of
unexpected, compulsive, and painful emotional conditioning that
we may have thought we had transcended; or our trouble spots may
lead us on to progression and transformation where we can enjoy
the deepening of our capacity for love and the expansion of our
consciousness, both personally and universally, without impediment. The direction of our movement is entirely up to each of us as
individuals.

Fear. The next contributing factor to obstruction is fear: it keeps us
from experiencing love and it keeps us closed as well as contracted.
If we cannot transcend fear, it is impossible for us to give or receive
love; we therefore miss out on giving and receiving nurturing
energy at a very deep level. Love is the softening of the heart and
transforming of the whole personality in which the energy and
consciousness of harmony, unity, oneness, and all-embracingness
flow out infinitely with total freedom, full strength, absolute clear
insight, and continual alertness. We know this from our direct
experience. This is the most powerful and important aspect of life.
How can the limited, separated self embrace or even approach that
which is most frightening to itself? Feeling small and standing in
front of something huge and powerful, a person with a sense of
separate self cannot help but tremble and feel afraid of death. Our
deepest fear is of love, and this manifests itself on many different
levels and in nearly every moment. There are many different types
of fear that we run into in our lives. The predominant fears are of
rejection, emotional hurt, inadequacy, offending others, loss of freedom, deep intimacy, and separation. These fears block us from
experiencing and expressing love; they hold us back from making
contact and letting ourselves be available. They create contraction
in our bodies and minds, paralyzing our actions and sensations.
Some of us become numb physically and mentally. We become
powerless to feel, sense, and think. In relationships this can lead to
dispassionate and energyless lovemaking. Fear of intimacy is very
prevalent among us.

   The fear of rejection. Now, let me elaborate on all of these
categories of fears mentioned above, beginning with the fear of

rejection. As far as I can see, all of us human beings carry around a very deep wound of deprivation and separation, the wound of desertion that began with being separated from our oneness and wholeness of being. As a matter of fact, this is the maturing factor in the evolutionary process of our consciousness. As we feel the urge to reach out to life and its abundance, we develop a sense of an individual self as a separate unit. In so doing, we move farther and farther away from the Dharma, Tao, God, Brahma, or whatever name you want to use. Through becoming a person or developing a separate reality, we get almost everything we want, but we also lose something tremendously precious: Total Freedom and the Wholeness of Being, including the Beyond. We pay a very high price for our development into a separate self. We do not realize what we've lost until we experience the feelings of rejection, abandonment, and desertion. This stirs up the fear of being alone in an isolated world of individuality. Deep down we always need companionship and partnership, which is really the need for love and emotional and spiritual nourishment. Longing for physical union with someone indicates the urge to return home, to rejoin the oneness consciousness. It is said in Taoism that living in the world, we are like a small river returning home. According to the Buddha, with the full realization of a separate self as illusion, we all melt and transform into becoming the Dharma (Dhammabhuta), the Absolute, Unconditioned Truth. The fear of rejection, or not being accepted, exists only on the self-conscious level, for, at the level of the oneness consciousness, everything and everyone is totally accepted as self and completely unified. There is no fear whatsoever. Love and freedom prevail and reign over the whole of life.

Because of the fear of rejection, we run away from closeness and availability. We try to avoid intimacy and do not wish to enter into any sort of committed relationship. Inwardly, we feel like asking for love from someone we feel sexually attracted to, or feel good with, yet we dare not speak up because of the voice of fear whispering in our ears that we may be rejected. "You might run into trouble again. You can't be sure that the person is going to respond to you positively." And so it goes. Our expectations and past experiences are so powerful in preventing us from reaching out for love that we become contracted and miserable. Pain and fear walk hand in hand as we continue living under the influence of the fear of rejection. We hide ourselves behind the mask of isolation and alienation, pretending to be okay. Because of this masquerade, depression sets in, making us feel sad at our loss of reality and angry at ourselves for not feeling we are okay. When worst comes to worst, our repressions burst out of their "holding tanks" and commit a "crime" of some sort. This behavior usually comes as a great surprise to everyone.

At this point, I want to make some suggestions to help those of us who fear rejection. Walk through that kind of fear gently but firmly. That is to say, be willing to accept any form of rejection from anybody. Learn to understand that it is not all of you that is being rejected; it is only a certain part, an action, a behavior, or a projection that is unacceptable. Realizing this, we are able to pay attention to the specific thing that is the target of rejection. With this practice, we transcend the fear, increase self-awareness, and bring the light of clarity into our lives. Then, we can reach out for love and share with many others who are also starving for love. We go for what we want and honor our feelings. Things, then, become simpler and we see fear as nothing special, just a contracting energy that our egos use to resist our creative movement toward love and full beingness. With such clear insight into the true nature of fear, we find our strength and gain courage to take full charge of ourselves, making direct contact with everyone and everything that can be a nurturing source of energy for us. At this point, fear of rejection can have no place in our lives; for we have risen above it and accepted it unconditionally. We have let go of this kind of fear completely.

The fear of getting hurt. Now let us explore the fear of getting hurt, which is similar to the fear of rejection as described above. Feeling hurt can result from feeling rejected as well as from broken promises. In the case of marriage or partnership, hurt feelings can arise when the partner fails to maintain fidelity. Sometimes, people may feel hurt because they are criticized or blamed. There are reasons for feeling hurt, but it is not our task to cite them all here. It will be more beneficial for us to look into how the fear of getting hurt arises. Again, we come back to the same basic answer, the *maintenance* of a separate self. It feels the need for protecting and defending itself. Underlying this situation is the longing for union and communion with the Origin through the feeling of being cared for and nourished by others. Getting hurt is very frightening to the ego and threatening to its plans for immortality. This is the main reason the fear of getting hurt is such a big problem in our human relationships. This fear of hurt is a mental process that is unpleasant and painful to the ego, but the ego must be hurt again and again until it can no longer stand the pain. Then, there is a chance for the ego to let go of the issues that cause it to perceive itself as hurt. When the feeling of hurt strikes, we must stay with it, living every second of it, without turning away from it or fighting against it. We must accept the hurt and all unpleasant feelings and sensations connected to it so that we can turn the situation into a positive and creative event for transformation and for opening our hearts. Then, we can remove all the armorings or bands that cover our hearts. In this way, we can walk softly and flowingly through the fear of getting hurt. It is identification with the ego that creates this feeling of hurt and perpetuates the weapon of fear as a survival tool.

What actually happens is that most of us do not want to experience the hurt, so we jump into anger instead. We complain "you hurt me; you abused me; you robbed me." This is because hurt burns our ego so painfully and at such a very deep level that we try to avoid going into it directly. It is much easier to feel anger; it gives us a sense of strength. Hurt makes us feel weak and pitiful, and we prefer not to show anyone our weaknesses. As a result, we may turn this energy inward and burn quietly, burying the hurt child in our psychic centers. The more we do this, the more the volcanic energy builds in strength. It can explode at any time without warning.

We see more clearly now that the fear of getting hurt is yet another powerful weapon that our egos use to keep us from diving deep down into the bottomless pit of our suffering. Instead, we stay on the surface with anger and complaints, making a lot of noise to keep from experiencing the depth of our hurt. But, without reaching the depths of pain and suffering, without having the full experience of it, there is neither total freedom nor enlightened wisdom. We must have enlightened wisdom for the utter destruction of *dukkha* (pain and suffering, fleeting pleasure, and dependent joy). In this connection, it is worth listening to the Buddha's statement, "The world of the wise is freedom from fear." In order to transmute the fear of getting hurt, we must open to it and allow ourselves to embrace the hurt fully with open arms, without any resistance or avoidance whatsoever. In this way we are in the position to transcend hurt and fear entirely. We also can gain precise insight into the whole structure of hurt and see clearly for ourselves what it means to experience hurt directly and totally. When there is no ego involvement with the experience, there is no trace of fear. Then, the event is just an event, the experience is just an experience, and the hurt becomes merely a feeling or sensation of mental discomfort. It is neither good nor bad, negative or positive; it is just a happening. In the Western expression, we say that the True Self, the Oneness Consciousness, never gets hurt because it doesn't identify with the fragmented parts. It is intrinsically whole. But, because of the very nature of ego, the self is fragmented and believes in a separate reality with identification, ownership, possessiveness, attachment, and dependence. Therefore, it suffers pain. When the ego feels attached and hurt or is driven by fear, it may run, fight, or become indifferent and detached. This process can even go to the extreme of catatonic schizophrenia.

Ego always wants to be the winner and in control although ultimately there is nothing to win and nothing to control. Without realizing this truth, ego just keeps right on deluding and deceiving itself. It is like the story of several blind people each touching different parts of the elephant and believing, as well as claiming, that they each know the "real" elephant, the "truth." They try to convince themselves and everyone else that each part is the whole without ever having seen the entire elephant.

The fear of inadequacy and self-worthlessness. Next, for those of us who try too hard to appear to be good and to please others, the fears of inadequacy and self-worthlessness arise. The "world" becomes the judge. If the world criticizes or lays blame, we fall apart and become, to varying degrees, non-functional. We may even feel that it is not worth living if we cannot be good and respectable in the world's eyes. We become so obsessed with this that we deny and learn to ignore our own feelings, becoming confused about our thoughts and feelings. For this reason we end up accumulating much repressed material and much frustration. We become very perfectionistic, demanding more and more of ourselves and everyone else. Underlying this compulsive psychological pattern of conditioning is the fear of being unworthy and inadequate. So, we think to ourselves, "I am not good enough. I am worthless." We feel, "Poor me!" If we look thoroughly into this way of thinking we see how ridiculous it is to berate ourselves over not gaining approval from the world. Meditate on these questions until you find the true answers through clear insight: What is the reason that the world rules my life? For what reason do I seek the world's approval? What purpose am I serving in doing this? How else can I fulfill this purpose in a more meditative, clear, and insightful way? Once we let go of our compulsive patterns of conditioning through the use of Vipassana, there is no fear of unworthiness. We can keep our left foot in the world while letting our right foot reach beyond. As the Sufi saying goes, "Be in the world, but not of it!"

The fear of hurting another's feelings. Before going into the deepest fear, that of separation, let us examine two other fears—hurting someone's feelings and being "swallowed up" by the world. When doing something we feel to be wrong, we say, "I don't want to hurt my wife's/husband's/partner's feelings so I will conceal my activities and keep secrets." This is not really our motivation. In actual fact, we are afraid of our own feelings and the other person's reactions. We do not want to face ourselves or them. The fear of hurting another person is a form of self-deception. We use this to justify our actions and hide from the real fear that is threatening us. Being real, open, and honest with ourselves and others requires a great deal of courage, the opposite of fear. "Good" intentions with false actions, as just mentioned, create more harm than good! When our dishonesty is found out by the other person, the hurt is only compounded. There is the hurt from our disapproved-of behavior heaped upon by the pain of our dishonesty and concealment. We have destroyed the basic trust the other person has so generously given us, and we may never be able to regain it. Yes, telling someone the whole truth when they are not ready to hear it can be harmful and unbearably painful, but if we are totally open, honest, sincere, caring, and loving in telling the truth, it will be more easily accepted and less hurtful. By behaving in this way, our courage will increase while our fear will decrease.

The fear of being "swallowed up" by the world. As for the fear of being "swallowed up," it is a matter of stinginess and discomfort in giving. Those of us with this character trait withhold attention as well as love. Showing love and letting it flow out to others implies an invitation to come into contact and to interact. When we are of this frame of mind, we fear giving and being available; we imagine and project that a person and/or the world is going to devour us. To avoid feeling afraid, we hide behind our "castle walls"; we withdraw and escape from people. Basically, those of us with this kind of problem do not want any kind of confrontation because it might force us out of our narrow little world. In such a situation one has to deal with all kinds of reactions: emotional, verbal, and physical. Because of this fear and withdrawal, the energy of love sinks to the bottom of the heart and disappears from the conscious level of existence. Whenever attention, the natural flow of love, is held back and lovingness unexpressed, we find it harder and more difficult to feel, to be in touch with our tender feelings. As a result, we stay aloof and remain distant, appearing detached or indifferent. Perhaps we even become mentally numb and insensitive. Apart from being deprived of love, we pay a very high price in many other ways for our psychological disorders and emotional problems. If we let ourselves go courageously into our fears, then we will have no debt to pay. Instead, love will naturally unfold itself, nurturing the whole of our being as well as radiating out to others, enabling them to be open to receiving it.

The fear of separation. The *greatest* fear that prevents us from loving is the fear of separation. We each have a deep, unhealed wound stemming from when we became separated from our Origin, the Oneness Consciousness. This wound constantly reminds us of our primal, deep, deep pain of separation; it is the constant nightmare in our unconscious mind. We must allow ourselves to love and be loved totally so that we can, through our direct experience, know that love means oneness, union, unity, and a sense of connectedness. But, since the original wound is not completely healed, we always suspect that there will be separation in one form or another. We feel no safety; we project the past unforgettable and unforgivable pain into the future. Anytime we are in love with or feel love for someone, the original chasm of separation vibrates deep down within us. We live in a constant state of *conflict* between love and fear. We are not at all sure of returning home safely. As a result, doubt dominates us, providing more energy for the passion of fear to exercise its power on our tenuous personalities. Thus the vicious circle of being locked within the boundary of the sense of separate self goes on and on. There is no freedom to love and the journey back home is postponed indefinitely. The effective way to heal this wound is not through seeking external union with another, but through the complete harmony and total integration within oneself that is brought about by the attainment of oneness consciousness.

We now have a better understanding of what happens whenever we experience physical and/or emotional separation from the people or the things we love; it can be terribly painful. Emotionally, we always long to be with them. The reason for this is that the blending of our energies on a very intense level reminds us of the oneness of Being, our intrinsic, real nature. For such a union creates a feeling of homecoming, while separation triggers our deep pain. It causes us to feel hurt and other unbearable feelings. For the ignorant, separation, pain, fear, and suffering may be used as an excuse for not entering into love relationships: the wise take hold of the situation and see it as an opportunity for finding a way to consolidate the feeling of connectedness and oneness with all. The wise ones can transcend the unpleasantness and pain of separation, for beyond the self-conscious level there is no feeling of separateness. Loving Oneness prevails.

The Error of Projection

Projection is also an obstacle to love, so let us look into it a bit further. This seems to be a compulsive, unconscious pattern with human beings. If we are not in the process of projecting a "bad" thing, then we project a "good" thing. Projection is a mis-location of an idea or fantasy arising in the mind. It is much more satisfying to pretend that what arises within belongs out there. For example, in a relationship we often project the essence of our yin energy (beauty, softness, purity, vibrancy) or yang energy (strength, handsomeness, powerfulness) onto the woman or man who in turn provides us with a clear mirror for our visual consciousness and perception. Instead of knowing that we are seeing our own projections, we mistake them for reality. When we project we don't look within; we abandon ourselves and concentrate our attention on the person with whom we are madly in love. During the "honeymoon" period, we are able to ignore all the discrepancies between our projections and the other person's real ego structure. But, when we can no longer deny these discrepancies, we tend to project in the opposite direction. We see the other person as a witch, a devil, a horrible person we never expected to encounter. Underlying the projection of a "bad" or "negative" experience is a lack of trust in oneself as well as fear of "the past repeating itself." It is true that lack of trust begets fear and fear increases doubt and confusion. So, projection goes on as an infinitely circular game constantly playing upon us until such time as we realize what we are doing to ourselves.

Projection itself is neither good nor bad; it just is. The way we relate to this process of projecting is what counts. We cannot relate to our projections realistically if we do not see them as they are. Attention is always required in every moment and at every point of contact. The moment we see with our inner eye of insightful awareness that this is a projection, we can then accept it and relate to it as we do to something in another person. In this way, there will be no further self-deception, and we can come to know more about the particular projection and the process of projection. We learn to live with illusion in full recognition of its true character. We can sing songs, write poetry, and make jokes about our projections. Our creative energy is mobilized and the Universal Life Force flows through us more naturally and more powerfully than ever before. With clear seeing, we drop our obstruction and interference. We then become free to be more playful with ourselves, our lives, and the infinite universe. The more playful we are, the more we can tune in to the rhythms and movements of life and of the universe in infinite, eternal flow; the more we *become* the infinite universal flow ourselves.

CHAPTER FIVE

Perception and Ideation

Perception and Preconception Versus Pure Awareness and
Immediate Insight

THE CONCEPT OF PERCEPTION, according to Western philosophy, is confined to the recognition of external objects experienced through our five physical senses—eyes, ears, nose, taste, and touch. It doesn't cover the inner sense of perceiving ideas, thoughts, and fantasies, let alone the world of our inner truth and emptiness (*sunyata*). As a matter of fact, *sunyata* in its full sense of a completely fertile Void is inconceivable; it lies beyond the thinking mind. *Sunyata* can be realized only by the wise through direct contact at the level of ultimate consciousness. This will be dealt with in some detail later.

Let us now return to this matter of perception, which plays quite an active part in our lives, particularly in the world of the senses. Generally speaking, we adhere to our perceptions much of the time, believing and assuming them to be true. Our sense perceptions thereby dictate the course of our actions and reactions in everyday living—how we relate to our environment and to the people around us. We act and react according to how we perceive at any particular moment and according to our preconceived ideas, which are involved with our perceptual memories. It is really a very rare moment in life that we are able to allow immediate insight and spontaneity to guide our actions. Worse still, the majority of us don't even see and cannot even imagine that there is such a thing as an insightful and spontaneous action. This is because most of us are so familiar with existing in the world of conditionality that our minds forget and become heavily conditioned by the law of cause and effect. This is the logical, reasoning, and rationalizing mind. To think and know things in the other way is considered naive and paradoxical and therefore unacceptable.

It may sound ridiculous to the purely intellectually intoxicated and thickly insensitive individual to hear the Buddha's statement that perception is like a mirage. What the perceiver convinces himself/herself to be real actually does not exist. This is similar to a dreamer believing everything to be real during the dreaming process, but after waking up and realizing that it was just a dream, she/he understands the world and self differently. So, it is very true to say that our lives in the world of perception are not so different from the dreamer in the dreaming state. Sometimes we have fun, but at other times things are unpleasant, painful, and frightening, which puts us into the world of fear, anxiety, worry, misery, and sorrow. As soon as these things, whether pleasurable or painful, have gone, we see the world in another perspective and conduct our lives accordingly.

When we free ourselves of all illusion and possess pure, clean awareness, we transcend the world of pain and its counterpart, pleasure. When we do this, we will be in an absolutely different state of being and our lives will have a different quality. We will transcend all the qualities we now know. Living through our perceptions is nothing more than a long dream for all unenlightened beings, while non-perception or perceiving without perception is the functional consciousness of the enlightened ones.

The Complex Kaleidoscope of Perception

Perception as Influenced by Feelings and States of Mind: A Reflection of Our Inner Conditions

In ordinary consciousness, with its psychological sleep, human perception is influenced and directed by feelings and states of mind. We perceive according to how we feel and according to our state of mind at any particular time. Feeling negatively about someone, we perceive him/her as an unpleasant, disturbing, and disgusting object. Whatever he/she does, or says, is annoying and seemingly ridiculous. Nothing is quite right about him/her. There is always something wrong somewhere within that creature. On the contrary, when feeling good and loving toward that same individual, our perception tells us a different story: now, this person is positive and pleasing to our eyes and ears and comfortably nurturing through physical contact. At this point, I would like us to look into these questions: Is the thing out there really good or bad? Or, is it the projection of the inner onto the outer? Or, is the response to the manifestation clouding and distorting our perception? What is the truth? And how can we find it? Can we rely on our perception entirely? Or, does it have the quality of a mirror or colored spectacles?

The perceiver, unaware ego, always perceives according to conditioning. Whatever we get from our perception is just a reflection of our inner conditions, such as knowledge, experience, skill, imagination, fantasy, and passion. The reason for this is that the perceiver is like a computer, working according to the dictates of the input. We have concepts and notions of things, people and the universe; whatever we perceive is related to, or associated with, a concept, notion, or idea in our heads. As a result, our recognition, which is the act of perception, of anything perceived is based on the dynamic process of similarity; this enables us to give it a name or put it into a form or structure. For example, when looking up at the sky and seeing certain shapes of clouds similar to a dog, an elephant, or a snake, we, the perceiver, already have a concept of such an animal in our heads so we quickly name it accordingly. This is a typical way of perceiving.

Perception as Time: Experiencing the Present in the Context of the Past

We notice that as children we learn to increase our word usage through the relations between what is being perceived and the notion or concept previously learned. The ability to relate the present to the past is an act of perception and is time. It is for this reason that perception is closely associated with time. In this connection, we may state that the information obtained through perception *could be* merely a knowledge of the past, which might be entirely different from the thing that is perceived. This means that the reality of the perceived is distorted without the perceiver's knowing it. Instead, we think and believe that we see the truth and get accurate information about the perceived. This is like a person walking in the moonlight and seeing a piece of rope lying on the ground and mistaking it for a snake. Or, like an ordinary individual looking at the moon, perceiving the shape of a rabbit on the surface, and taking it as reality that there is actually a rabbit hanging from the moon.

The Doors or Channels of Perception as Stated from the Buddhist Point of View

Let us learn more about the doors or channels of perception. According to the Buddha, our perception comes through six doors; the eyes, ears, nose, tongue, touch, and mind. These six sense modalities provide the channels for the arising and fading away of our perceptions. Described in more detail they consist of: (1) "eye perception": visible form, color, and light, as perceived through the eye channel; (2) "ear perception": sound (vibration) as perceived through the ear channel; (3) "nose perception": odor or smell as perceived through the nose channel; (4) "tongue perception": flavor or taste as perceived through the tongue channel; (5) "body perception": tangible objects as perceived through the kinesthetic senses of the body channel (touch); and (6) "mind perception": thoughts, ideas, dreams, fantasies, and all mental objects as perceived through the mind channel.

So, we see that the world of perception is quite a comprehensive one in which we encounter and know many different fields of experience including the world of phenomena, the world of maya or illusion, and the world of the Void. Realities as well as mistaken realities, at different levels of consciousness, continually present themselves to our "tools" of perception at many points of contact in both the waking and the dreaming states. It is really exciting, and at the same time very essential, to look into this matter of perception as thoroughly as possible. The direction of our lives, including our course of action, our ways of relating, and our ways of thinking, is more or less dominated by our perception. If we carry distorted perception, without knowing it, into our everyday life, we live in a world in which everything is upside down and all realities are distorted. On the contrary, if our perception is totally clear, clean, and precise and therefore impeccable, we certainly see things as they are and as they appear to be. Then, there is no distortion. Reality is viewed as reality, and unreality is viewed as unreality!

The Monkey Parable: An Illustration of the Effects of Distorted Perception. To illustrate this point, I would like to tell you the Monkey Parable.

A Chinese, Buddhist Master with his three disciples, Monkey, Sandy, and Piggy, were on a pilgrimage to India to find the Buddhist Scriptures. The Master was practicing a rather extreme, concentrative form of meditation in which he adhered strictly to the precepts and controlled his senses to such a degree that he turned off his insightful awareness of what was going on around him. Monkey was the only member of the group who maintained his awareness. He even felt the presence of the demons or evil spirits.

At one point in their journey everyone was very hungry, especially Piggy, who wanted to eat so badly that the Monkey disciple had to leave his fellow monks in search of food. Because he was aware that they were approaching the territory of the White Bones Demon who loved to eat all flesh, he drew a ring on the ground and asked his Master and the other two disciples to stay inside the ring. This way Monkey could leave and the Demon would not be able to get near the others. He emphasized that they must stay within the ring all the time, no matter what happened, until his return, as that was the only way for them to be safe during his absence. He stressed this very strongly. Then the Monkey disciple went off to look for food.

Shortly after Monkey had left, the White Bones Demon disguised itself in the human form of a young lady carrying a basket and walked toward the place where the Chinese Master and his two disciples were waiting. At first glance of her Piggy became very happy and excited! He believed totally that the young lady was bringing something for him and his party to eat. This is quite typical in the oriental culture; when monks see a layperson coming toward them with something in their hands, they immediately think they are bringing an offering. That was how it seemed to Piggy, the hungry one. In response to his perception and hunger, Piggy forgot all about Monkey's advice and ran out of the ring to help the seemingly devoted young Buddhist with the basket. The disguised Demon was a good actress and knew exactly how to entice Piggy, the Master, and Sandy. When she arrived at the ring she knew that it was a circle of power that could harm her if she entered it. As a result, she stayed outside and invited the monks out of the ring to join her. Due to their ignorance and completely distorted perception, they responded to her beckoning. At that given moment Monkey was clearly aware and knew that the White Bones Demon was attacking his Master and his friends. Using all his power he returned very quickly. Without a moment's hesitation he killed the disguised Demon with his magic wand. She then turned into dark clouds covering the sky and threatened them with lightning and thunder!

The Master was very upset that his Monkey disciple had violated the Buddhist precept of not killing. He became furious with Monkey and scolded him for his wrong action. Although Monkey was trying to explain to him that he didn't kill a human being but the powerful White Bones Demon disguised as a young woman, the Master was not convinced and spoke no further, keeping his anger inside himself. Thereafter, they carried on their journey with the Monkey disciple going ahead.

Each time Monkey was out of sight, something happened to the others. This time they encountered an old woman, who asked the monks if they had seen her daughter anywhere. Once again Monkey knew, through his expanded and ever-flowing awareness, of the danger approaching his party. He came back to them with all his might and found the same demon in the disguise of an old lady. He knocked her down, suddenly, with his powerful wand. This time the Master completely lost control. He dismissed Monkey on the grounds (of his belief) that his disciple had killed two human beings during the journey. (This is absolutely against the Buddhist discipline and code of conduct.) Monkey did not argue with his Master, apart from informing him of the truth that he only destroyed the Demon who was attempting to delude them and eat their flesh. He then left the group as his Master wished him to do.

The group traveled on in this way, without Monkey, until they were confronted with the most dangerous situation yet. In the end, they wished Monkey were there to help them, and in that instant he came and utterly destroyed the White Bones Demon, leaving no ashes behind. He saved his Master, himself, and his two other disciple-friends.

There are two main things that we see in this ancient story. The first is the sheer distortion of perception that dictated both Piggy and the Master to act in conformity with their preconceived ideas in regard to their emotion and hunger. Being heavily conditioned by the old, they cannot see the new as it is. Instead they experience it in the context of the old. This is how even factual reality can be distorted by our perception. Secondly, the monkey disciple was the only one that possessed the quality of impeccable awareness and precise perception. He was paying attention to his surroundings and was aware of the danger that would arise from the demonic consciousness during the journey. As a result, he was able to respond to the negative force precisely and with no hesitation, without falling victim to it.

This is also a good example for distinguishing awareness from concentration. Concentration shuts off direct contact with the obvious, or what is happening at the moment, by engaging the practitioner in ideal, preconceived notions and fixed objectives so that there is no room left for the new and the obvious to enter and make contact. Awareness allows us to be fully in touch with the Now, the creative present, so that the constantly aware person can know and see what is actually happening "in front, behind, and all around." For such an individual, there is no mistaking reality for unreality at any moment.

Pure Perception: The Act of Seeing Both Our Reflected Projections and Reality Simultaneously and Recognizing Both for What They Are

Now we have arrived at an important point in our discussion of perception. Most of us will wonder, "Is what I perceive always my own reflection or is it ever real?" When looking into a mirror or into clear, still water, what we see is our own reflection. We hardly notice the mirror itself unless we feel that our picture is not clear; then we become aware of the existence of the mirror. So, usually we just concentrate on what we want to see, our picture, and not on what is actually existing right here in front of us. In the case of the water, we may have a different objective. If we plan to look for something at the bottom of the water, we may see through it to whatever is underneath. But if our reflection is in the way, we cannot see past it. Very few of us can see both our reflection and reality simultaneously. This is because of concentration, which excludes the existence of things other than the fixed object. It is the limitation of the perceiver. With awareness, we see both the inner and the outer, the reflected projection and reality. Awareness constantly flows in and out between the internal and the external. In this way, both the perceiver and the perceived are seen precisely as they truly are: there is no distortion if awareness is present with perception in the moment. Such perception is total and without the interference of the perceiver. In other words, we say it is perceiving without perceiving. In such an act of pure perception there are no concepts, ideas, notions, images, or words. It is really beyond our cultural description because the description is not what is being described. It feels to us as if we are telling a lie, particularly when we feel that words are so inadequate for conveying the whole truth of what is realized through such ultimate perception.

Who, then, knows what is real? The wise see and know what is real and unreal within themselves. They live in a world of freedom from bondage and fear. Their senses are restful, tranquil, clear, and clean without any biases or dust. Restful and tranquil senses here refer to the state of being completely free from any interfering, disturbing, or interrupting influences. It is the state in which our six sense-modalities (through which our perceptions, feelings/sensations, and thoughts appear and disappear momentarily) become very calm, clear, and flowing, with no obstruction. In this state, we become totally alert, receptive, and responsive, and we recognize that which comes into contact with our senses. In addition, when the senses are at rest, they are in complete harmony within themselves and with the infinite universe. They shine forth vibrantly and radiantly.

If we encounter someone we don't know or someone we haven't been in contact with for a long time, our perception may tell us a truer story, provided that there is no projection of anima or animus. We are in a better position to see the real person through such non-contaminated perception. But, as soon as our memories, ideas, or opinions come in to cloud our minds, we perceive a different appearance; we see the old person once again with nothing really new about him/her. This is quite tricky, isn't it? If we have approximately five percent of pure and total perception in our perceptual world, our attitudes and responses to life situations and the world as a whole will be much healthier and more constructive. Such a clean and bias-free perception will not lead us into a jungle of distorted thoughts and views, mistaking the seemingly newly built road in the forest as a way back home, when it really leads to the devil's town. Obviously, a person lost in the jungle would be delighted if a road or path could be found. But, due to excitement and excessive delight, such a lost one would not bother to ponder if the road was real or built by devils. In this connection, we say that Mara, the evil one, the obstructing and deluding force, is always looking for a chance. Mara is similar to the Christian concept of evil, the devil, or Satan. The moment God is absent, Satan is in charge. In other words, Satan is the opposite of God.

The Buddha's Recognition of and Relationship with Mara As the Personification of Illusion/Distorted Perception/All Obstructing Forces

In the Buddha's life story, he often encountered the temptation, persuasion, and contradiction of Mara. He could, however, spot Mara immediately with his perfect awareness and total perception, so that the latter had to vanish without being able to carry out the Mara project and without choice. It was like the vanishing of darkness when light emerges and shines forth.

Once the Buddha was alone in retreat, the thought arose in him: "I am freed from that penance; I am quite freed from that useless penance. Absolutely sure and mindful, I have attained enlightenment." Then Mara became aware of the thought in the Buddha's mind, and he went to him and spoke these stanzas:

You have forsaken the ascetic path
By means of which men purify themselves.
You are not pure, you fancy you are pure.
The path of purity is far from you.

Then the Buddha recognized Mara and he answered him in
these stanzas:

I know these penances to gain the deathless—
Whatever kind they are—to be as vain
As a ship's oars and rudder on dry land.
But it is owing to development
Of virtue, meditation, and understanding
That I have reached enlightenment; and you
Exterminator, have been vanquished now.

Then Mara, the evil one, knew: "The Buddha knows me, the
Sublime one knows me." Sad and disappointed, he vanished at
once.

Another time, when the number of enlightened monks reached
sixty-one, the Buddha wished them to go out and teach the world.
He then addressed them thus: "Monks, I am free from all shackles,
whether human or divine. You are free from all shackles, both
human and divine. Go, now, and wander for the welfare and happiness of the masses, out of compassion for the world, for the
benefit, welfare, and happiness of gods and humans. Teach the law
that is good in the beginning, good in the middle and good in the
end, with the meaning and the letter. Explain a Holy (whole) Life
that is utterly perfect and pure. There are creatures with little dust
on their eyes who will be lost through not hearing the Law. Some
will understand the Law. I shall go to Uruvela, to Senanigama, to
teach the Law."

Then Mara came to the Buddha and they spoke to each other
in stanzas:

You are bound by every shackle,
Whether human or divine,
The bonds that tie you down are strong
And you shall not escape me, Monk.

I am free from all the shackles,
Whether human or divine,
Free from the strongest bonds, and you
Are vanquished now, Exterminator.

The shackle in the air that has
Its hold upon the mind, with that
I hold you bound for evermore,
So you shall not escape me, Monk.

I am without desire for sights,
Sounds, tastes, and smells and things to touch,
However good they seem, and you
Are vanquished now, Exterminator.

Throughout his life, beginning with the time when he started paying attention to himself and the world, the Buddha realized that Mara was right there as a tempter-self, an obstructor-self, and a contradictor-self. With this realization, the Buddha could extend his inner and outer perception by applying the flow of awareness, making distinctions between the real inner voice and the voice of Mara. In this very way, he saved himself from being a victim of Mara. He knew exactly and precisely when his whole being spoke through his heart and when Mara whispered in his ears.

The Danger of Falling Prey to the Appearance of Mara in the Form of Psychic Entities or Spirit Guides

For many of us, particularly those following our inner urgings blindly and dependently, there is a tremendous danger to the process of our consciousness evolution and the conscious evolution of those who depend on us for guidance. This is because Mara, or Satan, always follows us invisibly, looking for a chance to interfere and raise a convincing voice. Consider psychic entities. When we are guided with whole-hearted conviction by certain psychic entities or spirits, including a spirit teacher, our chance to escape from Mara's/Satan's interference is quite narrow indeed.

How can the dependence on a psychic guide block the growth of consciousness? It is similar to taking a psychedelic drug that can give us certain insights and clarity about some things, including a possible direction to pursue. We then build up the compulsive tendency of looking for help from "otherness" to direct the course of our actions, gradually neglecting and ignoring our own capacity to see and be clear through our own inward light and intuitive wisdom. When this intrinsic human resource is not used, it sinks down to the bottom of beingness and becomes dormant so that we lose touch with it. As a result, we are left entirely in the hands of the so-called guides. These come in many different forms such as an inner voice, an angel, certain entities speaking to us and telling us what to do and what not to do, tarot cards, and several other forms available in our society. In this way, we create a kind of hollowness and emptiness in which there is a lack, and we have a need to fulfill our hunger and nurture our lives. In other words, we feel more and more confined and limited in the world of psychic dependence. Sometimes we may even become ill psychically, emotionally, physically, or a combination of these. Such illness indicates a lack of balance in making use of energies and resources. With too much leaning on the psychic center, the creative energy for personal growth stops flowing forward toward our full beingness. When we do this, a dam is built by the psychic energy, blocking the natural flow of evolution and transformation forward. Instead, it becomes a whirlpool, a movement within the same level that will eventually lead to backward transformation (sickness, stagnation, etc.). At any rate, there is no freedom when dependence of any kind develops: our natural unfolding is hindered by leaning and depending on "otherness." The self, an organizing principle for inner growth and outward expansion, becomes dominated by the "otherness" that we invited to sit as a judge within ourselves, even though we gave it the nice, pleasant name of "guide." This word is, of course, more acceptable to our "spiritual" super-ego. Nevertheless, it is an ego domination and involvement.

"On The Invitation of A Brahma": The Buddha's Discourse, Which Illustrates That Once Ego Has Been Transcended, One Can Deal With the Spirit World Without Falling Victim to It. When the ego has been transcended, however, one can deal with the world of spirits without falling victim to it. We can master the spirit world just as the Buddha did when he visited the Brahma world and told this story to his monks:

"Monks, on one occasion when I was living at Ukkattha in the Subhaga Grove at the root of a royal Sala tree, there had arisen in the Brahma Baka a pernicious view (of his own permanence and absoluteness). I became aware in my mind of a thought in the Brahma's mind and I appeared in that world. The Brahma Baka saw me coming, and he said, 'Come, good sir; welcome, good sir; it is long, good sir, since you made an occasion to come here. Now, good sir, this is permanent; this is everlasting; this is eternal; this is totality; this is not subject to passing away; for this neither is born, nor ages, nor dies, nor passes away, nor reappears, and beyond this there is no escape.'

"Then, Mara entered into a member of the Brahma's assembly and he told me, 'Monk, Monk, do not disbelieve him; do not disbelieve him; for this Brahma is the Great Brahma, the Transcendent Being untranscendable, Sure-sighted Wielder of Mastery, Lord Maker and Creator, Most High Providence, Master and Father of those that are and ever can be. Before your time, monk, there were monks and brahmans in the world who condemned water, fire, air, beings, gods; there was Pajapati, Lord of the Race, who condemned Brahma through disgust with Brahma. Now, on the dissolution of the body, when their breath was cut off, they became established in an inferior body. Before your time, monk, there were monks and brahmans in the world who lauded all these through love of them; now on the dissolution of the body, when their breath was cut off, they became established in a superior body. So, monk, I tell you this, be sure, good sir, to do only as Brahma says. Never overstep Brahma's word; for if you do that, monk, then you will be like a man who tries to deflect a beam of light with a stick when it comes upon him, or like a man who loses his hold of the earth with his hands and feet as he slips into a deep abyss. Be sure, good sir, to do only as Brahma says. Never overstep Brahma's word. Do you not see the Divine Assembly seated here, monk.' And Mara thus called the Divine Assembly to witness.

"When this was said, I told Mara: 'I know you, Evil one; do not fancy that I do not know you. You are Mara, the Evil One, and Brahma and the Divine Assembly with all its members have fallen into your hands; they have all fallen into your power. You, Evil One, think that I have fallen into your power too; but that is not so.' When this was said, Brahma Baka told me, 'Good sir, I speak of the permanent that is permanent, of the everlasting that is everlasting, of the eternal that is eternal, of totality that is totality, of what-is-not-subject-to-passing-away, of what neither is born, nor ages, nor dies, nor passes away, nor reappears, and of that beyond from which there is no escape. Before your time, monk, there were monks and brahmans in the world whose asceticism lasted as long as your whole life. They knew that when there was no escape beyond, there was no escape beyond and that when there was no escape beyond, there was no escape beyond. So, monk, I tell you that beyond this you will find no escape and trying to do so will eventually reap weariness and disappointment. If you will believe in earth, in water, in fire, in air, in beings, in gods, in Pajapati; if you will believe in Brahma—you will be the one to lie near me, to lie within my province, as you will be for me to work my will upon and punish.'

"And I said, 'I know that too, Brahma. But, I understand your reach and your sway this way: Brahma Baka's power, his might, his following, extend thus far and no farther.' And Brahma Baka said 'Now, good sir, how far do you understand my reach and my sway to extend?' I answered:

> As far as moon and sun do circulate
> Shining and lighting up the four directions,
> Over a thousand times as wide a world
> Your power can exert its influence.
> And there you know the high and low as well,
> And those governed by lust and free from lust,
> The state of what is thus and otherwise,
> Arid creatures' provenance and destination.

Thus far do I understand your reach and sway to extend. Yet, there are three other main bodies of Brahma gods which you neither know nor see, and which I know and see. There is the body called Abhassara (of Streaming Radiance) whence you passed away and re-appeared here. But, with long dwelling here your memory of it has lapsed, and so you no more know or see it; but, I know and see it. Standing thus, as I do, not on the same level of direct knowledge as you do, it is not less that I know, but more. And likewise with the still higher bodies of the Subhakinna (of Refulgent Glory) and the Vehapphala (of Great Fruit).'

"And I continued, 'Now, Brahma, having had direct knowledge of earth as earth, and having had knowledge of what is not co-essential with the earthness of earth, I did not claim to be earth, I did not claim earth to be mine, I did not claim to be in earth, I did not claim to be apart from earth, I made no affirmation about earth. Having had direct knowledge of water as water . . . of fire . . . of air . . . of beings . . . of gods . . . Pajahati . . . Brahma . . . The Abhassara . . . The Subhakinna . . . The Vehapphala . . . The Transcendent Being (Abhibhu). . . . Having had direct knowledge of All as All, having had knowledge of what is not co-essential with the allness of all, I did not claim to be All, I did not claim to be in All, I did not claim to be apart from All, I did not claim All to be mine, I made no affirmation about All. Standing thus, too, as we do, it is not less that I know, but more.'

"'Good sir, if you claim to have access to what is not co-essential with the allness of All, may you not be proved vain and empty!'

The consciousness that makes no showing
Nor has to do with finiteness
Claiming no being apart from all:
That is not co-essential with the earthness of earth,
With the waterness of water, . . .
With the allness of All.

"And the Brahma replied, 'Then, good sir, I will vanish from you.'

"'Then, Brahma, vanish from me if you can.'

"Then, Brahma Baka, thinking 'I will vanish from the monk Gotama; I will vanish from the monk Gotama,' was unable to do so. I said: 'Then, Brahma, I will vanish from you.'

"I assumed the pose of a supernatural power thus: 'Just to the extent of Brahma and the Assembly, let them hear the sound of me without seeing me,' and after I had vanished, I uttered this stanza:

I have seen fear in every mode of being
Including being seeking for non-being.

There is no mode of being I affirm
Nor relish whatsoever whereto I cling.

Then, Brahma and the Assembly and all its members wondered and marvelled at that, and they said: 'It is wonderful, sirs, it is marvelous! This monk Gotama who went forth from a Sakyan clan has such great power and might as we have never before seen in any other monk or Brahman! Sirs, though living in a generation that delights in being, loves being, finds gladness in being, he has extirpated being together with its root!'

"Then, Mara, the Evil One, entered into a member of the Assembly, and he said: 'Good Sir, if that is what you know, if that is what you have discovered, do not lead your lay disciples to it or those gone forth, do not teach them your ideal or create in them a yearning for it. Before your time, monk, there were monks and brahmans in the world claiming to be accomplished and fully enlightened, and they did that; but on the dissolution of the body when their breath was cut off, they became established in an inferior body. Before your time, monk, there were also such monks and brahmans in the world, and they did not do that; and on dissolution of the body when their breath was cut off, they became established in a superior body. So, monk, I tell you this: Be sure, good sir, to abide inactive; devote yourself to a pleasant abiding here and now. This is better left undeclared, good sir, and so inform no one else of it all.'

"When this was said, I replied: 'I know you, Mara. It is not out of compassion or welfare that you speak thus. You are thinking that those to whom I teach this ideal will go beyond your reach. Those monks and brahmans of yours who claimed to be accomplished and fully enlightened were not really so; but I am, as I claim to be, accomplished and fully enlightened. A Perfect One is such whether he teaches this ideal to disciples or not, whether he leads his disciples to it or not. Why is that? Because such taints as defile, as renew being, as bring anxiety, as ripen in suffering, as produce future birth, aging and death, are in him cut off at the root, made like palm tree stumps, done away with, so that they are no more subject to future arising, just as a palm tree is incapable of further growth when its crown is cut off.' Since Mara had nothing more to say and on account of Brahma's invitation (to me to vanish) this discourse may be termed 'on the invitation of a Brahma.'"

So, the only way to be safe and free from any false as well as distorted inner perception and ideation is to be like the Buddha who remained fully awake and totally aware in every single moment. This is called "Buddha-Consciousness." It refers to one who is fully enlightened and completely liberated. With such ultimate consciousness there is no confusion to blind or distort the act of perceiving; all forms of sense perceptions and ideation are crystal clear and without flaw. All aspects of Mara, such as our (1) aggregates of existence, (2) impure, disturbing, unhealthy, and destructive influences, (3) beliefs in false deities and spirit guides, (4) superpowerful conditioning in the spiritual realms, and (5) deadening and desensitizing tendencies, are all utterly transcended and completely drained. If any of these appear in any form at any of the "doors" of our senses, including the inner sense of the psychic center, they are caught in the "net" of clear seeing and are seared by the flames of attention as illustrated in the Buddha's life story.

But, without precise, impeccable awareness of what is present at every moment, we may get lost in the realm of spiritualism, placing an unquestioning trust in the so-called spirit guides. Some of those entities might be as clever and as knowledgeable as Mara, testing and attempting to mislead us like the Buddha has shown in the story of the Brahma Baka. Nevertheless, we may experiment with such guides simply for the sake of experiencing and learning without falling victim to their powers; we need only to remember that they are not perfect and accomplished beings. Their power and knowledge are certainly limited. With this understanding and awareness, we need never be overwhelmed by the "spirit guides." Instead, we can make use of them for constructive purposes. In this way, we are not actually guided by them, but we can communicate with them so that we can make use of what they know. But to turn ourselves over to them totally is a way of ignoring and neglecting our inner resources and intelligence. This is very dangerous and destructive to the growth process and the "journey" to full enlightenment.

Developing Pure Perceptions: Transcending the Potentially Distorting Aspects of Perception While Expanding the Field of Pure Awareness

We have explored perception and ideation more deeply, have learned to recognize how they are influenced by our feelings and states of mind, and have seen, through the examples of the play of Mara in the Buddha's discourses, how both our inner and outer views of existence can become distorted and unclear. Yet, it is only when perception and ideation end, are cut at the root, reach complete extinction, that we can discover the ever-flowing stream of total awareness and ultimate consciousness. This ultimate freedom is discovered through some approaches to meditation practice. I will describe two in greater detail.

Nine States of Meditative Absorption (Jhanic Consciousness)

First let us turn to the various stages of samadhi-consciousness as clearly and accurately described by the Buddha as a result of his own experiences. This approach consists of nine states of *jhanic* consciousness or meditative absorption, subdivided into two sets of mental functions, each having four specific components or levels of awareness, and one stage of the experience of pure, non-mental consciousness. Thus:

I. Four Meditative Absorptions Existing and Roaming About in the Realm of Form

1. "Aloof from sense-desires, aloof from unwholesome thoughts (one attains to) the first meditative absorption which is born of non-attachment (freedom) and which has reasoning, reflection, joy and happiness."

2. "By suppression (elimination) of reasoning and reflection (one attains to) the second meditative absorption which is inner serenity, which is unification of mind, without reasoning and reflection, born of samadhi (a firmly and solidly stabilized state of consciousness), and which has joy and happiness."

3. "By being non-attached to joy (one dwells) in equanimity, mindful and aware, and enjoys happiness in body, (and attains

to) the third meditative absorption which the noble one calls: 'dwelling in equanimity, mindfulness and happiness.'"

4. "By the abandonment of happiness and suffering, by the disappearance already of joy and sorrow (one attains to) the fourth meditative absorption, which is neither happiness nor suffering, and which is the purity of equable-mindfulness."

II. Four Meditative Absorptions in the Formless Realms of Consciousness

5. The *jhanic* consciousness of the infinity of space.
6. The *jhanic* consciousness of the infinity of consciousness itself.
7. The *jhanic* consciousness of no-thingness or "nothing whatsoever."
8. The *jhanic* consciousness of neither perception nor nonperception, the state in which the perception or ideation becomes absolutely refined and therefore the cognition of any concepts and notions is almost impossible.

III. One Meditative Absorption of Pure Consciousness

9. The *jhanic* consciousness of attaining the cessation of perception, ideation, and feeling (*sannavedyitanirodha*).

Having achieved the extinction of the two groups of mental functions, there is no reactive response; there is only full consciousness with its high-frequency vibration and highly refined energy field. To put it in another way, we may say that in such a state of attainment all the patterns of perceiving, ideating, and feeling become completely suspended. This is the non-egoic state of existence. It is a matter of an experience at this level of higher consciousness. Its attributes last for a certain period of time until such energy fades away and disperses altogether. We then return to our ordinary state of consciousness and perhaps go into this ninth stage again as our mastery of attainment develops.

Such Samadhi-Consciousness is entirely different from Buddha-Consciousness. The latter refers to the state of everyday living through which the fully enlightened one conducts his/her life.

However, these nine stages and Buddha-Consciousness are not mutually exclusive. We can experience all of them simultaneously.

Three Forms of Contemplative Perception: The Process of Silently Looking into the True Nature of Things

Another approach to transcending the potentially distorting aspects of perception and ideation is to practice Contemplative Perception. This is the process of silently looking into the true nature of things. It consists of three forms:

1. the contemplative perception of impermanence *(anicca-sanna)*
2. the contemplative perception of conflict and dissatisfaction *(dukkha-sanna)*
3. the contemplative perception of the absence of an everlasting entity existing independently within or outside of humans *(anatta-sanna)*

By paying attention to the process of dissolution (passing away, disappearing, and vanishing of any processes or events in the phenomenal world), we get to know the characteristics of existence; everything is in a constant state of change and transience. Nothing remains unchanged or permanent in life or in the world. After our breath has come in, it goes out again naturally. With in-breath the abdomen and chest rise or expand, while they contract and fall when breathing out. This same nature of rising and falling, contracting and expanding, is applied to sensation, feeling, thought, and any other processes whether physical, mental, psychological, or spiritual. Looking at the clouds moving about in the sky, we see them form a shape, hold it, and change shapes again. So movement implies change and change provides space for eliminating the old and creating the new. Such is the nature of existence. From our keen and unmistakable observation of events and phenomena both within and outside ourselves, we clearly and distinctly perceive the three phases of: arising, existing, and passing away. These three phases manifest themselves consistently in every single thing with no exception.

With ordinary perception, we do not see the breaking up process of an event or a thing because of a limited view. As Gotama, the Buddha, pointed out, it is apparent *continuity* that covers up the impermanence. The ideas of permanence and eternity held firmly in the mind prevent us from seeing and accepting the truth of impermanence. For, this truth is quite threatening to our egos and, such an idea, which has no corresponding reality in this constantly changing world, is hard to justify. When the total perception of impermanence arises through our actual observation of the momentary existence of every event or thing in life or in the world, we are able to uproot the false idea of eternity, rise above the clouds of illusion, and enjoy the clear, blue sky. Furthermore, this pure perception of impermanence as the truly intrinsic nature of all existence can put us in a position of having the ability to dance even during life's storms when they occur. This is because true knowledge that springs from such impeccable perception always liberates us from imprisonments and obstructions. We then flow freely and smoothly in the streaming radiance of consciousness without getting stuck in the whirlpools of life.

The second form of contemplative perception is that of *dukkha-sanna* (the inner perception or ideation as regards conflict and dissatisfaction). From our experience of everyday living, we notice that one of the characteristics of our existence is the dissatisfactory nature manifesting in the form of conflict, pain, sorrow, and suffering, as well as in the form of fleeting pleasure and momentary joy. There is nothing that can be experienced as everlasting freedom from conflict and as a never-changing satisfaction. This is in accordance with the fact that whatever is impermanent and subject to change is also dissatisfactory and in a constant state of conflict. The change from a happy condition to an unhappy condition brings pain and suffering. As we are each a conditioned individual, brought up and trained through different backgrounds (culture, religion, tradition, and family rule) and systematic thinking, we very often run into conflict with one another. Conflict arises because we maintain different ideas and opinions about things; in other words, we perceive the world and view the facts differently. Conflict is inevitable. Conflict can get deepened by our attachment to our perceptual world and personal views that force us to ruthlessly build up support for whatever we maintain and perceive to be true. As a result, we are unable to listen to other points of view without digging into the conflict more deeply. This situation is obviously seen in all aspects of life, whether political, economic, religious, spiritual, social, inter-personal, or personal. Consequently, we create different systems of politics and economics, such as dividing the world into the communist world on one hand and the free world on the other. Both camps fight each other due to a constant conflict underlying the systems and ideologies. Instead of moving on toward the goal of freedom, harmony, peace, and understanding for all of humanity, we over-exert our energies in defending and protecting our holy systems and beliefs. This is the manifestation of conflict, isn't it? In the fields of religion and spirituality, we encounter different paths provided for achieving the same goal of total liberation, full enlightenment, and complete union or communion with God, Dharma, Tao. Again, our perceptual knowledge of the path and limited understanding of its implications lead us into conflict with one another, blindly thinking and believing that only our path is the perfectly true one; the other paths are false. Such false ideas and blind beliefs become a great obstacle to our universal human harmony and unity.

What I mean by the contemplative perception of *dukkha* (conflict, dissatisfaction, pain, suffering, pressure, stress, fear, guilt, anxiety, and so forth) is that we welcome and accept them as they arise or come to us. We fully acknowledge and recognize any negativity and destructive tendency that is being experienced at the moment. By maintaining an attitude of letting it be, by not resisting or becoming emotionally or mentally attached to it or obstructing it, by floating with its currents with clarity of mind and evenly hovering attention, we enable ourselves to inwardly relax into living with conflict, pressure, fear, sorrow, and all the rest of *dukkha*. This means that we allow ourselves to assimilate the *dukkha* process so that transmutation will take place: we then transform ourselves by moving on to another floor, another level of consciousness. In this way we will not get stuck in any form of pain and suffering or in any impermanent pleasure and joy. By living through any experience whether negative or positive, we allow the cleansing, eliminating process and the developing, growing process to operate full-scale, simultaneously. On the other hand, repression, suppression, control, avoidance, rationalization, taking mood- or mind-altering drugs, or conforming to compulsive patterns of conditioning can only deepen the *dukkha* process and therefore delay our journey to total freedom, integrated health, or holistic wellness. With the contemplative perception of *dukkha* we get to know and understand how it arises, which can help us go to the root and eliminate it entirely, leaving our body-mind clean, clear, and vibrantly alive so that we can fully live and totally enjoy our lives.

Arriving at the third contemplative perception, we have the most challenging Buddhist concept of *anatta*, no-self: it is very hard for our dualistically thinking mind to understand and accept this ultimate truth. Because I want to explore this matter of no-self and how to go about integrating it with the notion of self in another chapter, I will just briefly describe it here.

There are two ways of intellectually catching a glimpse of the Buddha's doctrine of *anatta*. One is the way of analysis; the other is the way of comprehending the law of conditionality. In analyzing our concept of a being, an individual, a person, a self, we see just a group of aggregates of existence. For example, human beings are comprised of five aggregates; body-form, feeling-sensation, perception-ideation, mental formation-conditioning, and consciousness. When these five groups of elements come together in a certain structure we call a human being, a notion of an individual, a person, a self, an ego, or a "me" consciousness arises. But by looking at this unit, its principle and its aggregates, we see that there is no such thing as a self, an entity, existing independently within itself or outside of the aggregates. This is like a notion of car: when different parts are constructed in such a shape as a car, the notion of car arises. Again, when the different parts are taken out and the shape of a car disappears, then there is no car but different parts with different names. Where is the car? Does it hide somewhere in the sky or under the ocean or anywhere else? It is just a name, a label, a word or a symbol, isn't it? This is the way of analysis by which a self or a sense of separate self is seen as merely a notion or an energy pattern operating within consciousness in our human evolution. Now, by looking into the law of conditionality, we see that everything is relative and conditioned by everything else. Things, including humans, are interdependent and inter-connected; there is nothing that can exist entirely independently. The whole world and the entire universe are completely related by way of conditions and energy fields. Anything that happens in any part of the world, be it physical, social, political, or economic, will set off a chain of events. For example, London Airport is covered with thick fog; a plane cannot take off due to the danger. A passenger, John Smith, has an important business meeting in New York City at a certain time. Because he is unable to take off for several hours, his business is not done, which causes a loss to his firm and/or to himself as an executive director. This is the matter of inter-dependence. When this happens, that also happens; when this ceases, that also ceases. It is a natural law of inter-relatedness. There is no such thing as an absolute being giving a command to the world to function and move in any way he wants it to. The world goes on according to the conditions by which it is influenced. It is poor thinking and primitive imagination to believe in an absolute entity existing somewhere above us, governing our direction and destination in life.

Let us take a closer look at what actually happens to us individually as a conditioned person. When we are insulted, we feel hurt and/or get angry and look for a way to retaliate so that we can maintain and justify our self-assertion. In this situation, we can see that our sense of a separate individual (which we identify as "me," "my," "I-am"), is the self that has a body, a feeling, a perception, patterns of conditioning, and consciousness. At the moment of feeling insulted, since the separate self is conditioned by the idea and notion of "I-am," "me," or "my," we feel hurt and humiliated. Furthermore, such a feeling causes the individual to perceive the situation as intolerable and unacceptable so that he/she thinks, "You hurt me, you abused me, you stepped over me," and so on. With such a firm grip on these thoughts, the individual re-enforces the building-up process to support his/her thinking, feeling, and perception. Consequently, the idea of retaliation occurs, leading him/her into taking retaliatory action. This is a process, and not a thing in itself. Looking at it superficially, we see an individual operating on his own, but with analysis and by investigating the details of how the action is taken, we see a process in which one thing is conditioned by the other, leading to the taking of action. In this way, we say that it is the unit or a heaping up of form that

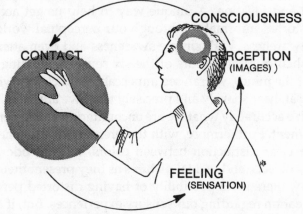

At the point of **contact** with an object through any senses there arise sensation or feeling, perception, and consciousness. **Feeling (sensation)** may be pleasant, unpleasant, or neutral (neither pleasant nor unpleasant). Dependent on the feeling arises **perception**, which creates an image for dwelling on—a solid, perceptual reality. This reality might be entirely different from objective reality. Conditioned by the perception arises a **consciousness** in which both the awareness level and the actual experience of an object manifest. And there is **awareness** as a *witness state*, which sees all of those things happening in their processes. Bear in mind that these experiences take place through our sense-modalities (eyes, ears, nose, tongue, body touch, and the mind or inner sense). This means that we come into contact with the outer world through our five physical senses and with the inner world, including ideas, thoughts, dreams, and fantasies, through our sixth sense of the mind. Also, it is essential to note that feeling, perception, and consciousness are interdependent and, therefore, they condition one another in their functioning.

---

prevents us from seeing the process or the no-self thing. If we simply stay with pure observation of the process and let go of the idea of an entity or a self, then we see things as they really are and not as they appear to be (or as we think they are). Thus is the perception of *anatta*, no-self: there is no independent agent with absolute power and everlastingness.

Now, we can see how much we are influenced by our sense-perception and how powerful the information processed by it is, regardless of truth or falseness. We can either be deceived and misguided, or safely and beneficially directed, by our sensory perception and ideation. A unique way to help us get accurate and non-distorted information through our perceptual world is to develop awareness. With simple awareness and even attention well established at all the doors of the six senses (including the inner sense of the mind), we can see impeccably and clearly what we are looking at, hear sharply and precisely what we are listening to, and recognize accurately what we are encountering and experiencing at the moment. Furthermore, with the presence of awareness we can make a clear distinction between colors, sounds, odors, flavors, tangible objects, and mental pictures as they present themselves. In this way, there is no possibility of having distorted perception or false ideation regarding our sensory experiences. But, if awareness is absent at the moment of perception, there can be any sort of distortion and wrong information because the patterns of conditioning *(sankkhara)* and reactive feeling cause us to process information inaccurately. This is a pivotal point in our lives. Most, if not all, of our perception and ideation is heavily influenced by our egoistic feelings as well as our compulsive patterns of conditioning. The only possibility for receiving accurate information from our sensory perception is to dissolve the potentially distorting aspects of perception and ideation at their root and keep awareness and attention flowing evenly and constantly in every moment.

CHAPTER SIX

Sleeping Dogs

Learning to Recognize Our Seven "Sleeping Dogs" of Attachment As They Are Provoked by Our Daily Life in the World

ANUSAYA IS THE PALI TERM for what I call here "sleeping dogs." Literally, *anusaya* means that which lies underneath. There are seven sleeping dogs within us that we need to watch and be aware of constantly. They refer to attachment to sensuality, hatred, wrong views, skeptical doubt, pride, clinging to becoming, and ignorance. These tendencies do not come up to the surface unless there is provocation and stimulation. That is why it is not so easy to see if the place deep down inside us is completely pure and clean until such time when we have a powerful, sharp insight into our whole story at all levels of our realities. This is also why we need to be in contact with life situations, or in the world of samsara (the nature of roaming about here and there both within and outside of us). This samsaric life or the cycle of existence is really full of testing situations where we can learn and see for ourselves if we are completely liberated, or just partly free and partly in the mud. Without samsara, a true platform of life, we cannot fully appreciate nirvana (eternal bliss and total freedom). This means that seeing the contrast intensifies the taste of Ultimate Truth.

Attachment to Sensuality

This is the first sleeping dog, which bites almost everybody in the world. It may be obvious, sometimes, that we are attached to sensual pleasures; at other times we feel that we can do without them. We can live our lives comfortably for a certain period of time with no longing for, or compulsiveness in, seeking a new sensation. Sometimes, some of us just cannot make it. It is tormenting when this sleeping dog wakes up and feels hungry. Sensuality is an English word translated from the Pali term *kama*, and not karma, although pronounced the same in English. *Kama* refers to both sensual objects and the impure, unhealthy, and defiled states of consciousness. The first part of *kama* includes all the objects of the physical senses such as form and color, sounds, smell, taste, and body touch. These sensual objects can demand attachment or dependence, particularly when they give us pleasantness and pleasurable sensations. The contaminating states of consciousness or defilements refer to all the negative, destructive, and disturbing influences of mind, including what Western psychology calls "emotions." Anger, resentment, hate, irritation, hostility, envy, jealousy—all kinds of feelings that are negative—are included.

By attachment to sensual objects we mean a constant demand and compulsive desire for pleasures and enjoyments of the senses. Otherwise, we cannot feel good. We think we need this attachment to feel alive and grounded to life. Without it, we become tense, uncomfortable, irritable, and dull. By compulsiveness we mean that you have to have it (whatever it is that you want) or else you will develop a personality conflict, neurosis, pain, and suffering. Attachment also means getting stuck and being unable to move on by letting go of either good or bad things. It is the matter of holding on and clinging to that which makes us feel good (high, secure, or safe) and to that which makes us feel bad (hurt, negativity, poor self-image) in order to sustain and retain the familiar self.

Three Categories of Relationship with Sensual Objects: Attachment, Liberation, Detachment. What we have to see clearly is our relationship with sensual objects, whether we are attached to them or free and liberated in relation to them. These two situations are our factual experiences with regard to sensual objects. There may also be a third fact: detachment. This detachment is defined here as a rigid rule of celibacy that we create for ourselves in order to suppress and control our feelings and need for sensual expression and enjoyment. In this connection, we may have a certain moral standard or even a solid image of a moralistic or holy, spiritual person who is bound by the ground rules of this detachment, thereby behaving in a certain aloof and detached way in regard to sensual objects. As a result, we try too hard to be all right while still feeling desire and an inward longing for contact and sensation. So, we are in constant conflict between who we imagine we are and what is actually happening in us. When attempting to exert too much energy in controlling the senses in order to maintain the rule, the discipline of moral code and the image about who we ought to be, we are restricting and blocking biological energy from flowing out naturally to reach and experience the world as it is. In this way, the natural rhythm of expansion and contraction in life, both at the biological and psychic levels, becomes disturbed and irregular or even confused. What follows is that the body has no choice but to create contraction and constriction and armoring in the musculature so that energy is locked in and held in certain parts of the body where it accumulates explosive strength. Consequently, one suffers pain, tension, tightness, discomfort, and freezing fears.

It is natural to our state of existence that biological energy assumes the function of flowing out consistently through our physical sense-modalities for the purpose of expanding and contracting rhythmically, reaching out for contact and joy. If there is a suppression of natural desire, or a control of biological energy, then we have to pay a high price physically, emotionally, and psychologically. Blockages of energy-flow and rigidity in both body and mind will dominate our lives as if poisonous snakes are chasing us. The conditioned mind often uses control over the senses in order to feel safe and secure within its walls of conditioning; this leads to suppression and neurotic detachment. There is, however, a natural, spontaneous control without overflowing, overdoing, or compulsively desiring instant gratification and fulfillment of all our needs. Such control comes about through the application of simple awareness and clarity of understanding, which transcends all forms of conformity. This is a natural flow of action and non-action with wisdom, love, and freedom.

If we can free our mind of conditions and impulses, there will certainly be freedom as well as love. It is not a fact that we feel totally comfortable all the time when living the samsaric life with all its stimulations, temptations, and attractions. People who devote themselves to working on themselves, in monastic and isolated settings, may feel somehow liberated while in such an environment, but when they return to samsara, to cities, towns, and to relationships with people of different levels of development, you may observe that they are not really comfortable. What they do is minimize the activities of their senses, controlling them as well as limiting their responsibilities to themselves and their community. They may just look straight ahead or keep their eyes cast down in so-called mindful ways. They must use this kind of technique or they will become victimized by the world. Therefore, they entirely depend on the control system and live by the rules and precepts.

This is very obvious in the Order of Buddhist Monks where they are taught to control all their six sense-modalities so that they will not get lost in the world of sense experiences. For example, the Buddha gave very strong advice to his attendant monk, Ananda, in regard to the relationship with women. He said: "Ananda, when coming across women, monks must not look at them. If it is necessary to communicate with them, just talk mindfully." In Buddhist countries such as Thailand, when monks go out for alms in the morning carrying their bowls in their hands or on their shoulders, they are all instructed not to look at the person giving them the food, but to cast their eyes down into their bowls. This way they control their sense of sight and never see the donor's face. Those who are willing to renounce the world, so to speak, to live the homeless life, must make rules a reality of their lives, accepting and surrendering to all the rules without questioning them. If they succeed, it is all right; if not, they return to the world, struggling with the samsaric life because the sleeping dogs are still biting them.

As I mentioned earlier, what matters are not the sensual objects and defilements themselves, but how we relate to them. If we find ourselves in attachment, indulging ourselves and having compulsive desire for getting satisfaction from sensuality so that we may feel good, happy, and high, this indicates that the first sleeping dog still bothers us. There are other forms of bliss and happiness derived from things apart from sensuality, which we can all experience. We must be free in relation to sensualities such as color, form, shape, landscape, the movement of the ocean, the flight of a bird, beautifully painted pictures, the dances of people or trees, striking music, lovely songs, the voice of a lover or beloved one, the smells of flowers, of earth, of spiritual perfume, the flavor of good food and the taste of a lover's mouth and lips, the loving, soft, and gentle touch of someone whom we love and admire dearly, or the gentle breeze and warm sun on our bodies, all of which could touch us with exploding ecstasy and orgasm. All of these might become a slaughterhouse for us if we get attached to them and are not wise in relating to them.

Experiencing and enjoying sensual objects with an open heart, true freedom, insightful awareness, and with no compulsive longing, will help us establish a liberated relationship with sensual pleasures. In this way, we will have no trouble either with attachment or detachment in regard to sensuality. We are open and available for whatever flows through us at any time. Then we can flow more freely with life situations without making sensual pleasures an end in themselves. When seeing in this way, we become flexible and are able to bend without denying or affirming anything regarding sensuality. As we know, the sensual things experienced with love, awareness, clarity of understanding, and freedom can give us a healthy and self-satisfied life, making us feel firm, strong, grounded, and united in our lives. We have to, however, keep an ever-watchful eye on attachment and compulsion. When we are totally clear and constantly aware of what we are doing, when we listen attentively to the wise one within us, the sleeping dog will turn into a faithful dog, taking care of us and keeping us company.

The Power of Passion. The other category of sensuality consists of impure and disturbing states of mind, like anger, hate, resentment, envy, jealousy, clinging, etc. We may state that all forms of passionate defilements belong to this category of sensuality. Passion is not something bad in itself even though religionists tend to condemn it. It is a strong and powerful energy within us that frightens most of us. Because of this fear of the power of passion, in the religious context, we find very heavy blame laid upon passion, the vital energy. It is blamed for being the downfall of the person who is supposed to stand above all kinds of passion. While he is being judged, the ordinary person falls into this unholy well. In this connection, what we can do is apply clear awareness and cope with this powerful thing so that the precise insight into the situation of our passions and disturbing influences will flow up to our conscious level more freely, giving us light and dispersing the darkness of ignorance. Even when we think we are free, we might sometimes experience jealousy coming up in a certain situation and just say, "Ah hah," or "Hello, jealousy!" Then we are in the position of being able to laugh with it. When it vanishes right on the spot, we may feel love and understanding, instead of jealousy. This means that we bring out our inner resources to nurture ourselves sufficiently.

Attachment to Hatred

This second sleeping dog is, in the Pali language, called *patigha*, which also refers to repugnance, irritation, and ill-will. It is a very subtle feeling within us. On the surface someone might appear calm, serene, peaceful, and even lovingly warm, but underneath there is a burning, and such a person is on fire with hate and aversion. When provoked or touched by a conflicting situation, it rises and bursts out in the form of hot anger or rage.

Sometimes, we feel like wanting to get rid of a certain burden within ourselves, and we even fantasize doing it in a destructive way. We want a person or a thing or a circumstance to be eliminated. It is a kind of vindictiveness. There is a tendency to punish somebody who rejects or hurts us. This sleeping dog is very much connected to certain ideas, standards, and rules of how things should be. When things do not go along with what we desire or expect them to be, then resentment and hate show up. For example, in a formal meditation, we want to have a quiet and peaceful atmosphere, but it turns out to be noisy. This goes against our idea and expectation. As a result we cannot take it as it is and become irritated, angry, or resentful. The idea of peace and quiet held firmly in our mind is actually biting us, making us angry and driving us crazy. Irritation may be manifested in such a way that we wish a person or a thing ill-will, perhaps taking revenge or acting out in retaliation. This is a reaction.

There are many levels of reaction: repugnance, irritation, ill will, resentment, anger, and hatred. All these are included in the family of the second sleeping dog. The cause is really very deep and subtle indeed. If there is no provocation, we do not feel irritation or impatience. We feel fine! This is the reason certain situations are needed to help us see when there are hidden tendencies somewhere in our psychophysical processes. What is actually lacking within us in regard to fostering this feeling of hate and anger is love, compassion, understanding, and unconditional acceptance for human beings, animals, and things. Basically, if there is contact with love, then repugnance cannot arise. For the energy of love is so healthy, so healing, so warm and loving that any negativity gets burned away instantly. It is impossible to feel negative feelings with love, including ideas about possessing or owning the object of love. This applies to impersonal (universal) love combined with a natural, free-flowing, open heart. Personal love, however, can still cause negative feelings of irritation and anger due to unrealistic expectations of the partner. This sort of love is not really "love" in its true sense of complete union or oneness consciousness (with no sense of a separate self). This personal love is merely an attraction or attachment, an emotional dependence.

Liberation and Transmutation Through Insight Versus the Power of Control. Many of us have been working on this category of sleeping dog—hate, resentment, anger, and hostility. We have found them hiding and locking themselves in different parts of our bodies, such as in the jaw, throat, chest, genital area, buttocks, groin, knees, calves, and ankles. When the holding point is touched or worked on either by the meditative energy, technically known as *atapa,* or by someone who knows the dwelling place of such a sleeping dog, it comes up by making sudden movements or noises due to the unbearable pain. When under the influence of such an emotional state, we feel easily irritated and angry with anything or anyone in any disagreeable situation. So, to be free of this sleeping dog, we first must clear it up and clean it out of our system by releasing all the negative energy of hatred, anger, and rage locked somewhere in our body, our minds, and our psychic center. In this way, there is no choice apart from going into all the situations of this kind in life, seeing them in full insight, living through them, and letting them transmute.

Only insightful wisdom can liberate us (not the power of control). Control may at best seem temporarily successful, but it is only on the surface for the purpose of keeping the self-image of a respectable person visible to the outer world; the inner state of affairs is still burning. So, if we clean out and clear up all the unfinished business connected with anger, hatred, resentment, and all the similar negative energies locked in our bodies, then we will certainly not become irritated or react so easily. If this kind of reaction takes place, we are able to see immediately how we come to be annoyed or impatient. We can understand quickly and precisely how not to let it get hold of us. Then, we let go of the ideas and principles behind our reactions, leaving ourselves free to relate to situations in new and fresh ways, with no interfering factors and with clarity of insight and impeccable awareness. As a result, we do not accumulate any more new karma, and all the old karma has been assimilated and worked through. Hence, we can be free. But, as long as the old stuff is not removed and cleansed, we can be easily stimulated and instigated by the attraction and distraction of the world. This is because the world is full of ideas and conflicts, and when something from the world comes in touch with our body and mind, then something inside us reacts and makes us feel uncomfortable, miserable, painful, and perhaps fearful as well. This means that the sleeping dog is still lying underneath and has not been rooted out. Conversely, if our body and mind are clean, clear, and pure, we will unfold ourselves freely, flowing and flowering with the movement of awareness and intuitive wisdom (the direct contact with reality). Along with this comes the natural flow of love and compassion as creative energy, which is always available, particularly when the blocks are released.

"Turning to the Source" to Transmute the Power of Anger. Very often such a question as this arises: "What shall I do with my anger when I feel it toward someone?" The steps are few: we take hold of that angry feeling and experience it fully without rationalizing or covering it up with any techniques or rules. We can just be totally open, allowing ourselves to be vulnerable to the emotion of anger, staying with it steadily without avoiding or turning away from it. In this way, we focus full attention on the anger and not on the object of it. Any object of anger is kept on the surface of consciousness and allowed to float and is used as an instigating factor for helping us dive deep down into the state of anger: the process of transmutation will take place naturally. Otherwise, we will explode or implode,

letting anger create havoc in our lives. We come to be grateful to the object of anger for assisting us in getting in touch with the real issue.

This is not a question of whether you should react, express, or control the anger. If our attention is focused on the object of anger, whether a person, animal, situation, or something else, we just provoke our anger and keep reacting to it without dealing with it directly. Such is the way of accumulating the karma of anger and of fostering it endlessly. More than that, our reactive mechanism gets stronger and becomes more powerful so that we become afraid of it and feel hopeless in coping with our anger reaction. By focusing attention on the object of anger, we step out of ourselves, emphasizing that something out there is the main cause of our anger. We do not bother to look into our inner situation where the real thing comes from. We do not see how anger arises and what lies behind it, feeding it with fuel. By turning to the source, we can see in perfect wisdom the whole structure of anger; then, what needs to be done will be done. We must just place complete trust in awareness and insight, so that we don't have to do anything special, apart from providing the hospitality of attention.

Adhering to Views

The third sleeping dog is like a jungle of life, the symbol of perversion or distortion of views—a person getting lost in a deep forest. We humans create ideas, opinions, and views about the world and about things in life so that we can complain about our pain, suffering, and confusion in being lost, as if in a jungle. The more views and opinions we acquire, the thicker and more frightening the jungle becomes, and the more work we have to do to cut down the forest without destroying any trees.

There is a story about a person lost in a jungle, wandering around anxiously, fearfully and in a state of confusion, not knowing how to find the way out. After a while, he/she comes across a beautiful road (built by so-called evil spirits or devils). Getting excited and feeling happy about this discovery, she thinks to herself that this road will lead her to a town or a city somewhere and eventually lead her home. Upon arriving, however, she finds that she has come to the dwelling place of devils and now has more trouble. Such a thing does happen in our own lives when we form views and opinions for abiding in and dwelling on. We become rigid and deeply attached to them, unable to move from point to point or to bend freely like branches dancing in the wind. The lack of this dance brings about a rigid inflexibility in living life and dealing with the world. Consequently, we suffer.

The Buddha was very much against any speculative views. I mean, he didn't encourage his disciples to speculate, but to see facts and realities as they are, without adding any opinions to them. If we speculate, we pull ourselves away from looking closely and seeing precisely what it really is. We just play an intellectual game to satisfy our minds, which constantly demand certainty and reassurance as well as definiteness about things. If we observe carefully, we will see that an individual who always has the tendency to create opinions and form views, who is swift to explain, to interpret, to make comments, and to put things into words, is, as a matter of fact, caught in the deep habit and compulsive pattern of avoiding going directly to the real issue of the challenge. This is the muddled way, leading us into the jungle. But the Vipassana way of life says to go right to the root and see it totally as it truly is. When there is complete seeing and understanding, views and opinions are not needed. The right, creative actions always take place spontaneously. So, adhering to any views, in other words, is a sleeping dog. The opposite to this is total freedom for being, dancing in complete harmony with perfect wisdom (samma-ditthi).

Attachment to Doubt

This term is used here to mean the state of indecision. Why does doubt become an obstacle or a hindrance to spiritual growth? As we comprehend it, indecisiveness is an aspect of ignorance or dark force, and clinging to views forms one side of that force. Because of not seeing clearly, as well as not understanding thoroughly, we cannot make a decision; we remain doubtful, uncertain, and even confused. Being in such an indecisive state of affairs is very painful, isn't it?

Do not confuse doubt with inquiry. Sometimes, some people use the word "doubt" in the sense of inquiring or an urge to know and see directly what the matter truly is. This kind of doubt doesn't become a barrier to personal development, but rather strengthens our wisdom and widens our insight. Inquiry means that we are totally open to deeper and broader understanding without creating any abiding point for ourselves; in other words, no conclusion. We do not set up any boundary to limit our knowledge and wisdom, but move forward openly and profoundly in all possible directions. With such an *inquiring mind* we never get stuck anywhere.

If we use doubt in the way of building up ideas, formulas, and theories for the sake of argument, and not for willingness to see the truth, then such doubt puts us in the position of a skeptic, and it becomes an impulse for more doubt, to which we will find no end. So, when doubt arises, we stay with it and get hold of it firmly to enable us to look at the doubting mind, in the doubtful matter, very deeply and totally. When the clarity of understanding of what we doubt comes into being, then doubt naturally drops away and we find ourselves in a clear space once again.

Attachment to Pride

The fifth sleeping dog is called "I-conceit." When pride is present, we feel and perceive a solid image about ourselves with a certain title and self-definition: "I am a spiritual person following an effective, powerful spiritual path under the guidance of a perfect master." "I am intelligent and wise, knowing what is right and wrong for myself and for others as well." "I am poor." "I am destructive and stuck." "I am in an equal position with a spiritual teacher, master or guru." We are proud of our images or self-concepts and therefore dwell on them. This is like digging a hole to live in. The symbol for pride or I-conceit, as used by the Buddha, is a "sandbank," which has nothing substantial.

Pride As Expressed Through Three Forms of Comparison: Superiority, Inferiority, Equality. Let us talk about pride in three forms of comparison: superiority, inferiority, and equality. We are proud to be superior and, unconsciously, we are also proud to be inferior because we like to play a comparing game. And certainly, we are proud to be equal, no matter what that means. This is another popular game people of the modern time are fond of playing. Pride is dangerous in the sense of solidifying the self-image and deceiving us by replacing the real with the unreal, as well as deepening the self-definition that we impose on ourselves. If we do not hold any self-concept and identification, we cannot have pride. That is why the Buddha called himself *tathagata*, which refers to nothing special; it is only a word for verbal communication when there is such a need. If we see ourselves in this way—as nobody in particular—we will not have trouble with a solid reality to hold on to or with images given to people we meet to make them higher, lower, or equal. We just see people as people, nobody special.

These days, there are many people who call themselves gurus or masters. If we try to live up to their images and reputations, we may be proud that we have somebody important and great in our life. We feel good and enjoy talking about this person, whom we follow and worship as a perfect master, an enlightened one, although we don't really know if she/he is actually as claimed or advertised. But, we believe it to be true for some personal reason and attraction. This is a subtle game of pride, a sleeping dog that keeps biting us unknowingly.

Ordination and initiation are not just ways of admitting someone into a particular organization, ashram, monastery, or religious order; they are also a deep and unconscious way of promoting pride, deepening I-am consciousness and self-deception, and creating more division in this already widely divided world. The reason being that the ordination or the initiation strengthens the pattern of self-identification. So long as there is an identification of self as someone who is identified with someone and/or a certain group, there is separateness and attachment to an individual identity and an organized, so-called spiritual movement, which leads to pride and self-delusion.

Once a certain image is established, the real person is lost. Then, relationships will be an image-to-image contact and not a person-to-person one. What we perceive in such a relationship and contact is a solid image, or a definiteness. In following a spiritual path, we think that we gain peace of mind, more understanding, more insight, more clarity, more bliss, and more ecstasy, and then we look down upon other people who do not achieve such experiences or know nothing about the spiritual path. In addition, we might even lay blame on them because of our spiritual pride. As a result, we become separate and divided and create disharmony by destroying the oneness of being and the universal unity among humankind. Among the so-called spiritual groups, we often hear such statements as these: "This is my method. If you want to follow me, you must come to me only. Don't practice any other methods. If you do other things rather than my method, don't come to me anymore." This is a matter of pride and stupidity, which disharmonizes humanity and hinders the natural flow of human potentiality.

So, pride in any form can cause us to get stuck in self-image, becoming isolated and divided, creating many different compartments of life, and the inability to flow freely into unrestricted and unlimited places through different paths. These paths are provided for us to make use of and to explore unobstructedly. Sometimes, in the monastic discipline, there are certain monks who feel themselves very pure, observing all the rules strictly; and then they look down upon other monks who are careless and break the rules very often. They, the so-called pure monks, hate to eat with the impure. This is a big ego trip with very strong pride. They just want to protect their purity without knowing in essence what it means to be pure. For, if we are really pure, it doesn't matter so much if someone not so pure is having a meal with us. We might be able to see the impurity in action more clearly and also test ourselves to see if we are still affected by the impurity acting out through our fellow beings. As pride is subtle, so it ties us up to the higher planes of existence. Only the exploding wisdom, or thunder-dharma, can cut through it, giving us total freedom of being and becoming, without taking name and form so seriously.

Clinging to Becoming

This sixth sleeping dog is similar to pride. The difference being that becoming is the process, while pride is a passion, the passionate energy of ego-consciousness. Becoming is also an ego trip in the sense of functioning and identifying with a role, position, status, duty, and image. When functioning in life and in society, we become somebody performing a certain task, bearing a certain title and having a label after our name. We just cannot ignore or deny the fact of being a wife, a husband, a cook, a secretary, a director, or a teacher when we function in everyday living. We cannot get rid of this becoming unless we want to be a rock—no more functioning. We might not become anything but the rock! Again, we cannot escape from becoming!

The becoming, by itself, is neither good nor bad; the *clinging* to it is destructive. The clinging keeps us confined to the narrow space of taking self-image or the role of functioning seriously, identifying ourselves completely with our functions or whatever we become, defining ourselves by what we do and nothing else. This is where the self-deception comes in. When I say that I am a cook, I merely talk about my function, job, or duty. But in essence I am not the cook. The most appropriate way to express this is that our function is cooking and not that we are the cook. Any job can serve as an example. The trouble is that we do feel ourselves to be whatever we identify with, which is a mistaken identity. More than that, we take this false identity as a solid thing, which is even worse. So, it is very essential to distinguish who we are from what we become. For the lack of such insight will inevitably lead to confusion, forgetting our real being or essence and getting lost in the comprehensive world of becoming.

When we know who we truly are and no longer take our functioning self so seriously, we may see our function of becoming somebody or something as a joke, a cosmic joke. This is when we become enlightened. We are just joking around in the world, and at the same time see clearly who we really are with no attachment and clinging whatsoever. This is freedom, the world of the wise, in whom no fear and bondage can be found. In life there is a need to become in order to function as humans, and this is not in conflict with being. They both serve as two levels of our reality. At the level of manifestation, we talk about becoming and doing different things to meet with certain needs and challenges; while at the "natural-flow-of-life-as-it-is" level, we use the terminology "totality of being" to express ourselves figuratively. So *being* is a delightful stretch of level ground, which provides a firm foundation for our becoming, functioning, and manifesting. It is our home where we can return constantly and relate through simple, clear awareness of who we truly are.

There was a story about the chief of a village in Thailand. Before being elected as village chief, he functioned as an ordinary citizen, with a family. Upon taking the position of the village chief, however, he put himself up on a pedestal and regarded everyone else as lower than himself, including his wife. He had to eat alone with food brought to him on a proper tray. His reason for doing this was that he had become a very important man in the village. He actually demanded this from his wife as well, and she did as he wanted for a while. But one evening the chief went to hold a meeting and came back late at night. Out of her intelligence and compassion for her poor husband, she plotted a situation to awaken him. That evening she went to bed earlier than usual and locked all the doors securely. When he came home, he found himself locked out and could not get in. He had to ask his wife to open the door and let him in. She then said, "Oh, you are now a very important person, as chief of the village, and I am just an ordinary villager. So, you see, the superior man cannot sleep with an ordinary woman like me!" That shocked his mind so much that he was awakened right there and realized what he had been doing. He gave it up right away, at that moment. So, with full realization of the whole truth, illusion is no more. Some people do need this kind of conscious shock because of their deep sleep.

Now, it is clear that becoming is just our temporary functioning, and being is the ground that flows deeply and eternally within us—the ever-flowing movement of life. Being can never be a static and stagnated state, but is a moving reality. So, let us all flow naturally together, with becoming and being, without dwelling on either one of them, so that "clear space and blue sky" may be seen and available for our attention always.

Attachment to Ignorance

This is the last sleeping dog. The term "ignorance" is used here in the specific sense of not seeing the truth totally, not in the sense of lacking knowledge and information. Doubt, uncertainty, perplexity, and confusion are all the symptoms of ignorance. Its opposite is wisdom and light.

The Three Worlds of Ignorance: The World of Unreality; The Phenomenal World; The World of Freedom and Emptiness.   Wisdom is a natural flow of being; ignorance is a mental creation and a condition for molding, shaping, and forming a life-style with its concomitant patterns of behaving and conducting life. When we move away from our natural state of being, we come to the world of phenomena, of change and impermanence, as well as the world of maya, of illusion, unreality, fantasy, and dream. Then we create things to satisfy our needs, our desires, and longings as well as create things to fulfill our thirst for pleasure, comfort, convenience, ideals, ideologies, dreams, and imaginations. In this world of creation we are busy and occupied with a tremendous load of activities. As a result, we become fire, always in a state of burning, rushing around without really being creative or even productive, dissipating and misusing our energies just to fill the day and to hide from anxieties and fears.

Look! In one meditation sitting, how many things we create, in the world of maya, by daydreaming and fantasizing or by planning, programming, and mapping things out in our heads. We must notice and acknowledge how often we live in the world of unreality and how often we appear in the world of phenomena, observing the rise and fall of our breath, thoughts, feelings, sensations, and mental activities as well as physical movements of our bodies, either internally or externally. In this world the wind blows, snow falls, trees dance, rivers flow, and oceans move. Apart from these two worlds, see if we ever drop into the world of freedom and emptiness, which has all the fullness and completion in itself—an abundantly rich and totally nurturing place where all things and nothing in particular are provided, and where desire, longing, demanding, and clinging are not around, even with their shadows, let alone ideas, thoughts, reactive feelings, and dreams. This is the completely fulfilled state of being where everything flows unobstructed.

When we have space, we are in touch with our freedom. Nobody can ever occupy such space; nevertheless, some phenomena might come through it without staying in it. This kind of space is not like the space between here and there, the external, material space in a room, for instance. It is inner and non-material space that we are talking about here. This inner space is freedom for being, sometimes called "Emptiness" or *shunyata*. It is empty in the sense that there is nothing special and familiar to us, no hanging on, no clinging, no desire, no deception, and no ignorance, but something absolutely free, natural, and unique in itself, the undefinable.

Being in such space without dwelling on any concept, notion, and idea, no matter what happens, we are permeated with total clearness, loving flow, fertile emptiness, and freedom. Nothing can affect us, we stay in it fully, dancing with it, moving with it, sitting, walking, running, and eating with it. In other words, we are *it!* This is the eternal *now*. Wherever we go, space is. Even when dreams and fantasies come, we still have space where we can look at them, seeing their illusion and unreality as well as accepting them unconditionally. We let them come and let them go and let them be as they wish; we are ever floating in space with complete freedom. In this way, there is no passion of ignorance.

The Fruits of Ignorance Ignorance only comes in when the truth is not seen. It seems that the more ignorance we have, the more we tend to search for knowledge and information in order to feel more clever and more intelligent than others. So, ignorance helps us create more activities, more theories, more philosophies, more ideas and opinions. The act of creation must be balanced with wisdom and a direct understanding of what we create so that we can avoid getting stuck and dwelling on our creations. Then, there will be an integration between knowledge and wisdom, the head and the heart. So, in a way, ignorance, as the main cause of suffering, is useful for helping us look and make use of our inner resources, allowing us to flow with ever-expanding life. Hence, when light appears, darkness disappears.

I should like to point out briefly that ignorance may be conceived of in many different ways, such as passion, obsessive and compulsive outflow, the inevitable condition for creating and forming our character structures and life-styles, the iron bar locking the gate to liberation, and a very subtle self-deception causing distortions of perception, thought, and views. The passion of ignorance provides colorful and beautifully painted energy for attracting us to the periphery and superficiality of things, causing us to confuse the inessential with the essential as well as blinding our consciousness and vision. It puts us into the position of abiding in our conclusions and dwelling on emotional and psychological levels of our realities without moving forward toward our full being and sinking down into the deepest depths.

The obsessive, compulsive outflow dominates or overrides our feelings, thoughts, patterns of conditioning, programming, behaviors, and the ways by which we react to the world and life situations. Look how we are driven by the impulse for acquiring pleasure and for becoming something or somebody. Constantly demanding, either of oneself or others, and dissatisfaction are the symptoms of the outflow of ignorance. All other forms of ignorance are quite obvious in themselves.

Have another look at two levels of our reality; the physical reality and the psychological reality. We must examine and see for ourselves how we hold our bodies and create blocks of the energy flow in them without any knowledge or conscious act. It becomes more complicated, when looking into our psychological state of existence, to understand how we ourselves, with our psychological mind, cause pain and suffering in our lives and to understand how we dwell on certain negative attitudes, self-concepts, and self-definitions that feed our negativity and deepen our habitual games and compulsive ego trips, which we always play without consciously knowing what we are doing.

Ignorance is the tremendously powerful and destructively dangerous sleeping dog, underlying all our negative and destructive actions, words, thoughts, feelings, and rigidly inflexible attitudes toward life, work, people, and the world in which we live.

CHAPTER SEVEN

Consciousness and the Core of Being

NOW, I WOULD LIKE TO EXPLORE WITH YOU, my reader, this vast subject of consciousness, to see broadly and clearly how it is manifested in our lives as well as in many other planes of existence.

Externalizing the Individual Process of Consciousness: Diverse Approaches to Common Goals Through the Formation of Social Groups

Generally speaking, consciousness is not just an individual process, but represents all the manifestations of humankind and the workings of our society, community, and various groups struggling to exist and to live in accord with the principles upon which their belief systems are based.

In the field of religion and that of spiritual movements, although we are divided into many different categories such as Hindus, Buddhists, Jews, Christians, Muslims, and so on, we all pursue the same goal of total liberation, full enlightenment, complete union or communion with the One, Ultimate Being, or call it what you will. That may be termed "religious energy systems within consciousness" as it manifests in our religious beliefs and faiths, as well as in our spiritual pursuits, the search for purity of heart, love, compassion, and the oneness of being.

At political, economic, and social levels of existence, we attempt to accomplish stability, peace, security, prosperity in its fullest sense of no-starvation and no-poverty at any corner of human society and in any parts of the world, understanding and harmony in living, or peaceful coexistence within the framework of our differentiating systems, which means unity with diversity.

Coming to the group level, we see that each group with its members and followers is trying hard to preserve its identity as well as prove to themselves and others that their path is right and direct to the final destination, no matter what happens to the rest of the world. We all walk together, in the sense that we are following one another as well as conforming to ideas, ideals, beliefs, ideologies, and systems of thought and philosophy. As a result of this conformity and compliance with group beliefs and the group's methods for achieving its objectives, as group members we become narrow in our perception, vision, and thinking so as to close ourselves off from the rest of the world by ignoring what others are doing out of disinterest in understanding them. That is the disease of ignorance and arrogance, which can be easily found in any group, be it political, economic, religious, or spiritual.

So, we are not really different from each other in terms of our manifestations, although we (and our groups) have different approaches, ideas, and options about things in life and in the world. All of those that we maintain and attempt to put into practice are nothing but the manifestations of our consciousness as it expresses itself in different circumstances and situations of life and of the world. In the Buddha's words: "We are what we have been; and shall become what we are."

Examining the Contents of Consciousness as They Affect Group Behavior

Externalizing Our Yearning for Continued Parenting and the Illusion of Safety Within the Family Unit: The Need for Leadership and Symbolic Power

Let us look into our general human situation. As we are all brought up in a particular family, with its rules, and within certain cultural and religious beliefs, as well as trained in a certain system of education and tradition, we do appear different from each other on the periphery, but we are the same in the practice of life. That is, we all follow leadership with its authority and symbolic power, starting from our obedience to our parents and doing what they say without questioning. We imitate them, taking in certain patterns of their behavior and trying to live up to their expectations so that we may get affection and love from them. Also, we want to feel the satisfaction of being like the people we love and admire and to feel a sense of belonging and participation.

When deprived of warmth and affection, we feel loneliness and lack a secure psychological sense of safety. Lacking a secure sense of belonging, we may build up the habit of holding on to someone to lead us and to provide us with some assuring idea and a solid system for coping with life situations, both external and internal, as well as with the world of an opposite camp. This *rigid* identification with a group isn't as likely to occur in people who have found love and support in personal relations, especially in family life. We form our group or party to preserve our belief system and to strengthen our identity as well as to protect and defend our territory. Although each group has its own consciousness resulting from the contents emphasized in the operation of the group, the basic elements of conflict, power struggle, and infighting for personal achievement within the group remain the same. There is usually a superficial harmony within groups; it is just a show for the purpose of winning the game against opposing groups.

How the Illusion of a Separate Self, Fueled by Its Manifestations of Greed, Hate, and Delusion, Creates Social Fragmentation

The fundamental contents of our consciousness take root in greed, hate, and delusion, which spread their diseases and evil spirits through different ways and levels of manifestation. Sometimes, these are seen in forms of nationalism, tribalism, patriotism, and guruism, for the so-called spiritual people. The simple reason for this is that our human consciousness bases itself on division and separateness, which may be termed "self-consciousness" for convenience in communicating here. So, all the manifestations through activities, speeches, and thoughts, which come from, or originate in, such self-interest and the dividing principle, result in deepening and supporting such division, the departmentalization and fragmentation of humanity. Consequently, violence, cruelty, and ruthlessness follow us, dictating and contaminating our minds to think, act, and speak in such a way that division and separation between groups, tribes, societies, nations, and the worlds (as in the so-called free world and socialist and communist world) can become more distinct and evident to their members, followers, and citizens.

Wherever we look in the world we encounter wars, disputes, and crises, or at least tensions in various groups of people of all categories, with no exception. This observable fact shows us repeatedly that when we start with an unhealthy and destructive beginning, the end result is our destruction and perishability. In order to change the currents of events, we have to go to the root to enable us to destroy the center of its operation utterly.

Consciousness has many different names because of the contents from which it arises: consciousness arising from greed is called "greed-consciousness," consciousness arising from hate is called "hate-consciousness," just as a fire burning with wood is named "wood fire" and fire burning with ore is named "ore-fire." Without content, there is no consciousness as we can conceive of in our brain-mind, or computer-mind, so to speak.

As we all know, a computer can work out or function only with what is already put in, the input. When there is no information available within it, the computer cannot work. Similarly, human consciousness proceeds in almost exactly the same way.

Take a close look at those believing in church and going to church regularly; they form a church-consciousness, manifesting themselves according to the teachings, faiths, and dogmatic assertions contained in the church-consciousness. Whatever the church says is fine and, therefore, very often we witness the conflicts and contradictions between churches of the same religion. Some maintain that their God is the only real god; and only by placing a complete trust in that god can people reach the kingdom of heaven and become liberated from sins. Although to some of us this sounds quite ridiculous, there are a number of followers adhering to such a belief, and that same statement sounds very true to them. Obviously, it is man who creates God, and not the reverse. The God-minded people need such a Being to look after them and save them from going to hell as well as from remaining sinners forever. The way to increase their followers and members of their faith is to make that God more powerful and more perfect than other Gods created by other God-minders. Then their concepts of Gods are further made to be in conflict with one another, fighting for the position of the "True God."

The same thing happens to guru-minded people. At first, somebody makes himself a guru, an enlightened master, trying to gather disciples by some personal charisma or magnetism, seemingly wise speeches, and psychological tricks. Then, all his disciples are molded into a consciousness in which worship and total surrender is required as the practice for their liberation. In some guru-worshipping consciousness, it starts off with worshipping the master who is supposed to be a perfect one. Then the acts of worship extend to all the activities in everyday living. By this way, the guru-consciousness can be maintained and the disciples can deepen their dependence on, and bondage to, their guru and all the energy and power that he is believed to possess. This seems like many beautiful birds in an enchanted garden where a princess is obsessed by grief and threatened with death if she refuses to marry a giant who constantly demands her marriage to him.

The category of guru-consciousness is built into a heavy, total commitment to the master who functions as an absolute authority. Any words or statements that come out of his mouth (or sometimes as somebody puts them into his mouth) become a rule, a guideline, or a matter of truth for all his disciples to follow without question. For their consciousness always dictates that the guru can do no wrong and that he is an all-knowing master who can never make any false statement or lead them to a harmful, useless end. He has so much power over his followers!

Because of the total commitment on their part, the disciples live under the influence of fear of breaking such a commitment so that they must close themselves off from the rest of the world and, therefore, can never open themselves up to anything else, particularly to the things or people that might threaten their commitment.

Here we see why the so-called spiritual community formed around a guru becomes, in actual fact, very narrow minded and almost blind to the outside world. Because they are a small minority with a very limited boundary, they feel a great need to assert themselves and consolidate their existence and identity. Thus they are likely to become ruthlessly aggressive and emotionally violent with those whom they perceive as their enemies or as barriers to their expansion and security. They become even more isolated from others. The vicious circle goes on and on. Perhaps they think that a controversy and conflict with other members of the world community could keep them awake and alive to constantly remind them of their survival as a separate and unique community. Being small, they feel more need for protection as well as recognition so that their small minority and small nation can survive and possibly prosper in their own way and within their territory. This is just like a person falling asleep, having dreams and nightmares, thinking that he is awake; for he fights a great deal with monsters and demons wherever he happens to be.

The Matter of Conflict: The Mask of Insecurity and Fear Within the Divided Self

Let us look into this matter of conflict a bit further. Why is there conflict at all? Or the proper question is; how does conflict arise either in an individual or in a community? To such a basic question, perhaps we may find a very simple answer.

It is characteristic of human beings that we do not want to deal with what is actually happening as it is, but habitually tend to create the opposite, something other than what *is* at the time. So, the "what is" and its opposite become a dichotomy of the mind, an insoluble problem. With such a dividing and dualistic thinking conflict arises; the conflict between what *is* and what *should* or *ought* to be. For example, I am afraid of being devoured by someone who appears much more powerful than I am. Instead of just giving all my energy and total attention to the fear of being devoured in order to open myself to the full experience of such a fear, I think that the other person *should not* attempt to swallow me up and that I *should* be respected and given compassion and loving care. Or another way of avoiding that kind of fear is to convince oneself that if one becomes open and loving to people at all times, one will eventually get swallowed up by them. With such a conviction, one just withdraws from openness and lovingness and tries to hide in one's own world, keeping away from people. Then, conflict arises between one's fear of being devoured and the ideal of being open, loving, and available for people's needs. If one were to deal with the fear directly and completely, then there would be no conflict. For the opposite would, and need not be created for the purpose of escaping fear.

The problem of conflict can be solved easily if we are truly willing to overcome it. The process of dealing with conflict is first to look into the nature of the conflict itself, to see clearly what kind of conflict it is, and secondly to find out how it arises or what the conditions and causes are that give rise to it. It is very important to take the first step of understanding the entire structure of conflict with an open attitude of accepting and welcoming it, and not with the intent to fight or crush it through a negative response. By welcoming the conflict, we relax our inner tensions and calm down our minds so that a clear space is created for us to be and to relate to the conflict more at ease and perhaps more freely. With the clarity and space provided, we are in a better position to get to know the conflict more precisely, enabling us to grasp its structure and associated factors that contain, as well as support, the conflicting energy.

With such comprehension of the whole issue related to conflict, we naturally minimize complication and confusion. Under these conditions, conflict can be transcended without too great an effort. However, if we look for a solution without sufficiently understanding the structure of conflict, then it will become more complicated and harder to overcome. Just as in anything else, the solution to a problem actually lies within the complete understanding of the problem itself. This particularly applies to inner conflict with which we are all confronted from time to time in our lives. As for the outer conflict between groups or nations, it might take more time and energy to bring a solution to it. This is because such a conflict is involved with practical matters that the two parties need to agree upon through their real willingness to settle the conflicting issue together. Otherwise, the crisis of consciousness will go on and, therefore, deepen the persisting conflict to the point of destruction.

When looking into individuals and the world around us, we come across the crises of consciousness taking place within individuals, in relationships between partners, married couples, friends, colleagues, neighbors, groups, communities, and nations. Conflict, a common content of consciousness, is often seen as a basic element in creating and manifesting a crisis of human consciousness. With conflict as a starting point of all crises, there comes into operation other destructive contents of consciousness such as aggression, hate, resentment, fear that something bad is going to happen, or of being attacked or destroyed. As a result, an individual builds walls around himself/herself, thinking that he/she might live safely and securely within those walls of protection.

As a nation, various kinds of weapons are made for killing humans and fighting wars as well as for settling any crisis either within its own country or in neighboring countries, including allied nations. The initial intentions sound good and make sense to a majority of the population because, as individuals, they are facing personal crises and conflicting interests similar to those faced by their governments. Those in power say that dangerous weapons and defense systems are built for the purpose of protecting their country and their peoples as well as for defending themselves against their enemies or even for forcing the other superpowers to come and sit down at the negotiation table for arms control.

The words sound acceptable and comforting. But the driving forces of fear and self-interest contained within such consciousness are working behind those seemingly beautiful words. Therefore, we meet with more crises of delusion and ignorance, which put us to sleep with our belief system of defense and protection. We then follow the leadership that appears strong and brave on the surface without realizing that underneath such leadership is insecurity and fear, the cause of human destruction. As a matter of fact, behind fear and a sense of insecurity are delusion or ignorance in the sense, on the one hand, of not understanding the whole issue of crisis, and, on the other hand, of attachment to the idea of survival and to the belief system.

These two, the failure of genuine understanding and attachment to ideas and belief systems, function as the building up process for re-enforcing the ideas and beliefs of the leaders and their advisors. There is no wisdom or even intelligence when overruled by fear, ignorance, and attachment. So, it is absolutely harmful to place trust in those whose consciousness is full of crises. Most of the time, it is not easy to see if there are any crises operating in the consciousness of our leaders, for they train themselves to hide them well by learning how to tell lies, and we ourselves are driven by similar crises within our consciousness, do not care to look into them, but expect our leaders to pacify and settle all the crises for us. See how the vicious circle works!

Focusing on the crises of consciousness within an individual, we see that in actual fact there is no such a thing as an individual's consciousness, although some more mature individuals can function from their own centeredness. Nevertheless, their culture, religion, and family background still raise voices to frighten, withhold, and confuse their perception and cognition and shape their movements in carrying out their activities and the life-styles that they believe to be correct and healthy.

The Illusion of Free Will

We all have to deal with our internal crises almost all the time, for within our consciousness there are so many contents derived from various sources in this lifetime as well as accumulated through centuries. Parental authority, religious power, and cultural command, plus influences of ideas, philosophies, systematic thinking and models, pouring into us through our education, training, and personal experiences, dictate the course of our action, forming our views and opinions about different issues in life, in society, and in the world. Consequently, our thought and reaction to what is going on in our lives and to situations and crises in the world are heavily conditioned and thickly colored by the input or contents of consciousness that form the core of personality. Within this unit of personality a solid structure of character is built from which we manifest ourselves. All our movements in life, in society, and in the world spring from and comply with our character structure, which is in fact our organizing agent, which has all the power over our perceptual and conceptual modalities. Where then is our free will?

Will is just a small part of the organizing principle, which contains many other factors and elements, such as contact, mental impact, feeling, perception, ideation, fixated purpose, determination, and fixedness of mind. All these together with will or intent are inseparable properties common to our ordinary, human consciousness. So, there is no room for free will at this level of our working consciousness. It is merely an illusion, or a narrowing of perception, to put it in better terms, when people say that they exercise their free will on certain issues.

What do we do when confronted with challenges? We respond to them according to the contents of consciousness. If you are brought up in democratic society, you take an action in accordance with your democratic principles and ideologies. If you are trained and educated in the communist or socialist system, you react to challenging situations in conformity with communism or socialism. In the religious field, if you are Hindu, Buddhist, Christian, Muslim, or Sikh, you automatically respond according to the principles, dogmas, and beliefs of your religion. If you happen to be a nonbeliever, skeptic, scientist, or anarchist, you certainly react and behave in compliance with the system and assumptions that you perceive within your field of knowledge and limited experience.

Coming to this point, one would raise a question: where is true freedom of action and freedom for being? At this level of ordinary consciousness operating within the world of relativity, there is no absolute freedom, the totality of being free in doing and non-doing. What people call "freedom" is just a relative term for conveying the meaning of action and thought that is born out of the self-centeredness of an individual who is relatively free from psychological and social conditioning at a time. This means that such a person acts, thinks, and speaks from the center of his/her own gravity, personal power, and visionary insights into the matter concerned. Still, the freedom born of these sources is limited to and can be measured by knowledge and the degree of the individual's development. That means that the individual's actions can, nevertheless, be predicted from an understanding of his/her personal history. But true, total freedom is immeasurable, absolute, and born of clear, empty space, or of nothing whatsoever. In other words, there is no underlying principle causing such freedom to occur. What is called "clear and empty space, or nothing whatsoever" here simply refers to a figurative expression of a delightful stretch of level ground. Certainly, the consciousness flowing with such ultimate freedom is not the one that we have been discussing here up until now, but ultimate consciousness itself. There is no way to understand it unless one has fully evolved into such consciousness.

Levels and Planes of Consciousness as Described in the Buddhist Texts and Elaborated Through the Archetypes of Buddhist Mythology

The Four Main Levels of Consciousness

The preceding chapters of this book have discussed, in some detail, the first two of four main levels of consciousness. The four are:

1. Consciousness operating in the world of pleasure and pain (Kamaloka).
2. Consciousness functioning in the meditative, spiritual sphere of form (Rupaloka).
3. Consciousness manifesting in the higher meditative, spiritual sphere of formlessness (Arupaloka).
4. Consciousness transcending the worlds of pleasure, form, and formlessness, culminating in *shunyata*—the Void or Complete Emptiness—in which what we are familiar with does not exist. Instead there is a Fullness of Being where God, Dharma, Tao, and Brahma can no longer be found (Lokuttara Citta).

Now let us delve more deeply into each level, respectively, using the mythological archetypes of Buddhist theology as keys to enhance the analytical process. (See Chapter 8 for a discussion of archetypes in Jungian psychology.)

Archetypes are apparently collectively present dynamic patterns of energy. Each culture and each religious tradition has described the activity of these patterns in a unique, poetic manner. Throughout the body of this chapter I will use the mythological archetypes of Buddhist theology and show, through pertinent examples, how its seemingly exotic and mysterious characters and their behavior successfully describe subtle and complex experiences in our everyday life and in the experiential process of our transpersonal (spiritual) development.

Level I: Consciousness Manifesting in the World of Desires/Pleasure-Pain (Kamaloka)

The first level of consciousness, consciousness operating in the world of pleasure (and pain) operates in three planes of existence:

(a) the plane of non-progressive beings such as those living in hells on earth; the animal kingdom, hungry ghosts or evil spirits, and demons. (This is the realm of misfortune.)

(b) the plane of human beings.

(c) the plane of *devas*—shining beings, dwelling in heavens.

These planes of life are confined to the dictation of desires so that beings in the lowest plane suffer tremendously both day and night, while beings in the highest plane enjoy the pleasures of the senses to their extremity. The middle plane, of humans, fluctuates, swinging back and forth between hells and heavens, experiencing both pain and pleasure from time to time. In another way of explanation, we say that the above-mentioned three planes of existence are involved with sensual pleasures in which pain and suffering are included as an inevitable experience through the senses.

Plane 1: The Non-Progressive Plane of Misfortune: Living Hells on Earth.
Let us elaborate on these three main planes of existence as governed
by the first level of consciousness, operating in the realm of desires,
beginning with the non-progressive plane or the realm of misfortune. In this plane of life, we find four categories of beings living
their lives as already mentioned. The concept of a hell or purgatory
state in mythology refers to different places under the earth where
sinners or those committing different degrees of bad karma, after
death, have their rebirth. By re-experiencing and reliving their
karma until it is all over, they become cleansed of such karma
accumulated in their human form of existence. In actual life situations, this hell or purification simply means our regression, in which
we go back to our early childhood experiences; this is a reversion to
a chronologically earlier or less-adapted pattern of behavior and
feeling. Regression is seen in the therapeutic process when those
driven by pain and suffering, either emotionally, physically, or both,
work as well as live through different incidents of their unpleasant
and miserable past. Everybody regresses or transforms backward
in order to cleanse their unfinished business with their parents and
those who interacted with them in negative or destructive ways,
causing a volcanic, explosive energy to be stored up or be buried in
their psychophysical processes, or "body-mind." This state of affairs
is very obvious to therapists and psychotherapists as well as to those
who have undertaken the therapeutic process in their lives.

During the time that we exert our energy to resolve all the
possible situations in our early lives (and perhaps some from previous lifetimes), we go through, and live in, various hells, according
to the degree of pain and suffering resulting from the negative
karma accumulated by our own behavior and the actions of others
toward us (i.e., inappropriate actions by our loved ones that blocked
our growth instead of nurturing and supporting us). Sometimes our
experiences in these hell realms are unbearably painful; other times
they are bearable and less sorrowful. Some processes take so long
that we begin to think they will never be finished in this lifetime;
others pass by quickly. Their duration is unpredictable.

When investigating human life experiences, we often see our
fellow beings, including ourselves, of course, going into hell and

coming out of it in everyday living. We suffer losses, greater and lesser, of our businesses, our beloved ones, our friendships, and relationships of love and marriage. When things go wrong and we are unable to put them right, we go into a hell emotionally or psychologically. All unpleasant, fearful, miserable, and unsatisfactory experiences in life, which fill our days, however long each experience might take, are our hell-dwellings.

During such a period of time, there is nothing progressive you can do at the material level. All you can do is suffer and torture yourself. You have no choice until your bad karma or deposited conditioning of pain, fear, confusion, rage, and suffering is eliminated, or temporarily suppressed and controlled by Western medicine (drugs).

In this way, we see hell as an experience through one of our six senses: eyes, ears, nose, tongue, body touch, and the mind (perception, cognition, and consciousness). Whenever sense impressions, or mental contact with thoughts, ideas, dreams, or fantasies, are disagreeable, unsatisfactory, agonizing, miserable, depressing, resentful, hateful, frightening, and fearful, confusing as well as unclear and doubtful, conflicting and perplexing, distorting and displacing, we are in hell at that moment. Certainly, the duration of the experience and degrees of misery vary. Nevertheless, from being in hell we gain insights into our life stories, seeing profoundly and thoroughly the causes of pain with all its dramas and episodes, so that we can free ourselves and transform forward to the level of happiness, peace, harmony, love, clarity, and wisdom. For this reason, we say that the experience of hell awakens us!

The animal kingdom. The animal kingdom suffers dullness, while the predominant state of consciousness of those living through hell is *dosa*—hate, aversion, resentment, anger, repugnance, envy, jealously, and things of that nature.

It is quite evident to all of us how animal life is. All the animals just live their lives according to the instinctual drives of fear, hunger, and sex. They cannot make much progress in their lives, particularly when compared with human beings who are fully equipped with a highly developed physical form and six senses, brain and mind.

Their primary goal of life is survival. Even so, they cannot do much about preserving and prolonging life due to their stagnated and tremendously limited state of existence. *Moha,* or dullness, a major content of animal consciousness, governs their lives. They have no choice but to live through such a state of misfortune until they die. This is another way of endeavoring to clean out certain karma that had accumulated in a fragment of consciousness during a lifetime of taking a human form. It is actually a form of lifetime regression!

The experience of being a certain animal such as a cat, a tiger, or a snake is not uncommon to us humans during a phase of our therapeutic process. Even in our day-to-day living we may have an awareness of animal consciousness in our minds. Apparently, some element of the animal consciousness exists as a residue of karma within the human state of existence. Therefore, we cannot be completely differentiated from animals and insects; all are merely manifestations of consciousness.

Hungry ghosts. Considering the realm of unhappy, hungry ghosts *(petaloka),* we see *greed* as a predominant factor of their consciousness. Beings in this realm, technically known as *peta* in the Pali language, or *preta* in Sanskrit, are said to be in a constant state of greed (hunger), trying to fill their stomachs.

In mythology, there is reference to the body of a hungry ghost as huge as a mountain, with a mouth as small as the hole of a needle. Imagine how much and how often a *preta* has to eat in order to sustain such a gigantic body. Because they are constantly driven by hunger, those beings roaming about in the realm of *pretaloka* become very aggressive in their attempts to get food, to feed themselves. Aggression and hunger go hand in hand, driving all the hungry ghosts crazy in their struggle for survival. Inwardly, they always feel insecure and threatened that they will not have enough to satisfy their hunger. Consequently, they end up eating compulsively so that their bodies can become bigger and more powerful in the world. All the activities in their lives are organized around the sustenance of their physical form. That is why we hear stories about hungry ghosts or evil spirits demanding offerings and sacrifices from human beings with a certain threat: if they are not sufficiently fed, some disaster and/or illness will befall those humans who live near them. If anybody enters their territory without offering things such as food and drink, the ghosts get furious and become extremely cruel.

Demons. Now, turning to the realm of the Asura, demons, we find they live under the influence of fear. As a result, they often involve themselves with fighting and making wars both with human beings and *devas*, heavenly gods. It is quite common for demons to attack humans and gods without giving any notice, as soon as they become suspicious and feel frightened or insecure. This sort of action is what we normally call "back biting" or "blackmail" in the human realm, since it is not an open and honest action. Due to the dictation of fear, they carry out their activities in a very hateful, resentful, and angry way. It appears that they are always ready to crush and destroy their enemies with no mercy. Outwardly, they act brave and appear strong, but inwardly their lives are dominated by fears for their safety and security and by the fear of death. Surprisingly enough, they possess a great deal of power, but are not wise.

For example, in a Persian story a demon named "dajit" used this method of getting a young girl from a village: he ordered the villagers to perform a festival once a year and gather all the young women together to enable him to pick the one he liked most.

One day, a young stranger entered the village. Out of curiosity about what was going on, the young man approached the village chief and inquired into the reasons for their joy and happiness. He was told that on the contrary, they were not at all happy, but only pretended to be. They were under the power of the demon who commanded them to arrange a seemingly happy festival to provide him with a young girl from one of their families. They had no choice, but did it so that they could get on with their lives without too much trouble from the demon.

Upon hearing this story, the youth asked if they could present the demon to him so that he could make some direct inquiries into the state of affairs. They agreed and informed their demon that a young chap from a strange land visiting their village wanted to have an interview with him regarding this unusual wedding procedure. Out of pride and self-delusion, the demon agreed.

At the meeting the young fellow told his host, the demon, that in his civilized world the groom must demonstrate his power as a mature family leader by accomplishing certain tasks before having the bride with him. The demon, being proud of his superficial power and guided by ignorance, determined to show his honorable guest any power that his visitor wanted to see. So, the young, wise man put his *tarisma* into the water in a glass to diminish the demon's power and asked the demon to drink it before putting himself into a barrel and trying to get out of it. In his belief that he still had all his power, the demon threw himself into the barrel and struggled to come out with no success. Then, the young man set fire to him and burned him up.

Plane 2: The Human Plane of Existence. As for the human plane of existence, we find ourselves wandering around in a fluctuating place, somewhere between those four realms of misfortune and the planes of fortune, although in the final analysis we are included in the latter. As a matter of fact, we humans embrace both categorical planes of fortune and misfortune as our life experiences tell us time and time again. We go back and forth, up and down, between happiness and unhappiness, between sorrow and joy, between pain and pleasure, etc. Sometimes, we fall down to a purgatory state, submerging ourselves in pain and suffering; other times, we climb up to a heaven, enjoying all kinds of sensory pleasures as we find them in such a heavenly state of existence. This simply refers to the sensory experiences in our everyday living. Our eyes, ears, nose, tongue, body touch, and mind bring us both pleasurable and painful experiences at different degrees and for various durations of time, facts that we directly experience as well as witness throughout our lives on earth.

Because we are fully equipped with these six sense-modalities—eyes for seeing visual objects, ears for hearing sounds and vibratory things, a nose for smelling, a tongue for tasting, body touch for contacting tangible objects, and a mind for thinking, imagining, inventing, dreaming, fantasizing, and communicating with the internal world of ideas, thoughts, and psychic phenomena, as well as with the external world together with five other physical senses—we are in a position of meeting with all forms of challenges and information pouring in through our sense-impressions. Each sensory experience, whether good or bad, pleasant or unpleasant, agreeable or disagreeable, inviting or uninviting, immediately sends us to a certain plane of life within a certain level of consciousness and energy field. Then, we leave, shift, or die from our previous state of experience and are born or transformed into a new consciousness with a new experience produced by such a sense-impression and sensory awareness.

For example, one morning while enjoying your favorite breakfast with your wife or partner, she unexpectedly brings up the bad news that she has been having an affair with another man. Under the influence of anger and jealousy, you might just throw your plate and smash the dining table, your body shaking and your mind getting burned with powerful negative feelings. Are you in hell at that moment? Before that, were you in a state of heaven? Joy as a content of consciousness manifests in you and through you while in the former state of enjoying your wonderful breakfast; then, anger, supported by jealousy and/or possessiveness, forces you to descend to enter hell, a realm of misfortune, an unhappy state of existence. This is how varying sense-impressions produce different planes of life in which the appropriate states of consciousness manifest themselves accordingly. Just observe your life experience through the contact of senses, and you will gain deep insights into the situation of sense-impressions where heaven and hell exist.

Human beings manifesting animal consciousness. Apart from those categories of hell and heaven, we humans could possibly become animal-like beings in terms of a manifestation of consciousness. For we possess all the instincts, emotions, and passions, including *moha* (dullness), delusion, or lack of insight, which are the predominant factors of consciousness in the animal kingdom. When entering an animal-human state driven by instinctual forces supported by delusion and dullness or muddledness, we become very cruel, violent, and without any compassion for our fellow beings who are needy and/or helpless. We just sleep with our selfish desires for producing more and having more merely to increase our comfort, prosperity, wealth, and fleeting pleasures. It doesn't matter to us what happens to others and to the environment in terms of pollution, destruction of beauty, clean air, and so forth. We close our eyes and confine our minds to our own world within the community or group that shares our interest in group survival and self-prosperity.

In the history of humankind, we observe that uncultured humans or animal-humans fought in disputes and wars between tribes, killing one another. The English killed the Scottish when conquering their kingdom. It was said that thousands of children were slaughtered in order to destroy the Scottish descent or tribes completely. For the same reason, Hitler mercilessly killed the Jews. Fighting and killing between tribal people has been quite common throughout our prehuman and human history. Even now, in our so-called civilized world where technology is highly advanced, some of us still carry within ourselves the animal consciousness of guarding territory and protecting a community and allied interest: we are actively indulging in building up a nuclear arsenal that could destroy us all, including our children. Such action is taken because ignorance, the predominant content of animal consciousness, operates in the political arena to create policies based on fear, aggression, and destruction. Many of us who are still ignorant and asleep, identify blindly with patriotism and nationalism and enthusiastically support such attitudes. We continue to act foolishly and irresponsibly despite the lessons that history has taught us.

We had better wake up from ignorance and nightmares to the truth of life; to illimitable, unconditional love and the awareness of how great compassion can work in the world to bring the universal unity of humankind into existence. Animal consciousness can be transformed, for the opposite of ignorance is wisdom, in which we also find the natural flow of undiscriminating love and impersonal compassion.

Human beings manifesting hungry ghost consciousness. Now, let us discuss the consciousness of hungry ghost-humans, in which *greed* is contained as a predominant factor. Observe what actually happens to our world today. Our environment and the beauty of nature are being destroyed in almost every part of the industrial world. Big businesses are created to invest millions and billions of dollars on the same basis: having more and producing more. That is a greedy consciousness, isn't it? For those who are dictated to by greed and are hoarding wealth, there is no mercy for nature and no sense of natural beauty and a healthy environment. In other words, they just don't care for such things; their only concern is doing business and making money. The greedy, selfish people show no compassion to the needy and the helpless such as those who live in poverty and starve, the handicapped and elderly. Worse still, they even want to get rid of such innocent people because they are no longer useful to productive society. See how immoral and cruel people can become when driven by greed: they resort to stealing, robbery, taking advantage of others, and trying to get ahead of others in jobs as well as in politics with passive aggression or even by violently destroying those standing in their way. All of these things, obvious in our human society, result from our greedy consciousness, which is originally rooted in the realm of hungry ghosts. Thus, many of us are still the hungry ghost-humans that walk the earth.

Human beings manifesting demonic consciousness. When human beings manifest demonic consciousness, their bodies and energies really appear like demons. A smoky, misty atmosphere appears around demon-humans from the anger and fear devouring them. They lose their radiance, or a clear, clean, and loving expression. In neurotic cases, the demon-humans are actually very afraid when friendliness, gentleness, tenderness, and warmth of the heart are offered to them. They even interpret such beautiful energies manifested in others toward them as some sort of phoniness and unrealness, for they can never place trust in such friendly and loving people, however real they may be.

This brings to mind the story of a demon who lived on a diet of *anger*. After some years of consuming human anger, he thought to himself that the anger of *devas* or heavenly beings (gods and goddesses) might have a different flavor. So one day he disappeared from the human world and arrived in one of the six heavens, *tavatimsa*, where there lived thirty-three deities headed by Indra, the king of Tavatimsa heaven.

Upon getting there, no *deva* was present in the assembly hall. So the demon went in and sat down on Indra's throne, waiting for food. Not long afterwards a few deities came in to have a regular audience with their king. Instead of meeting with their loving, wise king, they encountered a demon with all his dark, ugly, and disgraceful energies vibrating and flying around him and in the beautiful hall. They immediately got angry and became absolutely furious with the demon. They yelled at him: "How dare you come and seat yourself on our king's throne?" "You bastard demon! Get off of the throne right now!" All the nasty words that serve the purpose of expressing their anger came out of those *devas'* mouths. Then, more and more *devas* entered the assembly hall, and they were all angry at the unexpected demon seated on their Indra's throne.

But the demon was very happy that there was plenty of food for him, more than he anticipated. He then ate and ate until all the thirty-three *devas'* anger became completely exhausted. A big feast for him! Thereafter, Indra came in. He knew exactly what was going on. So, instead of sending out angry energy, he starved the demon by offering him friendly energy with a hospitable kindness. He said to his guest: "Hi demon! How nice to see you here with us in our heaven! What should we offer you, our honorable guest? We have some special drinks of *amarita* and *soma*. They are both very strong and palatable as well as good for getting high, energywise!" Upon hearing such beautiful words and encountering the unexpected friendliness, the demon was caught by his fear and distrust. Instead of opening himself to receiving and accepting Indra's loving gesture, he sank down, deep down into the throne, and vanished then and there, without a word to Indra.

Being under the influence of demonic consciousness, one tends to act brave and appear strong. But inside of such demon-humans there is a great deal of fear and feeling of insecurity. Sometimes, they behave themselves with warmth and a nice manner outwardly, while inwardly they are burning with hate and anger. Such warm and tender behavior is adopted for the purpose of wanting to be liked by others in contact with them. Also, some demonic people like to fight a lot, either against an authority (including authority figures) or with themselves in terms of struggling, pushing, and trying hard with very little learning. For this reason, they suffer tremendously in their lives, and perhaps one may say that they actually specialize in the matter of suffering. I am sure that pain and suffering are the path of demonic humans toward final liberation. They certainly know a great deal of misery and sorrow and can conceptualize them well. As a matter of fact, without *dukkha* (dissatisfaction, suffering, and changing conditions of life) there would be no total freedom and full awakening for us sentient beings that walk on earth. So, it is not bad at all to suffer for any reason, or for no reason whatsoever, if one understands the implication of such an unpleasant or even unbearable experience. For it always points to learning as well as obtaining wisdom and gaining insights into the true nature of life with its situations. In other words, one may say that suffering, whether we like it or not, is our "awakener" who wakes us up from our psychological sleep to the truth of Total Freedom. For any time when awakening emerges through suffering of some sort, there is transformation, the definite movement toward our *full beingness*.

Truly human humans: a joyful marriage of heaven (yang) and earth (yin): the union of opposites. Turning to the unique consciousness manifesting in our real human form of existence, we have a category of truly human humans whose intrinsic nature is the state of balance and union of heaven and earth. We humans, when keeping ourselves flowing evenly and creatively within our excellent form of life, free from influences of lower as well as higher states of consciousness, are a meeting place or a point of equilibrium between yin (an upward moving form of energy—earth) and yang (a downward movement of energy—heaven). Whenever heaven comes down and earth goes up, merging with each other at a point of complete harmony, a real human being is born and lives his/her human life without any perversions and contaminations.

For this reason, true humanness is nothing but a joyful marriage of heaven and earth, and the moving apart, the departure, or the separation of heaven and earth creates crises in human consciousness. In such a state of disintegration and separateness between heaven and earth, human form still exists in its built-in structure, but the human consciousness is no longer unique, being torn into different fragments by the crisis of the two energy forces.

So now, a question arises as to what is it that pulls heaven and earth away from each other? By their true nature, the earth energy ascends, while the heaven energy descends. They are certainly meant to meet somewhere in between, a middle place between their two poles. There is no way for them to miss the meeting point, unlike parallel movements. Once they have met and become unified, they should be able to stay together as partnership forces of creativity and receptiveness. For they both always move toward each other, attracting themselves endlessly, and for that matter there is no room for them to be otherwise. So, one wonders about the causes and conditions that separate them as well as a unique principle that can keep them in their full union. There must be something wrong somewhere, and there must be a right thing for eradicating such a separating cause.

To find the answer to this question, we have to look into ourselves and our human situations, for what I have called the movements of heaven and earth are just symbolic gestures, helping us to form a creative imagination within ourselves, so that we may bring together in harmony the scattered, fragmented energies both within and around us. If both are done, that is, the inner work of balance and the outer work of living and existing together peaceful- ly and harmoniously, then heaven and earth as a universal life energy available both within an individual human being and in the entire universe will dance together in complete harmony. Then healing, if necessary, takes place, and there emerges the wholeness of being, a total union of opposites.

The crisis of consciousness that acts as the unbalancing factor in human beings. Now, let us return to the basic question of what it is that breaks down the natural union of heaven and earth within each of us as well as among us human beings. It is the crisis of our consciousness that disturbs and destroys the harmony and the dance of heaven and earth. As a matter of fact, we humans tend to create an opposite to *what is*, which we are experiencing at the moment. Out of fear and pain, we avoid a direct experience of it by turning our attention away and focusing it on something that is in opposition to the happening. Therefore, we inevitably get into conflict, both inner conflict within ourselves individually and outer conflict with the world, or that which is in front of us and is obviously challenging us. This is the beginning of our crisis within human consciousness.

Take a look at a very simple situation of pain, be it physical or emotional. Instead of opening ourselves to fully experiencing it with all our attention through accepting and welcoming it as we do with pleasant things in life, we automatically jump into the idea of killing it or getting rid of it with our little, logical thinking mind, which dictates that pain is unpleasant and disturbing and should be eliminated at once. So we take pain-killing pills or resort to alcohol or drugs to put us to sleep so that we may forget all about our pain. For this reason, the crisis of pain accumulates more explosive strength and rapidly expands into more inner tension and addiction to alcohol or drugs, physically or psychologically, or both. As the crisis of our consciousness gets bigger and bigger through neglect of direct work on the thing itself and looking for an opposite, a compensation, an easy way out of a challenge, we pay an even higher price than we originally anticipated. The crisis becomes more complicated. Instead of simply dealing with the pain only, we now must put a great deal of energy and time into reducing stress that has accumulated through our inner tensions and coping with our addictions. And yet, that pain is still there as an explosive energy (in case of a negative feeling) that is ready to burst out and erupt at any moment, the timing of which we have no idea. This means that there will be more work to do and a greater price to pay for such a little thing as the original pain.

As we go on living our lives unaware, compulsively endeavoring to accomplish our material success, fulfilling all the tasks in the world out there, no matter what happens to our inner world, we create more crises in and through our consciousness. Then we complain that life in the world is full of conflicting situations and is terribly complex.

We don't really want to know how such things as conflicts and complexities of crises come into being, but try harder, while groping in the darkness of ignorance, to resolve all those problems that face our humanity. Is it possible for an act born of unawareness or ignorance such as the passion of fear and clinging to put an end to a crisis within our human consciousness? Such an act will certainly lead to more complicated crises and eventually to the destruction of humankind. For only light can bring about more light. The darkness will only darken itself more deeply.

Unless we humans realize the truth that all our crises are basically the outcome of the lack of awareness, the full contact with what is going on, we will never be able to bring to a complete stop the crisis that we face within ourselves individually as well as collectively in the world of human society. With total awareness of life and of the world, we will find out together the causes and conditions giving rise to any crises, whether within individuals, between and among individuals, and in the entire world. With such a clearly and impeccably aware action in every movement of life and of the world, we shall certainly be able to shape them into harmony, peace, and integration and, therefore, keep heaven and earth together in complete union, both within each of us and all around us. All the crises of consciousness will just vanish like a disappearing illusion when the actual seeing of the whole truth arises.

Before going into some details of how to keep the balance of, or to neutralize the opposing forces of, creativity and destruction, let us elaborate on the matter of conflict and how it spreads into various areas of our lives. When taking a closer look at the origination of conflict, we find that it is closely linked with our dualistic thinking, for in such a way of thinking, we create concepts, ideas, and notions in opposition to one another. Good-bad, right-wrong, true-false, moral-immoral, violent-non-violent, peace-war, love-hate, relative-absolute, body-mind, subject-object, and so on, are in themselves nothing unique or special but the products of our dichotomies, dualistic thinking. Once the world of duality is created, we take it so seriously, that is, attribute to it reality, an independent existence, that such a concept or a notion weighs heavily on our human mind. We then become like an elephant in a mire. We cling firmly to the meanings of the words interpreted by our computer mind, which has nothing really new to say but repeats endlessly that which has been already put in such a computer—the input, so to speak.

Very often, some so-called deep thinkers in their search for truth try to bring out the meaning of concepts and notions as used by certain philosophers, mystics, and religious masters. Those taking a firm grip on words and their meanings without directly experiencing the truth beyond them often get into conflict with others who use those same words in a slightly different context. For example, the word "God" can be used in a variety of ways by different people. Some use it to mean an old, wise gentleman in the kingdom of heaven, who is a Creator, while others employ it to refer to the most powerful, male, spiritual energy available in the entire universe, an energy that has a descending movement. Between those two kinds of people, the former are religious, while the latter are spiritual scientists. They certainly do not agree with one another; therefore, there is conflict between them, and all that is merely in their minds with their belief systems and subjective experiences to support their maintenance of the word "God." With a deep clinging to, and blind belief in, the concept and notion of God, those believers can argue with non-believers forever, attempting to prove that they are right and others are wrong. Worse still, some believers even maintain that their God is the only true One, and that the God maintained by other believers is false. Hence, we see in an obvious way the crisis in the consciousness of religious people. This implies that such people's minds get narrower and narrower to the point of closing themselves off from seeing what is going on outside of their own boundary. When such a mind dominates our perceptions and points of view, we are farther and farther away from reality and, therefore, submerging ourselves in the world of illusion without even realizing that illusion envelopes us, closing our hearts and blinding our minds, let alone our spirit and soul!

In this connection, Gotama the Buddha said: "In the beginning there is the mind." Mind is the chief: all conditioned things are made by mind. When one's mind is in crisis one speaks or acts and is followed by conflict in the same way that the wheels of a cart follow the footprints of the oxen that pull it. If, however, one speaks and acts with clarity of mind, a mind devoid of crisis, happiness and joy follow like a shadow that never leaves."

So, all is in the mind, and everything expressed in thought, action, or speech does originate in the mind, does it not? Ninety-nine percent of us walking on earth do believe in whatever the mind says. The mind becomes an ultimate authority, which has all the power to dictate, control, and manipulate almost all of us in all the activities carried out in our lives as well as in the world. Very few of us question the mind, for we are brought up to think logically, to reason, to rationalize, and to intellectualize, working things out through it. If anything appears illogical, unreasonable, irrational, disagreeable, or unable to be proved scientifically by our systematic thinking, it is immediately rejected and put down. It is the mind that makes decisions and judgments on any matters concerning life, death, and world affairs. Without this computerized mind it seems as if we might not be able to function adequately. For this reason, the mind becomes a boss, a master of all our human affairs. We then become totally dependent on the mind. So there is no freedom on our part unless the mind, itself, is free and liberated.

Letting go of conflict: dropping off the mind. As we understand that all is in the mind, if we change the mind, emptying it out of all the conflicting ideas, thoughts, principles, philosophies, theories, belief systems, etc., everything will be fine. We will no longer be in conflict with anybody or with anything, for the pure light of wisdom arises in such an empty and luminous mind.

Just experiment with dropping something off your mind and letting it be free of any contents, particularly of those that put you into conflict with other fellow beings and/or with the world. Then, see what happens. Proceed from there. To a petty mind that always holds on to some things to provide a false sense of security and an illusion of safety, a suggestion such as this sounds quite frightening, doesn't it? Where is conflict when the mind is free and fully understands things as they are without any prejudices, any biases, and any distortions? The Buddha used to say that he was not in conflict with anybody, but someone might be in conflict with him. The reason for his statement being that the Buddha's mind was totally free and absolutely clear, as well as empty, so that he could not find any conflict anywhere within himself. But for those of us who haven't freed our minds, there is a chance for getting into conflict even with the Buddha or with Christ. In actual fact, the unfree mind is influenced by fear and rooted in ignorance and therefore finds itself in a constant state of conflict, which as we have seen, is the root cause of all the crises in living and existing.

One of the habits of mind is that it tends to set up in advance an unrealistic situation for suffering, although sometimes an actual experience of pain and misery does take place. But before that happens, the mind has already created it by anticipating, or getting painfully anxious about, the actual experience. Such a mind simply cannot let things be, nor can it open itself to welcoming and accepting the world as it comes. It always wishes the actual situation to be other than it is. Hence, the mind compulsively creates and looks for an opposite—the cause of conflict.

For example, you have an appointment for an interview for a job that you desperately need. Before the appointed time for the interview, your mind is driving you crazy, thinking, imagining, and inventing all sorts of possible melodramas that could happen at the interview with your prospective boss. You might not appear capable and intelligent enough for the job. You might not be able to answer certain questions adequately, so your boss-to-be would consider you unsuitable for the job. There would be many more intelligent and capable people, lined up for such an interview to get the job that you want. You might be very tense and nervous, or even fearful, in front of the interviewer, so you would have failed to win the race before it had actually begun.

These things in your mind put you into suffering for many hours or perhaps several days before your interview takes place, and you might suffer even more during the actual interview. However, if your mind is clear and free of anticipating the occurrence of such unpleasant things and then remains unmoved as well as prepared to meet with any challenges, your experience of yourself and of your mind before, as well as during, the interview will be entirely different. That is to say, you will relax into talking and exchanging your views with the interviewer, dealing freely with whatever happens during such a period of the interview. Perhaps you might just enjoy the occasion of meeting with another human being, which you would take as an opportunity to learn about yourself, the other person, and the business. Here it is very obvious to us that the open, innocent, and youthful mind works differently from the closed, old, and heavily conditioned mind—the computer mind that we discussed earlier.

In a way, it is very simple not to enter into conflicts in living and in interacting with the world, including our human relationships and our relational contact and movement with regard to objects. The simple thing we have to do is not fill our mind with any opposites but let it be so free and empty as to enable us to face any challenges just for what they are. By so doing, we will allow ourselves to fully experience what is, with all our attention and creative energy. In such a way of being and acting, we neither look back, nor do we look for anything else apart from being totally in touch with and looking at what is being experienced at the moment. So, there is no divided attention, nor is there distracting consciousness when we can wholly be. In such complete beingness there is tremendous power and ever-flowing energy with all its movement, freedom, and insightful wisdom. Included in this movement is love, peace, intelligence, harmony, beauty, strength, and vibrant aliveness.

It has become clear that personality crises, as well as conflict with others, the family, the group, the community, and the world at large, are manifestations of the crisis of consciousness. Realizing how much burden there is in carrying in our mind the conflicting things that lead to crises of our consciousness, the starting point of all our troubles, difficulties, and problems in conducting our lives and the world affairs, we have no choice, if we really want freedom and peace, but to turn all our attention to seeing and thoroughly investigating the workings of our own minds, exerting all our energy into letting go of all the conflicting elements that have been put into this computer mind of ours. Then, our consciousness will surely be free from crises and, therefore, return to its intrinsic, true nature of purity and luminosity. But as long as our attention is divided and we are fragmented and our lives become compartmentalized, there is always room for a crisis and conflict to occur and to burn us with the fire of pain and suffering as well as that of fear, anxiety, and distress. As a result, we live our lives under pressures, threats, and insecurities so that we compulsively think that we must build a strong defense system for protecting ourselves, our nations, and our allies or, for that matter, for destroying our so-called enemies. The more and stronger the defense system, the more enemies appear and the more the arms race is intensified, like the shadow that never leaves. More conflicts and more crises follow us and put us in a constant state of tension, personally, nationally, and internationally. The perceived danger and potential destructiveness get bigger and bigger. This destructive element does originate in a petty, insecure mind, a mind filled with ignorance (unclear seeing) and fear.

At a personal level, when under stress, pressure, threat, and a sense of insecurity, we automatically put up psychological defenses as well as physical ones. That could result in a psychological and emotional breakdown when a personal crisis gets worse and defense mechanisms become totally rigid, unbending, and inflexible. But remember that *all is in the mind*. When the mind is put right and redirected toward unconditional love, natural understanding, peaceful living, harmony, and alive oneness, there is nothing to defend and to protect. Hence, once and for all, we free our consciousness of all the crises.

As stated earlier, the problem of conflict arises as the outcome of our dualistic thinking, which always creates an opposite. Underlying such a way of thinking is craving, a driving force to get that which is pleasurable, a desire for becoming better, or becoming other than what one is, or that which is being experienced, which is dissatisfying and unsatisfactory. This power of craving supported by clinging, its building-up process, takes control over our thinking mind, dividing its attention and tearing down its inner focus. As a result, our thinking mind produces the opposite in complying with the craving for the satisfaction of the self.

Thus goes the story; we create the world of duality whereof comes the conflict, the starting point of crisis within our consciousness. With the invention of dualistic concepts and notions, we struggle to find where the truth really lies. Perplexity arises as the truth is not to be found in the world of duality (except the conventional, relative truth). We inevitably get into conflict with what is absolutely true, the ultimate truth to which there is no opposite. As far as our dualistically thinking mind can conceive, there is no such thing as absolute truth unless one just assumes and believes that there is, which is not the truth but a faith, for anything that comes into existence within the network of thought is a thought. Therefore, thought cannot go beyond duality and is bound to having an opposite. Producing the opposite through our dualistic thinking not only creates conflict, both inner and outer, but prevents us from seeing the whole truth. For in order to realize the totality of truth, one has to transcend the world of duality and, for that matter, bring to utter destruction all the opposites, the elements of conflict. Nevertheless, words, concepts, and notions still can be used, not for implying the opposites but purely for conveying and describing the matter of an actual experience. In such communication, both the speaker and the listener must be in the same level of consciousness with all its energy fields and vibrations, in the act of making things common together.

Before our departure to *deva* consciousness, I would like to make a final point here that real humanness, which is nothing but the manifestation of our unique human consciousness, is the state of balance, the harmony of the negative and the positive. At this level conflict is not yet transcended, but by accepting and letting be what is, it is possible to live with it healthily. That relationship to conflict is based on simple awareness and understanding or insight in action. Whenever such awareness is lost and insight into reality not actualized, there is a dropping off and falling down from the state of true humanness to the archetypal lower forms of existence as already described.

Plane 3: The Plane of the Devas: Shining Beings Dwelling in Heavens. We turn now to *deva* consciousness, which manifests itself in the fortunate plane of sense-experience *(sugati-bhumi)*; let us look at the map of mythological heavens as described in the Buddhist texts.

It is said that there are six classes of heavens lying on top of one another. Beginning with the lowest class they are:

1. the heaven of the four kings who take their positions at the four quarters of the firmament;
2. the heaven of the thirty-three gods headed by Indra;
3. the heaven of the Yama gods (the governing gods);
4. the heaven of Delight;
5. the heaven of the gods who rejoice in their own creations; and
6. the heaven of the gods who make others' creations serve their own ends.

Bear in mind that all the *devas* or heavenly beings still enjoy sense-pleasures, even more than we humans do. They do not believe in celibacy yet, and there is no monastic institution offered to them as an alternative. So, they spend their lifetimes consuming the pleasures of the senses with great rejoicing. Due to the (temporary) absence of suffering as a challenge, they don't seem to make any further progress in their lives in terms of spiritual development or material production. It seems as if they are stuck with sensual pleasures until the extinction of their ages has come and they disappear from their heavens. I wonder if anybody wants to live in the form of a *deva* life for long?

The only chance for the gods to be transformed is when a Buddha appears on earth so that they may take an opportunity to go and listen to his Dharma talks, or to ask certain questions. In this connection, one of the Buddhist texts mentioned that in the second watch of the night (ten PM to midnight), every night, Gotama the Buddha made himself available for the *devas* (gods) to have audiences with him. On such occasions, he answered their questions or gave them appropriate talks to enable them to shift the level of their consciousness and become enlightened.

Because of the incompleteness of their development, there was an incident expressing a consciousness crisis even in the world of *devas*, beginning with the thirty-three gods in their heaven. For a period of twelve years, they had been thinking about and discussing the issue of the nature of a blessing. During that time, they divided into three groups: the first group believed that whatever forms and colors please the eyes are blessings *(dittha-mangalika)*; the second maintained that whatever sounds pleasant to the ears are blessings *(suta-mangalika)*; and the third concluded that all inner experiences achieved through sensing and knowing inwardly are blessings *(muta-mangalika)*. Finding it impossible to come to agreement among themselves, they appointed a certain *deva* as their representative (envoy) to come down to the Jeta Grove where the Buddha was staying to ask him the question of blessing. The Buddha did respond to the *deva's* request by delivering a discourse on blessings *(mangala-sutta)*, which settled the dispute so that all the *devas* could once again live in peace and in harmony with one another.

Considering the *deva* consciousness in general, we can say that it is not so different from the higher state of human consciousness. As a matter of fact, when the beautiful, good contents of human consciousness have reached their full development, they become the contents of *deva* consciousness. This level of *deva* consciousness is a resultant form of consciousness that bases its station in a realm of happiness that lasts for a limited period of time.

Like any other form of fragmented consciousness, it becomes exhausted and runs out of energy eventually. Then it is born again with a similar content transmitted from death-consciousness. This is like flames dying and providing a condition for giving rise to one another as long as there is fuel to feed the burning. So, the fuel for a *deva* consciousness is the full development of human consciousness carried out through the human form of existence on earth; for instance, this arises when a human being is cultivating such states of consciousness as self-esteem and full acceptance of the consequences of one's action whenever performed, as well as a clean livelihood. As soon as these three states, to mention the least, have been fully developed, they naturally become the contents of a *deva* consciousness. This means that a certain *deva* is born, although a person is still living in a human form. At the end of the last breath and after the physical body breaks up, that person dies with all his/her consciousness and other aggregates, but the energy of those three states of consciousness is transferred to a rebirth-consciousness. Conventionally, or as a way of speaking of this matter, we say that such a person who has brought those states to full development is reborn a *deva* in a certain heaven. That is not to say that there is an entity that is reincarnated or takes rebirth, but it is the evolutionary process of consciousness that undergoes transformation from one floor to the other until it reaches the ultimate goal of Shunyata— the Complete Emptiness—in which God, Tao, Brahma, or Dharma no longer exist. Such is ultimate consciousness itself. Once the evolution process has reached such a culminating peak, the journey has been completed.

There was another mythological story told in the Buddhist scripture about Magha, the Youth. He possessed a Bodhisattva consciousness in which compassion and love for humanity are predominant. Magha, the Youth, started a development project building a road for better communication in a rural area. In that project, he also included the digging of a well and the construction of an inn for the travellers to stay overnight and have water to drink.

He had thirty-three people who volunteered to work with him for this project. The work was done as charity. Magha himself had four wives. Three of them participated in his project, while the fourth one thought that whatever her husband did would also benefit her. So, she decided to do nothing to help with such a charitable project but beautified herself satisfying her husband's sense pleasure.

Each of the three wives carried out a specific decorating project. One made a beautiful botanical garden; the other had a pool built for swimming; and the third wife devoted herself to having a meeting hall constructed for conferences. Out of these meritorious deeds, Magha, the Youth, was, after his death, born Indra, the king of *devas* in the heaven of thirty-three deities. This indicates that all the thirty-three volunteered men were born *devas* to join him in that heaven, which is named after that number. Also, his three wives took their rebirth there to continue being his consorts. But the fourth one missed her chance due to her wrong way of thinking and not performing a good deed. Instead, she was born a beautiful white bird living by a lake.

Indra was said to possess a thousand eyes and be very closely connected with the Buddha. One day after surveying his small but beautiful heaven, he realized that one of his wives was missing, so he used all of his eyes to look and find out where she was. Then, he saw her existing in the form of a lovely bird. He immediately vanished from his heaven to visit with her and help her work out a certain karma, so that she could be reborn in his heaven to join him and the three other wives there. When Indra revealed himself to her, she was delighted and wanted to be with him as he lovingly asked her if she would. He then gave her a precept of not killing. She could only eat a dead fish but not a live one. The white bird observed that precept so strictly all her life that love and compassion grew in her.

Once Indra wanted to test her sincerity and conscience. He came down to the lake where she lived and pretended to be a dead fish. When she picked the fish up with her beak, he made movements to show her that he was still alive. With her realization that the fish was not dead, she let him go into the water. Indra then revealed himself and told her that the seemingly dead fish was himself in disguise to test her. With deep appreciation of her, he brought her to his heaven, and they lived happily together there. That means that after a time, she was born a female *deva* in Tavatimsa.

Such is *deva* consciousness. Indra did not seem to have a problem admitting a bird to his kingdom of heaven. In a way, he gave her time and a precept for developing her soul so that she could join him in the heaven of thirty-three. That implies that when one comes in touch with one's soul, the gentle, softly touching kind of energy like that of the heart, one enters the realm of heaven.

It is quite interesting to note here that what we call "soul" in the West is not monopolized by human beings only. As we understand it, the soul is nothing but the essence of yin (female form of energy) that exists in all beings and in all things without discrimination, regardless of sexes and forms. However, in certain structures and in the male sex, yin is less than yang, her counterpart, in both quality and quantity. Similarly, the essence of being, or soul, however deeply dormant it may be in a lower form of life, can potentially manifest itself when a proper contact is made, as demonstrated by the story of the white bird, Indra's former wife.

Another story related to *deva* consciousness is about the Buddha's mother, Siri Mahamaya. After seven days of giving birth to her special child, Siddhattha as he was originally called, she died and was born immediately in the heaven of Delight (Tusita) where all the Bodhisattvas or the Buddha-to-be Beings live and wait for the right time to be reborn in the human form. Because she did not want to give birth to another child and therefore kept her womb pure just for the Buddha-to-be child like Siddhattha, she died and waited there to welcome him as the Light of the three worlds: the human world, the world of *devas* and the world of Brahmas.

The Buddha went up to visit his mother and preached the higher doctrines, the philosophical and psychological system, to her and a hundred thousand *devas*, for a period of three months. To be exact, according to what is written in the Buddhist literature, the Buddha actually went up to the heaven of the thirty-three where Indra lived and where there was a large, proper assembly hall for him to have audiences and to teach the Dharma. His mother, who then was a male *deva*, came down to visit with him, her son, the Fully Enlightened One, known as the Buddha. She listened to his talks on the teachings of *abhidharma* for the entire period of three months, and as a result, became enlightened in front of her own son. It was also said that the real purpose of the Buddha's visit to that heaven for such a period of time was to pay off his debt to his mother, and that his selection of the *abhidharma* (literally: Extraordinary Dharma) for preaching to his mother and all other *devas* was done solely for helping her attain full enlightenment. That truly served his purpose. More than that, many thousands of *devas* at these gatherings became enlightened as well. For this reason, the Buddha bears the title of the "Master of gods and men" (*Sattha devamanussanam*). He did work very hard in his lifetime, endeavoring to help both men and women as well as gods and goddesses be free and liberated.

The interest in "spirit guides" and "channeling" as related to the place of the devas. I am wondering how many enlightened *devas*, or whether any at all, have been left in stock in the heavens these days, for it has been over twenty-six hundred years since Gotama the Buddha passed away and as the ground rule says, all the *devas* without exception are unable to accomplish by themselves any spiritual (or material) goals of life unless they get direct help from a Buddha, the Fully Enlightened One. The simple reason is that they do not have the means to further their development. They do not possess physical bodies as we humans do, which are very essential parts of spiritual development. That is why we encounter some spirit teachers borrowing certain human bodies to function in rendering their services in the human world.

Whether a true or false belief, this interest in spirit guides is now becoming more and more widespread in the Western world. People in the East have had experiences in this field for quite some time, and the majority of them do not take it so seriously. But in the

West, people are better organized, so that the work of spirit guides is disseminated rapidly through efficient organizations or services. There is nothing really new as to what those spirit guides say and do, but people's psychic centers get stimulated and inspired by the invisible forces so that this phenomenon is gaining interest, not only among those believing in superstition, but also among the people who understand the growth process. These people believe that whatever is advertised and sounds helpful should be brought into experimentation and exploration. This is an open attitude of finding out and of seeing it for yourself, before affirming or denying what is available in your society.

We will find in our encounters with spirit guides that we all have those messages and healing energies *within each of us*, and that we are all capable of receiving the universal life energy and of channeling it into healing and helping both ourselves and others seeking our assistance. Realizing this truth, we can free ourselves of dependence on the external guides, be they humans or spirits. Then we are able to tread the spiritual path by making use of all our human resources through looking, listening, and sensing very deeply as well as with all our attention. In this way, the natural unfolding and transformation will keep revealing and exploding to us endlessly as the ocean full of movements, depths, and infinity, constantly undergoing changing form and producing form. As we reconnect ourselves with the ever-flowing, big stream of consciousness, we can never get caught in our personality, but flow with our pure light, love, immeasurable freedom, illimitable compassion, and impeccable awareness with its profound insights into the true nature of things, including our own real nature.

So, what I have been attempting to say up to this point is that all the *deva* consciousness and so-called spirit guides are already here within our human form of existence. We do not have to travel very far to find out who we really are and what we actually have. If we truly want to go very far, we have to begin very near, that is, from where we actually are. In the words of the Chinese saying: "Ten thousand miles of the journey begin with the first step."

Once again, let us return to those six classes of *devas* as mentioned earlier. The first and lowest class is the four kings, each taking control of one quarter of their heaven. The second class is the heaven of thirty-three (Tavatimsa) headed by Indra as previously discussed. The third class is the heaven of Yama, the governing gods. As far as I know, there is not much written about those gods. Perhaps we can compare them to a government body or administration of a country in our human world. I will call it here "the consciousness of politics."

Let us observe how those in power of running their countries do their jobs. Ninety-nine percent of the government programs are carried out for the sake of politics or the self-prosperity of the politicians. Their main consciousness is focused on how to get support from the public. They do anything and everything possible to foster public opinion. To reassure and soothe their supporters they give superficially beautiful speeches in seemingly soft, calm voice, while acting outwardly brave and confident. Those who know well the machinery of politics and how to make it work can stay in power longer and become successful. With the understanding of how the consciousness of the governing politicians manifests itself through their activities and responses to various situations and/or crises, both national and international, we shall comprehend more clearly how the Yama gods become conscious of things and conduct their lives accordingly. It must be for this reason that we sometimes encounter certain bully gods acting out through a shaman or a medium. Some of them become very forceful, or even cruel in conducting their business in helping those seeking their help. They materialize themselves and carry out their healing or therapeutic activities in a dark room, for instance. Such spirit guides as these must come from the heaven of Yama. We may say that such consciousness expresses itself through the use of power or a power of sub-personality that runs the show.

Now coming to the fourth class, we have the heaven of Delight (Tusita). This seems to be a special station for the wonderful and highly developed beings such as Bodhisattvas to live and fill themselves with joy, bliss, ecstasy, love, and compassion. They are genuine helpers and pure in their heart's desires. If we come across any one of them either in our dreams or through a medium, we feel especially peaceful and loving; for they have tremendously abundant and beautiful energies to share with those in contact with them.

In addition, they are also very intelligent and wise *devas,* the best of all the six classes, I believe.

The fifth class of *deva* consciousness belongs to those who are creative, artistic, and so psychically rich that they can create anything to rejoicingly entertain themselves. This might be called "the full manifestations of psychic consciousness" from which are derived many different forms of healing arts such as inner journey, Reiki, psychic reading, past life therapy, and so on. We see all of these healing arts being conducted in both the Eastern and Western worlds. So, this consciousness is very common to all of us who are actively involved in the field of healing and helping many others free themselves of their karma, illness, emotional difficulties, and psychic troubles, including personality crisis. In such work as this, we draw tremendous energy out of the psychic center as well as making this center a better and better channel for the passage of universal life energy existing both deep down within us and outside of us. At the time of functioning as healers, shamans, psychic readers, and inner journey facilitators, we are actually manifesting this class of *deva* consciousness, technically known as Nimmanarati, which means "rejoicing in one's own creations."

Now, it has become clear that all forms of heaven are really found within us humans who exist in the comprehensive world of consciousness. Some of us can make use of the healing energy through our own psychic channel, while others are prone to act as mediums through whom the heavenly beings or gods or spirits materialize themselves and function as helpers, healers, teachers, etc. Perhaps, many of those who are qualified healers, clairvoyants, and prophets actually come from heaven number five. Nevertheless, what I am saying is that *devas* are both inside and outside of our human form as energy fields and stations of consciousness (Vinnana-thiti). Comprehending this, we shall never be surprised when being exposed to the medium, the shaman, or the psychic healer through whom a certain *deva* or spirit guide is manifesting and offering services out of love, caring, and compassion for humanity. But at the same time, we should investigate the qualities and the teachings as well as the acts of those spirit teachers or spirit healers so that we will understand what class of heaven they belong to. This will help us see more profoundly what kind of consciousness is manifesting and at what level it is operating. To do so is nothing but the study of consciousness, by direct observation, at many different levels through its actual manifestations at the moment.

The last class of heaven is that of those *devas* who make others' creations serve their own ends (*paranimmita vasavratti*). This, I think, refers to the consciousness of those deposed monarchs, retired leaders of nations, rich or poor, who do not have to do anything to earn their living, for they have accumulated much wealth, whether properly or improperly, during their time of being in power. After having retired, they still go on enjoying their wealth and have others to serve them. Such is a heaven on earth in a material sense. There is little record of this class of heaven, so we just have to understand its manifestation on the human plane.

Viewed from a more timely concept of psychological theory, all *deva* consciousness may simply be referred to as the *deva* subpersonality operating within human consciousness

Level II: Consciousness Manifesting in the World of Form (Rupaloka)

Now, we arrive at the level of consciousness operating or manifesting in the realm of form (Rupaloka) where those beings who achieve different grades of the Meditative Absorptions, technically known as *jhana*, delight in the *jhanic* bliss, transcending sensual pleasures.

Archetypes Symbolizing Four Planes and Sixteen Grades of Jhanic Bliss (Meditative Absorptions): Altered States of Consciousness That Transcend Sensual Pleasure. The beings living in this realm of consciousness are named "Brahma," and they are divided into sixteen grades according to the four stages of *jhana* as follows:

I. The Plane of the First *Jhana* comprises three grades of Brahma, namely:

1. the realm of the Brahma's Retinue (Brahma Parisajja);
2. the realm of Brahma's Ministers (Brahma Purohita);

3. the realm of Great Brahmas (Maha Brahma).

II. The Plane of the Second *Jhana* also comprises three grades of Brahma, namely:

1. the realm of Minor Lustre (Parittabha);
2. the realm of Infinite Lustre (Appamanabha);
3. the realm of the Radiant Brahmas (Abhassara). It is said that the rays of light, like lightning, are emitted from the bodies of the radiant gods.

III. The Plane of the Third *Jhana* consists of:

1. the realm of Brahmas of minor aura (Parittasubha);
2. the realm of Brahmas of infinite aura (Appamanasubha);
3. the realm of Brahmas of steady aura (Subhakinha, lit. "good light," meaning a mass of steady light emitted from a body).

IV. The Plane of The Fourth *Jhana* consists of:

1. the realm of Brahmas of Great Reward (Vehapphala—abundant reward, resulted from the *jhana* practice);
2. the realm of Brahmas without ideation (Asannasatta);
3. the realm of the Pure Abodes (Suddhavasa), which are further subdivided into five:
   a. the Durable or Immobile Realm (Aviha);
   b. the Serene Realm (Atappa);
   c. the Beautiful Realm (Sudassa);
   d. the Clear-sighted Realm (Sudassi); and
   e. the Supreme Beings of the Highest Realm (Akanittha).

According to the Buddhist texts, when one practices a form of concentration meditation, known in the Pali language as Samatha, one will attain one or all of the four *jhanas* (meditative absorptions, *recueillement*, ecstasies). The stereotypic formula that describes the first *jhana* in the Pali *suttas* reads as follows: "Aloof from sense-desires, aloof from unwholesome thoughts one attains to the first *jhana* which is born of detachment and which has reasoning, reflection, joy and happiness." The formula describing the second *jhana* is: "By the suppression or elimination of reasoning and reflection, one attains to the second *jhana* which is inner serenity, which is unification of consciousness without reasoning and reflection, born of concentration, and which has joy and happiness."

As for the third *jhana*, the formula of description reads as follows: "By detachment also from joy, one dwells in equanimity, mindful and aware, and enjoys happiness in body, and attains to the third *jhana* which the noble ones call 'dwelling in equanimity, mindfulness and happiness.'" The *sutta* passage that describes the fourth *jhana* is as follows: "By the abandonment of happiness and suffering, by the disappearance already of joy and sorrow (one attains to) the fourth meditative absorption, which is neither happiness nor suffering."

What we classify into different grades and realms of Brahmas are nothing but different levels and varying, altered states of consciousness as we evolve and develop our consciousness. As clearly described in the Pali texts as quoted above, we see that as consciousness shifts from one level or stage of *jhana* to the other, certain factors or states of consciousness are transcended or left behind, just like leaving one floor with its scenery, the aggregate of features that give character to that floor. Then, with a new level of consciousness, there come the names and qualities of beings dwelling in the new floor as described in the sixteen realms of *rupaloka* (The World of Form).

One more thing that needs my mention here is the different grades of Brahmas who have achieved the same *jhanic* consciousness. The reason for such a classification is that the dwellers in such a realm excel others in happiness, beauty, and age limit because of the intrinsic nature of their mental development. So the first grade of each plane is assigned to those who have developed the *jhanas* to an ordinary degree, the second to those who have developed the *jhanas* to a greater degree, and the third to those who have gained a complete mastery over the *jhanas*.

In the eleventh plane, called Asannasatta, beings are born in the realm of meditation in which the mind with its ideation is completely absent. Here, we see that only a material flux exists in a very subtle form of the body energy as well as in the physical form with its normal structure. The mind is temporarily suspended while the power of the *jhana* lasts. But at our ordinary level of existence, body and mind as psychosomatic processes are inseparable. By power of a certain state of meditation where the powerful energy both from inner and outer merges, permeating the whole of our psychophysical system, the mind is completely blown away until such power of meditation fades away. Then, the mind returns with a new quality of more purity, more clarity, and more freedom. So, during the time of abiding in such a meditative experience, Asanna-satta is born as a form of Brahma consciousness resulting from the fourth *jhanic* meditation. This is common to those meditators who have mastered the meditation practice, although it is unusual or even abnormal for ordinary persons who are ignorant of the experiences in meditation.

The Pure Abodes of Suddhavasa are exclusive planes of the Never-Returners (Anagamis). Other beings are not born in these realms. They are provided for those attaining *anagami*, the third stage of enlightenment, only. Those never-returning beings (this simply means that they do not come back to be reborn in a human state of existence) complete their final stage of *arahatship* there and live in those planes until their life term ends.

Level III: Consciousness Manifesting in the Formless Worlds (Arupaloka)

When consciousness develops and evolves further, we reach the other four planes called Arupaloka, the Formless Worlds. Here, Buddhists maintain that there are realms of existence where consciousness alone exists without form or matter. For in the *arupaloka*, matter or physical body doesn't exist. In this connection, Kassapa Thera wrote: "Just as it is possible for an iron bar to be suspended in the air because it has been flung there, and it remains as long as it retains any unexpended momentum, even so the formless being appears through being flung into that state by powerful mind-force, and there it remains till that momentum is expended. This is a temporary separation of mind and matter, which normally coexist." It should be mentioned that there is no sex distinction both in *rupaloka* (The World of Form) and *arupaloka* (The Formless Worlds).

Four Planes of Formless Jhanic Consciousness. The *arupaloka* is divided into four planes according to the four *arupa jhanas* (formless *jhanic* consciousness). They are as follows:

1. The Sphere of the Conception of Infinite Space (Akasanan-cayatana),
2. The Sphere of the Conception of Infinite Consciousness (Vin-nanancayatana),
3. The Sphere of the Conception of Nothingness (Akincanna-yatana),
4. The Sphere of the Conception of neither Perception and Idea-tion nor Non-Perception and Non-Ideation (Nevasanna nasan-nayatana).

This is not to say that the Buddha attempted to expound a cosmological theory. The essence of his teaching lies in the truth of development and evolution of consciousness through the most effective tool—meditation. He had accomplished this evolution and development through his training and learning from his two dis-tinguished teachers prior to his attainment of full enlightenment, and he played with those *jhanas* as his spiritual sports, although they are not necessary requirements for achieving enlightenment or total awakening.

Before our departure to further levels of consciousness, I would like to reiterate that what we have discussed up until now are nothing in essence but various states of consciousness as it (consciousness) shifts from level to level. In every detail of the shifts there are mythologies and cosmological implications involved as part of sharing knowledge and explaining the journeys through consciousness. This is the reason there are descriptions of different planes of existences with their beings, whether hungry ghosts, hell-beings, demons, *devas*, or Brahmas. All these notions and con-cepts arise from the mythology in a culture. The actual process can be lived through in our actual experiences, through both our per-sonal and transpersonal journeys in this very life on earth. All the archetypes and mythologies are merely the symbols of various states of consciousness or energy patterns manifesting both within us and in the external world. As symbols they are man-made things; for our human mind is clever enough to create and make anything either out of actuality or imagination. "All the conditioned things are made by mind," declared Gotama the Buddha. For this reason, we humans are inwardly very rich in having the opportunity to experience and understand the living truths manifested in consciousness, which appear outwardly in different cultures and traditions maintained by different peoples of different developments at different parts of the globe. Also, it is our task, as we further our development and evolution and learning, to transcend, as well as uncover, all the coverings of reality, so that there will be no conflict nor contradiction left in our minds.

Level IV: Transcendental or Supra-mundane Consciousness (Lokuttara Citta)

What we have discussed up to this point are the different classes of mundane consciousness, which could be summarily classified and divided into two categories, namely, lower consciousness (belonging to hell-beings, the animal kingdom, hungry or unhappy ghosts, and demons) and higher consciousness (belonging to *devas* and Brahmas right up to the formless realm of consciousness). Human consciousness is between these two categories and at the same time embraces all of the lower and higher states of consciousness, including supra-mundane consciousness which we are going to discuss now. This beyond-the-worlds-consciousness is so named for the simple reason that it transcends all the three worlds of Kamaloka (the world of pleasure), Rupaloka (the world of form—the lower *jhanic* consciousness), and Arupaloka (the formless world—higher *jhanic* consciousness). This transcendental realm or level of consciousness belongs to the enlightened beings, beginning with the Stream-Enterers right up to the Arahants (the totally liberated ones).

As we evolve through self-transformation and self-transcendence as the results of our learning and development, we purify our minds, liberate our consciousness, and transcend the sense of a separate self, cutting through our confusion and illusion about self and otherness. We return to our Origin where there is no boundary, nor is there separation of any kind, only fully alive and loving Oneness or Wholeness of Being. This level of consciousness is called Enlightened Consciousness.

Enlightened Consciousness does not belong to any particular plane of existence. Any beings, in any plane of life, can achieve supra-mundane consciousness as a result of their evolutionary process. However, as human beings, with our unique form comprised of physical, sensate, emotional, and mental attributes, we seem best suited to accommodate it.

From our knowledge and experience of consciousness development, we observe that the higher consciousness evolves, the more refined and the more radiant and free it becomes. It peels off and eliminates all the impure, contaminated, and disturbing conditions and influences, technically known as karma "energy patterns" and "blocks," so that the real, intrinsic nature of consciousness is revealed and emerges into actuality. Then we say that enlightenment is attained and that all the influxes that block the natural flow of Freedom, Love, Strength, and Insightful Wisdom are removed and uprooted with no trace.

The First Floor of Enlightenment: "Stream Entrance." This we shall see from the level of Stream Entrance where certain blocks are cleared away. They are our illusion about the sense of separate self, all kinds of doubt, and blind faiths, beliefs, and assumptions (transcendence of superstitions, dogmatic assertions, and cultural boundaries). In place of maintaining the existence of a separate self is oneness consciousness and the experience of connectedness; in other words, the boundary of self and other has been diffused totally. Clear insight into things as they are takes the place of doubt, while the natural confidence and trust in Truth, as the direct contact with It confirms, replaces the blind faiths. This is actually a very big step toward the fullness and complete mastery over enlightenment or total freedom, for the course of moving on with certainty and clarity is irreversible.

The Second Floor of Enlightenment: "One Returning." Arriving at the second floor of enlightenment, the other two main binding fetters that tie us up to the lower world, are considerably reduced. They are attachment to sensual pleasures and hateful feeling, the real emotion of hateful consciousness. This means that the negative and destructive, imbalanced states of feeling are becoming more balanced so that one has more power to let go with immediate, clear seeing at the moment. The chance of becoming a victim of such an emotion as hate, including resentment, anger, envy, and jealousy, is much less, while the chances for freedom and wellness increase. This is called "Once-Returning," which implies the possibility of coming back once in a while to the humanness, instead of staying divine all the time. This enlightened being knows exactly what it means to be human and how to become divine, saint or sage. There is no problem of switching. Those who do not know always get confused about the human and the divine because they try too hard to draw a dividing line, the boundary between humanness and divinity, without understanding that the dividing line is in fact the union of opposites.

The Third Floor of Enlightenment: "Pure Abode."   Shifting to the third floor of enlightenment, one further frees oneself completely from those two reduced dispositions (attachment to sensual pleasures and hate with all its family unit and the whole structure of it). There is no return to the lower world of sense-desires and disturbing feelings at this point. That is why the plane of existence for those attaining this level of enlightened consciousness is called Pure Abode (Suddhavasa) as previously described in the realms of Brahma Consciousness. This is not final, yet, for the Non-Returners are still bound to the higher world, the more refined states of consciousness, which is to be liberated by the power of thunder-wisdom at the fourth floor of enlightenment (Arahantship).

The Fourth Floor of Enlightenment: "Arahantship."   The completion of development of the enlightened consciousness brings to utter destruction, without ashes, the remaining, subtle fetters tying us to the higher world of self-consciousness. They are: clinging to form at the *jhanic* level of consciousness where many beautiful, ecstatic states or higher and altered states of consciousness are overwhelmingly experienced and clinging to the formless realms of infinity regarding space and ever-expanding consciousness and those of nothingness (Nothing whatsoever) and neither ideation nor non-ideation, a sense of "I am" or I-conceit (the false conception of self), restlessness (scattered, agitating energy within), and ignorance (absence of clear seeing and knowing directly). Complete enlightenment totally blows up (eradicates) a sense of separate self with all its sensations and feelings, leaving no illusion about the notion of self behind. The primary boundary of self and other no longer exists in such fully enlightened consciousness. This is unlike the earlier stages of transformation and transcendence such as the Stream-Enterer, where there is still a sensation and feeling of "I am," although one realizes in profound wisdom, fully and clearly, that there is no such thing as "I am." This means that a sense of familiarity with the idea of self still goes on as long as the aggregates of existence are kept alive together in their functions as a personality in time.

Now, it has become clear to us that the final evolution of consciousness has reached the Origin, the Upstream, or the Real Intrinsic Nature of Consciousness, which is total *freedom from attributes; emptiness, luminosity,* and *complete radiance.* Here the number of concrete processes are reduced to a minimum. There is unity, illimitable Love, non-attachment, but no differentiation, dependence, and encumbrance. In negative terms, we talk about the complete "extinction" of all the conditioned states, concepts, notions, and ideas. It is Emptiness beyond the notion of emptiness, where there is no God, Tao, Supreme Identity, or even Dharma, in the Buddhist terminology.

So, God-Consciousness, Supreme Identity and Oneness with Tao, or Dharmakaya is not yet Ultimate Consciousness, for each of these still contains and retains an idea, a concept, and a notion of God, Identity, Tao, or Dharma. What we call *sunyata* is the complete emptiness of those notions and of all other conditioned states or, for that matter, of any states whatsoever. Therefore, Ultimate Consciousness is Supra-mundane, Absolute, and beyond our adequate description in words because It is undefinable and cannot be reached by our linguistic conception and systematic thinking, or systems view of reality. "Hence, earth, water, fire and wind gain no foothold; here long and short, fine and coarse, pure and impure, here name and form cease without trace," as stated in the Buddhist text of Digha Nikaya.

In Conclusion: A Summary of Consciousness

Consciousness, as we have discussed throughout this chapter, can be summarized as follows: It is consciousness, with its conscious and unconscious elements, that characterizes our human mind as manifested both in individuals and in human society. Collectively, consciousness operates and actualizes itself in our cultures, organized religions, faiths, spiritual movements, social institutions and establishments, political structures, and economic systems. As we unenlightened humans are divided by differentiated belief systems and limited visions as well as views of realities, our collective consciousness is also divided into various fragments according to different sectors, groups, political parties, social systems, the communist world and the free world, and so forth.

The contents of consciousness, be they philosophies, ideologies, belief systems, dogmatic assertions, assumptions, or speculations, indicate the types of consciousness manifested collectively in different categories of peoples maintaining and following the structural systems with all their theories and ideals. For that matter, consciousness acts as a social unit, a group personality, or an active agent in the processes of death, birth, decay, and continuity through modifications, changes, and adaptations in accordance with the changing conditions of society and of the world.

The same is true with individual human consciousness. That is to say, consciousness becomes the core of personality, the carrier of karmic energies, sub-personalities, and creating forces, enabling an individual to manifest himself/herself in everyday living. Furthermore, with consciousness and its contents, one learns, grows, develops, evolves, as well as renews and transforms, both forward and backward, maintaining a sense of self, struggling and moving on from level to level until the evolution process is completed and Ultimate Consciousness reached.

With each self-transformation, consciousness becomes cleaner, more refined, purer, and freer. The inner space within an individual consciousness widens as choiceless awareness enlarges so that more insights and transcendental wisdom grow with greater clarity and luminosity. The creating processes with all their dispositions and energy patterns acting as contents and shadows of consciousness reduce their functions until they eventually become empty. At this point, the individual consciousness is liberated and reunited with the Origin of the eternally flowing Upstream, with Total Freedom and everlasting Enlightenment. At that peak of consciousness, there is no crisis of perception, no crisis of consciousness itself, and no crisis of view. All is in complete harmony and equilibrium. A dynamic balance occurs in which there is no place for higher or lower, just a delightful stretch of level ground where both the personal and impersonal centers are utterly destroyed. Thus ever-enlightened consciousness flows eternally with no obstruction.

LEVELS OF CONSCIOUSNESS

Supreme Consciousness Level
(Transcendence)

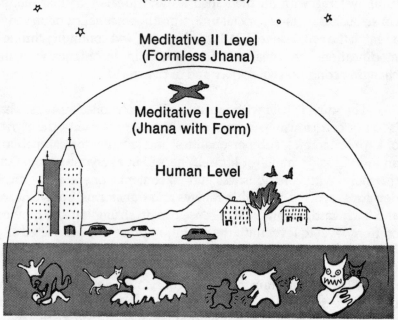

Meditative II Level
(Formless Jhana)

Meditative I Level
(Jhana with Form)

Human Level

Non-Progressive Level

CHAPTER EIGHT

Oriental Meditation and Western Psychotherapies

O RIENTAL MEDITATION AND WESTERN PSYCHOTHERAPY
have similarities and differences in both theory and practice.

Clarifying the Goals of Oriental Meditation and Western Psychotherapy

Oriental mediation places its final aim in the attainment of Total
Freedom and Enlightenment, the state of complete liberation from
greed, hate, and delusion, as well as the utter ending of suffering
with all its causes. This goal also includes the complete purification
and refinement of consciousness, in which all the conditioned states
or creating forces, both conscious and unconscious, cease to influence the human mind. Ultimate, supra-mundane consciousness,
with all its radiance and luminosity, is reached. At this peak of
enlightenment, samsara (the processes of rebirth and death) is broken up, and nirvana is realized.

In discussing Western psychotherapy, we confront a complex
situation. There are many schools of thought, many approaches. We
cannot offer a statement of the aims of psychotherapy that represents a consensus of views. For example, Freud described the aim
of psychoanalysis as the replacement of neurotic suffering with
ordinary human unhappiness. Other therapies seek the maximiza-
tion of individual potential for psychological growth, while still
others regard it as little short of immoral to set any goal other than

the remission of symptoms. Thus, to speak of the goals of Western psychotherapy requires that we throw a cloak over these differences and seek a statement broad enough to cover them; regrettably, such a general statement fails to do justice to the differences the adherents of these therapies regard as vital to their work.

We can at best speak of some Western psychotherapies as having the aim of healing and curing neurotic pain and suffering, of building up and strengthening the ego-self in order to function properly and efficiently in the world, and of creating and expanding the boundaries, especially between self and other, so that one's primary boundary is clearly marked, fully recognized, and well protected. In this process it is expected that there will be learning, growth, development, and maturation, as well as the elimination of the confusion and illusion that cloud the mind.

Generally speaking, both Western psychotherapy and Oriental meditation have the same quest and aim: for the cure of psychological illnesses, pain, and suffering both at the psychological and bodily levels. Though it would be difficult to find explicit statements by psychotherapists to this point, many would probably agree that their efforts, as is the case of Oriental meditation, are in favor of wellness, health, harmony, peace, love, and understanding, both at the individual and community levels.

We can speak of common goals for Oriental meditation and Western psychotherapy, although aspects of the final aim are differently emphasized. That is to say, Western psychotherapy lays its emphasis on the maintenance and development of the self, fostering and strengthening ego-consciousness for the purposes of functioning and performing one's duties well and of relating freely and autonomously to other individuals in the society in which one lives. The emphasis for Oriental meditation is on the renouncing and transcending of the illusion of self, dissolving all the boundaries that are falsely created between self and other, organism and environment, etc. In this connection, the notion of ego is totally eliminated and not fostered at all; for in the ultimate sense and at the absolute level of truth, there is no ego, nor is there self apart from the processes conditionally rolling on in the relative, interdependent, and interrelated world of existence. In the Absolute, all is totally *empty* (meaning, all the creating processes within consciousness are reduced to zero). And such Emptiness is a Complete Fullness of Being (not *a* being, but *beingness*).

It is a difficult task to bring together and integrate the concepts of the two cultures, for it seems very impractical, even undesirable, for the Western mind to admit and accept the radical idea of self-transcendence and egolessness and find a place for such awareness in its practical world. The basic question that is often raised is: How can one function in the world if self and/or ego is not at work? When the functions of creative and dynamic processes within one's consciousness are reduced to zero, is it possible for such consciousness to manifest itself as the active agent of personality in time? If the answer is negative, then the whole world will stop, and there will be no more production. In actual fact, as we all know it, if there is no hunger, then food is not needed. This kind of questioning is on our human mind, particularly on the Western mind, which emphasizes the practical matters in everyday living. So, we shall attempt to find a practical answer to such a basic query throughout this chapter.

Exploring Some Principles and Methods of Oriental Meditation

Let us first begin with exploring the principles and methods of Oriental meditation so that we can throw some light on both the theoretical and practical aspects of this seemingly mysterious-sounding thing.

In general, we understand meditation as something confined to monks who are supposed to renounce worldly responsibilities and undertake monastic disciplines and to those who wish to become sages, not wanting to live in society any longer. From this impression, we assume that meditation has nothing to do with the actual life in which we have to produce material things and enjoy our sensual pleasures, having a good time and raising a family, etc. It sounds rather lofty and, therefore, incompatible with our mundane level of existence.

As a matter of fact, there is some truth in such an assumption, for a certain form of meditation does lead the practitioners to what may be called here "a neurotic detachment and turning away from the world" *(samatha)*. Such a technique of meditation lays a strong emphasis on attaining bliss and ecstasy through developing a highly concentrative mind with an absolutely firm control over the senses. As a result, those practicing this sort of meditative technique tend to indulge themselves in getting "blissed out" and becoming indifferent and negative about world affairs. In fact, there are quite a number of immature meditators who possess such an unhealthy attitude of misusing meditation as a substitute for drugs. This incorrect application of meditative practice gives a false idea to, and has a negative impact on, the uninformed public. Therefore, there is a lot of misunderstanding as to what meditation is all about, particularly among uneducated and/or incorrectly educated people. To clarify all of the misunderstandings and to clear away all the wrong impressions about meditation and its use, I will make a short but precise survey of Oriental meditation, particularly the Buddhist methods of meditative practice.

According to the Buddha-Dharma, we find two main forms of meditation: Tranquility *(samatha)* and Insight (Vipassana). The former is the way of mind training, while the latter moves directly into development of Insight through the constant application of simple, impeccable *awareness*, actual living in the timeless time of the here and now.

Techniques Used in Tranquility (Samatha) Meditation

Tranquility meditation has developed many different techniques for training the mind to be firmly one-pointed with the chosen subject of meditation in order to achieve various stages of meditative absorptions or ecstasies, technically known as *jhana* (see pp. 154–162).

Concentrating the Mind on a Fixed Object

Following the breath. This way of practice begins with concentrating the mind on a fixed object, for example, the breath. In this case, a student of meditation, or yogi as he/she is called in the East, focuses his/her mind on the inhalation and exhalation by following the breath closely and precisely. When breathing in, the beginning of the breath is felt at the nostril, the middle of the breath is perceived at the heart center (middle of the chest), and the end of the breath is experienced at the navel. When breathing out, it is opposite, that is, the beginning of the breath is at the navel, the middle at the heart center, and the end at the nostril. So, a meditator follows the breath very strictly whenever it touches those three points, one after the other, without missing any one of them at any point of contact and without getting distracted by any other event or object either in the external world or in the internal environment. Using this technique, as time advances, the meditator's mind is totally fixed with the breath and becomes one-pointed with it to the extent that only the breath exists, nothing else.

From that point onward, the first stage of meditative absorption develops, along with certain factors of reasoning, reflection, joy, happiness, and unification of consciousness. If such a developed state of *jhanic* meditation is maintained and increased, the yogi will certainly attain the second, the third, and the fourth *jhanas* respectively. Bear in mind that these achievements take a lot of practice and total dedication in which tremendous amounts of time and energy are consumed. Absolutely solid and firm concentration is required, and it must be sustained for a long period of time before a *jhanic* state arises. A practitioner of Tranquility meditation must always maintain such a concentrated state of mind without wavering; otherwise the attained *jhana* could collapse and lose all its power. Remember that in all the above-mentioned *jhanic* states, all the hindrances (e.g., negative feelings, fears, and morbid states of mind) are not uprooted but suppressed and could resurface and exercise their powers at any time when a yogi's consciousness becomes distracted and gets diffused by a stimulus or a tempting object in the external world.

Counting the breath. Another popular technique of Tranquility meditation is "breath-counting." In this practice, the meditation student sits in a cross-legged position with his back straight and all parts of his body in complete alignment, fixing his mind exclusively on the breath, counting "one" when breathing in and out, then "two" with another in-out breath, then three, ... four, ... up to five.

Thereafter, such a novice must begin counting one to five again and again while keeping his concentration sustained unwaveringly on the breath. This is to be practiced repeatedly until the state of one-pointedness of mind is reached.

Mantra repetition. In the case of using a mantra (a short phrase, a word, or a sound), a meditator of this type may repeat the mantra vocally or silently until her mind is filled with the given mantra, or she becomes one with it. Consequently, the meditator feels good or becomes relaxed, physically and mentally. The highest results may be the attainment of meditative absorptions, mystical experiences, and altered states of consciousness, but if insight is lacking, intensive exercises of this type of meditation may cause psychic problems. For this reason, one must always seek guidance from an able teacher when following this form of practice.

Forty subjects of concentration as outlined in the Buddhist texts. In the Buddhist texts, there are forty subjects of concentration, or techniques of Tranquility meditation (*samatha*):

Ten *kasina* (devices): earth, water, fire, air, (the colors of) blue, yellow, red, white, light, and enclosed space.

Ten *asubha* (repulsive things): swollen corpse, bluish corpse, festering corpse, fissured corpse, gnawed corpse, scattered corpse, hacked and scattered corpse, worm-eaten corpse, and skeleton.

Ten *anussati* (recollections): the Buddha, the Dharma (teaching and path), the Sangha (an enlightened person and a community of monks), morality, liberation, *devas* (radiant beings), death, respiration, what belongs to the body, and peace.

Four *brahmavihara* (sublime states of mind): loving-kindness, compassion, sympathetic joy, and equanimity (or even-mindedness).

Four formless states of meditative absorptions (formless *jhanas*): infinity of space, infinity of consciousness, the state of nothing whatsoever, and the state of neither perception and ideation nor non-perception and non-ideation.

One perception of the loathsomeness of food.

One analysis of the four basic elements of extension, cohesion, heat (temperature), and motion (vibration).

A detailed description of the use of color kasinas and mandalas in Tranquility practices. Of these forty subjects, possibly the best known and most frequently practiced of the external *samatha* techniques are the four color *kasinas* (blue, yellow, red, and white). In this connection, the Venerable Saddhatissa wrote: "The practice of kasina meditation involves first constructing one's kasina." The ancient meditation manuals explain the exact quality and tone of the stipulated colors. They also describe how the would-be meditator should fashion his *kasina*.

As is done in the Zen tea ceremony and flower arrangement (which developed later historically), the preparation of the *kasina* should be part of the meditation itself. Every action should be carried out with quiet awareness and fixed precision.

The size of the *kasina* may vary: some say that the diameter should measure the same as the hand span of the meditator plus the width of her fingers; others say that the size of the *kasina* should be modified according to the degree of concentration present in the meditator. Those of dull concentration use larger discs and those whose concentration is sharper may use smaller ones. The disc is set up at a reasonable distance from the meditator. Here, again, the sources differ as to the distances they recommend. About ten to fifteen feet is satisfactory. The center of the disc should be slightly lower than the horizontal eye level of the meditator when he is seated in front of the *kasina*.

When the *kasina* is built and placed in a good position, the meditator sits before it and starts the meditation. The gaze should focus on the disc without staring or straining the vision at all. After a few seconds, the eyes are closed, but the concentration remains fixed on the memory of the disc. If a disc appears while the eyes are closed—as we look at the moon for a second and then close our eyes—the meditator should concentrate on that until it fades. The process is then repeated until the allotted time for the meditation session is over. Sometimes the meditator will find that she can hold the image of the disc much longer than at other times. This should be noted and after some experience it will be found that it is possible to relate the various states and sequences of one's meditation session to one's habits and character traits.

A more elaborate form of *kasina* meditation is the mandala. A mandala is a symmetrical pattern that is used as an aid in concentration in much the same way as the *kasina*. Mandalas are generally many colored and often show symbolic or mythological figures arranged in an intricate and stylized pattern. Many of the Indian and Tibetan works of art currently on display in the West were made as mandalas and were used by monks in their meditation practices (*The Friendly Way, Journal of the Buddhapadipa Temple*, October 1982).

Tranquility meditation as it is expressed in other world religions. Tranquility meditation is popularly known, both in techniques and in practices, among the people of all religions. Christians call it contemplation and contemplative prayer, the prayer of the heart, while Hindus categorize it into different forms such as *bhakti* yoga (devotion), *pranayama* yoga (breathing exercises based on control and manipulation), *siddha* yoga (intentional identification with the spiritual teacher), and samadhi (Raja yoga). Included in this tranquility path (concentration techniques) are the Krishna consciousness movement, transcendental meditation, and Sufi meditations.

A Thai practice of Buddha visualization. One of the most respected practices among those following Tranquility meditation is *visualization* as generally described in the *kasina* and mandala techniques. But I should like to share with you a specific Thai method of visualization practice.

A student of meditation is instructed to sit in a meditation posture in front of a Buddha image and try to remember different parts of the Buddha's body until the whole physical structure and color are fully memorized. Then, the practitioner closes his eyes and attempts to visualize the Buddha's body. If any part of the body is not clear, if he can't remember it precisely, the meditator must open his eyes and look again, trying harder to recognize the part of the body; then close the eyes once again. This is repeated again and again until the image is acquired. The meditator must keep the acquired image sustained without wavering until it is firmly fixed and absolutely clear, as if the body with all its parts is seen with the open eyes. Thereafter, the meditator is taught to invite the Buddha to come and sit on his head, visualizing him (the Buddha) seated there. When that is successful, the meditator should invite him to come down to sit inside his throat, then down in his chest (the heart center), and further down in his stomach, on top of the hara where the Chi or ki energy operates.

When the Buddha is invited to "sit" in the meditator's stomach and the conceptualized image is stabilized, *patibhaga-nimita*, the third degree of samadhi is reached. This is the most powerful state of meditation. The practitioner directly experiences the Buddha, shining with complete radiance, illuminating with golden light and beautiful colors. (I carried out this practice to its full extent when still a novice in a monastery in Yasothorn Province in Thailand.)

According to the *samatha* system, in visualization meditation there are three stages of samadhi (one-pointedness of mind or unification of consciousness): the preparation stage (*parikamma*) trying to memorize the visual object set for meditation; the acquired image (second stage); and the conceptualized image firmly established (third stage). (Thus, the stability of the conceptualized image is actually the *jhanic* state, ecstasy, or meditative absorption.)

Concentrated visualization as an aid to the healing process. Visualization meditation can also be used to assist a healing process. In this connection, the person involved should obtain precise and clear instruction from an able mentor who has practiced visualization meditation. Two approaches may be followed. First, accurately locate the organ or part of the body you wish to heal and focus all your attention on it. Then visualize it and mentally remove the disease, or the unhealthy part, replacing it with a new healthy one; or actively imagine it becoming healthier and healthier until it eventually returns to its normal state. This practice should be done very concentratedly for ten to fifteen minutes twice a day.

It is not the purpose of this book to elaborate all the practices of Tranquility meditation; I just wish to share some popularly known techniques. For those wanting to pursue the tranquility path, the following guidelines may be helpful in choosing the subjects of *samatha* that are most suitable for them according to their temperaments or inclinations:

Choosing a suitable subject for concentration based on your temperament. The ten repulsive things *(asubha)* as mentioned on page 170 and mindfulness of what belongs to the body are appropriate to those possessing the temperament of lust *(raga-carita)*.

The four sublime states of mind *(brahma-vihara)* and four colored devices *(kasina)* are good for those having the temperament of hate *(dosa-carita)*.

Mindfulness of breathing is good for the temperaments of delusion *(moha-carita)* and obsessive thinking *(vitakka-carita)*.

The first six recollections *(anussati)* are good for temperaments of faith.

Reflection on death *(maranasati)*, recollection of peace *(upasamanussati)*, analysis into four basic elements *(catudhatuvavatthana)*, and the perception of loathsomeness of food *(aharepatikula-sanna)* are good for temperaments of intelligence *(buddhi-carita)*.

The six remaining devices *(kasina)* and the four formless states of meditative absorptions *(arupa-jhana)* are suitable for all temperaments. That is, these practices help to reduce certain neurotic patterns or tendencies and may be seen as having a therapeutic effect.

A guided meditation with love as the fixed object of concentration. One adaptation of *samatha* technique is to design a guided meditation that focuses attention on a specific subject and explores it in depth. Following is an example of a guided meditation with love as the fixed object of concentration. I use these techniques as part of the format in an extended retreat.

Prior to the session the participants have completed extensive work on their emotions and on the process of opening their heart centers. They have participated in both intensive sittings and expressive bodywork designed to release energy blocks in specific parts of the body. The guided meditation is used to complete the processes of release and integration.

When leading the meditation, the guide should speak in a firm, gentle, compassionate tone of voice, allowing adequate time for the participants to absorb and integrate their experience. The participants should wear loose, warm clothing and be in a comfortable posture, either seated or reclining, depending on their physical abilities. It is essential that the room be kept comfortably warm and that there are no disturbances during the session.

The meditation is divided into five sections:

1. Relaxation, Awareness, and Receptivity
2. Opening the Heart Center
3. Exploring Loving Consciousness
4. The Releasing Power of Forgiveness
5. The Loving Embrace

Following is a brief description of the essential components of the meditation:

1. Relaxation, Awareness, and Receptivity

During the opening phase of the meditation, the guide gently leads the participants into a state of deep physical relaxation and receptivity. Normal, relaxed breathing is stressed and non-judgmental awareness of one's total being is suggested.

2. Opening the Heart Center

Attention is gradually focused on the heart center, located in the middle of the chest, with an emphasis on feeling the sensations of expansion and contraction that arise naturally through the movement of the breath. While maintaining an attitude of choiceless, non-judgmental attention, any sensations and feelings that arise, as the heart center opens and becomes more pliable, are allowed to float freely into the meditator's field of awareness. (These may include sensations of warmth, frozenness, constriction, expansion, spaciousness, etc.)

3. Exploring Loving Consciousness

After having passed through sensations and feelings, the body and mind become calm and quiet. The participants are ready for the inner journey into heart consciousness.

The leader now guides the whole group to feel loving energy in their heart centers, to emanate it and radiate it outward through various parts of their bodies and to bathe their minds in love.

The following statements are made as the journey continues. "The action of love is giving. The more one gives, the more love flows, and the more one receives. Love is found within the heart. There is no end to love. It flows eternally both within one's heart and outward to all beings without discrimination. In love there is no separation or division. Oneness and all-connectedness prevail.

"Love of self is the greatest love. There is no selfishness in self-love, for love of self is the fountain spring, the origin of love, the source of the love that flows outward to others. Without discovering this unlimited well of love within oneself, one cannot actually love others. Staying outside the energy field of love and trying to practice love or loving-kindness is like a child crying for the moon. So, bathe yourself in the warm ocean of love, then spread it out to the entire universe. With open arms embrace all beings and all things with no distinction."

4. The Releasing Power of Forgiveness

The leader now strongly and firmly suggests that the participants let go of all that they have held against themselves, whether it be self-hatred, self-punishment, or a negative, impoverished self-image.

"Forgive yourself for all your mistakes and wrongdoings—for what you have done to yourself and what you have done to others.

Repeat to yourself, 'Forgiveness is the greatest gift I can ever give to myself . . . forgiveness is the greatest gift I can ever give to myself . . . forgiveness is the greatest gift I can ever give to myself. Forgiveness is the act of letting go with clear seeing and non-attachment. There is no merit in holding on to a past that is unhealthy and destructive to my self-growth, self-development, and self-transformation. Forgiveness is an act of love.'" (Sometimes it is very painful to forgive oneself because the ego is deeply hurt as a result of its intense clinging to negativity and that which causes suffering.)

5. The Loving Embrace

Now all the participants should be directed: "Open yourself up to more loving energy and a feeling of home-coming. Embrace yourself completely and unconditionally. As the abundance of love overflows, reach out and share it. Picture your parents in your mind, regardless of whether they are alive or dead. When you sense them clearly, bring them to your side—your father on your right, your mother on your left. Mentally hug them and hold them with warmth, tenderness, and love. Deep in your heart forgive them for any of the painful or unpleasant actions that they may have done regardless of their reasons or ignorance at the time. Expand all of your love toward your parents. Experience a deep bond of sharing, forgiveness, and connectedness."

As the power of the loving energy increases and loving consciousness expands within the group, its radiation is now directed toward a loving universal embrace. All are encouraged to increase the scope and power of their loving, forgiving transmission to include all their family members, husbands, wives, children, intimates, friends, and colleagues, to all the people they know who personally touch their lives. The expansion continues in an ever-increasing circle to include all human beings, regardless of race or nationality, rich or poor, free or unfree, healthy or unhealthy, happy or unhappy. Everyone is equally and unconditionally embraced with warmth, forgiveness, and love.

Finally, all beings and all things, visible and invisible, throughout the entire universe, throughout the history of humankind are embraced unconditionally and bathed in the boundless love of Oneness Consciousness.

Vipassana (Insight Meditation)

A General Description of Vipassana Practice. This type of meditation is unique in its method. Strictly speaking, it does not require a technique.

The object for Insight meditation can be *any* and *every* thing that is distinct and evident at the moment. In this connection, a student of Insight Development is instructed to be constantly aware and mindful of whatever is arising in or entering the consciousness and body, knowing them for what they are without conceptualizing, labeling, or analyzing things into categories. This is the way of openness, alertness, and clarity of mind. Here there is no question of thoughts, breath, energy flow, or blocks. In short, both conscious and unconscious processes of mind-body *(nama-rupa)* are welcomed in the constant movement of simple, clear awareness and bare attention.

Because the primary aim of this practice is to see things as they truly are, one needs to bring with oneself and apply all the time this impeccable tool of choiceless and desireless awareness with the arising of ever-flowing insights into realities and unrealities. The actual living, reliving, and working through one's pain and suffering, including confusion and fears, without avoiding, denying, despising, suppressing, repressing, or ignoring is an essential part of Insight practice. For in the way of Insight, *precisely clear seeing* and *unconditionally accepting* go hand in hand. Freedom, in the true sense of the word, is the only structure of Vipassana.

Vipassana practice is like taking a journey through life; what we come across depends upon our own conditioning. If we are afraid of unpleasant experiences, or if we expect only what is "positive," then we shall have more difficulties in practicing this meditation. As in life it is a journey of *discovery*. People have talked about hidden human treasures or potential, but until we discover what we really are, we neither accept nor reject such things. We just leave things as they are and continue to travel through ourselves because our intrinsic, true nature is not realized through ideas such as those that arise from evaluating or judging our experience.

The process of discovering what *is*, and accepting it as it unfolds, is basic to Vipassana or Insight. There is an element of desire in the spirit of inquiry, in the sense of an urge to know, but this is balanced by open-mindedness and the acknowledgement of uncertainty.

When we do not think obsessively that we *have* to know, we are able to tolerate not-knowing with the patient and dispassionate approach of science in its purer aspects. Yet, this kind of science does not work in an ivory tower, disregarding the possibilities brought by knowledge, or the reality of subjective experience. To be truly objective we have to take our own inner life into account and see more clearly what is happening there, without being afraid of our subjectivity. If it is dismissed or denied, our dynamic internal world does not go away—it becomes more explosive and frightening. As a result, we look at it even less, which is tremendously dangerous to our development and evolution.

The cycle of fear as well as the cycle of desire have the same effect: the *narrowing of our attention* into a more limited field, in other words, concentration. Methods of concentrative meditation can produce mental illness, hypnosis, and psychic powers, and at lower intensities many forms of control and success, because they work by excluding what is not wanted. But the nature of the mind is such that it has to flow, and if it is continually channelled in a narrow direction, or blocked, its energies eventually emerge in a destructive way. Psychosomatic disturbances give warning signals of this situation, but for a long time it was not seen that the mind affected the body in this manner. Investigators turned their attention outward instead of observing their own inner states and their physical effects. It is not only the "experts" who are afraid of looking within—it is nearly all of us. We must look, above all, at this fear—the state of being afraid of what is happening, or of what might happen.

During meditation, what arises may be neither particularly pleasant nor unpleasant, but we are impatient, that is to say, we cannot wait if there is nothing interesting. As soon as feelings of impatience and restlessness arise, we must look at them—so that what is subjective is made the object for Insight meditation. We do not look *for* anything; we just watch with bare attention, which is different from the concentrative state because it flows with what is arising without getting stuck. When we look in this way, we shall see. It is the same in daily life: we shall hear what we hear, feel what we feel, and see what we see.

Concentration can produce knowledge and power, but not *insight* because insight is not "produced"—it arises naturally when non-interfering and non-judgmental watchfulness has allowed all the veils to be fully seen through.

When the conditioned mind can lose what has been accumulated and come to the *unconditioned*, without dwelling on any ground or center, it ceases to take refuge and is open to the flow of insights, containing only what is needed at the moment until such a need is transcended altogether.

Emptiness of the mind does not mean that anything is lacking. All that is needed is there, or available, like an open hand awaiting our attention when we are in need of help, and because everything is allowed to pass, according to the laws of change and impermanence, this opens the way for what is fresh and relevant to the next moment. Nothing is out of place, and all things can serve their proper purpose if we cease to interfere, just letting them come and go like breathing.

The Domain of Vipassana Meditation. We may summarize the principal factors of this practice into five areas as follows: (a) exertion of energy, (b) clarity of consciousness, (c) choiceless and desireless awareness, (d) letting go, and (e) non-attachment.

Exertion of energy. As far as the exertion of energy or personal investment is concerned, we simply mean the act of constantly putting energy into living in the now-moment, in which both past and future things are allowed to pass through, without our getting caught or stuck in them. They are seen as passing events as they float along in the currents of consciousness. With the practice of disidentification, one is able to experience them more objectively and therefore see them for what they are, without adding any opinions or views to them. At the same time, there is more open space within so that things of the past and future may find their way through more easily. Because they are operating, by nature, within the law of change and impermanence, they are transmuted and alter their forms as the development process goes on. An inner process of reorganization and realignment regarding our conditioned states takes place naturally as we perseveringly exert energy into living life fully in every vital moment, regardless of anything and everything, whether pleasurable or painful, that comes along within its currents.

When energy is mobilized like a constantly flowing river, there is no lack of power and strength. In such a flow, power, either for creating or for destroying as is appropriately needed, increases as more strength comes from behind and the flow continues with its eternal movement and creative action. Thus the processes of elimination and purification, development and growth, come into operation. It is the ripening and fruition of these processes that constitute the meditative procedures for enlightenment and liberation.

The type of energy produced and mobilized in the meditative process is named *atapa*: it diffuses all the disturbing, negative, and destructive influences within our psychophysical systems (commonly known as body-mind). *Atapa* clears away energy that is trapped as a result of repression. Such suppressed energy blocks the flow of life as it is, hinders our natural process of unfolding, and prevents us from living in an ongoing state of freedom. The other function of *atapa* energy is to accelerate the growth and manifestation of insight, peace, love, compassion, stillness, and clarity of mind.

At the healing level, *atapa* acts both as the inner source or healing agent and as the connecting field of the universal life force that is available both inside and outside each of us. When a person sits in the meditative posture for a certain time, *atapa* surges through his/her body-mind processes, doing healing work quietly or noisily, depending on how deeply rooted the aspect to be healed is. Sometimes *atapa* causes an individual to adopt an awkward physical position that is so painful it cannot be maintained. At other times, it causes the individual's hand(s) to press the specific location on the body where energy is blocked. This *atapa* directed pressure may be firm or gentle. It functions to release the energy and promote healing and psychophysical integration.

The spontaneous activities of *atapa* energy can occur at any time. They are not restricted to sessions of sitting meditation. In fact, *atapa* sometimes wakes a person in the middle of the night so that he/she can work with it. The individual must be prepared to provide hospitality at any time so that the releasing and healing work can successfully take place.

The duration of each session is also determined by the energy itself, and not by the person under care. If one stops sitting before the fixed time is over, one could suffer by becoming more negative and more unhappy in life; and when getting back to the inner work, pain, whether physical or emotional, could become more unbearable. There is a need for a complete surrendering on the person's part so that the work may be done more smoothly.

The body and the mind are totally interdependent in their functioning as a living organism. Bodily processes and mental activities mutually affect one another. The mind is in the body, and the body is permeated by the mind's control and manipulation. When the body surrenders and opens up to release and cure, and the mind lets go of interference and truly believes in such a form of remedy, the healing work is very powerful. When both the helper and the receiver have a strong belief in the same method of remedy, they provide the best channels for *atapa* and life energy to flow freely, and the healing process is profound.

The *atapa* energy produced through the meditative process works in the form of self-healing without a healer or helper, apart from the person who receives the healing. Sometimes, a guide is necessary to provide comfort and encouragement, especially when fear is a predominant factor in the person under the care and treatment of the *atapa* energy. However, once complete trust in the process is established, there is no need for a guide to be present; for in trust, the inner guru has been found. All the guidance and direction will come through with the process, as clear awareness, insight, and intelligence work together in complete harmony with the *atapa* energy.

Clarity of consciousness. This is the second principal factor required for Vipassana practice. It simply refers to our clear seeing of what is going on, or what is happening at the moment.

The student of Insight development must look, listen, and sense precisely and constantly what is within the field of consciousness, be it visual consciousness, auditory consciousness, or inner sense consciousness as well as the other sense-modalities where consciousness arises and manifests itself, including body consciousness in terms of touch or contact and sensitivity. Without this precision and clarity of seeing through the inner, all-seeing eye of Insightful Wisdom, there is no learning, no development, and no evolution. Self-transformation doesn't take place. In order for radical change to come into effect, clarity of consciousness, as the powerful eye of insight, must be cultivated and constantly applied both during meditation sessions and in everyday living. There must be constant awareness of the interflow between one's internal and external environments, and between self and other.

Figuratively speaking, consciousness is like inner space where anything can be filled in or emptied out in the same way that breath flows in and out of our physical bodies. Internal (mental) activities fill up consciousness and command it to manifest according to their plans, desires, and attributes. But when awareness flows in with penetrating insight into what is going on within the world of consciousness, the activities (arising from our conditioning and habits of mind), slow down and decrease to allow inner space to appear.

When the activities of thought and reflection (*vaci-sankkhara*), and those of inner perception and sensation or an imbalanced state of feeling (*mano-sankkhara*) are reduced, consciousness returns home to its own intrinsic, true nature of luminosity and radiance. This enables it to connect with the more refined fields of energy of peace, stillness, love, and oneness with all, without discrimination. At this level of natural unfolding or inner explosion and eternal flow of the

Upstream, there is no boundary to be found anywhere. Even the primary boundary between self and other disperses. It is *sankkhara*, internal activity, that creates the boundary, which is an illusion after all. The complete reduction of the *sankkhara* states gives total freedom to consciousness. Flashes of insight, the capacity to see things as they are, as well as Thunder-Wisdom (Vajira-panna) flow through swiftly and naturally with no obstruction. Clarity of consciousness is nothing but the insightful eye of seeing things as they are *(yathabhutam pajanati)*.

Choiceless and desireless awareness. As discussed in the preceding general description of Vipassana meditation, "choiceless and desireless awareness" is the ancient, golden key for discovering, developing, and moving on toward full awakening. It also functions as an element of stabilization when a meditator's conditioned mind attempts to grasp peak experiences and build a structure of value and attainment around them.

With choiceless and desireless awareness, one does not make any programs for experiencing, achieving, or attaining anything. It is a light and free journey for discovery, for uncovering the covered, making known the unknown, and bringing the unconscious into the conscious through awareness so that there is nothing hidden in any parts of our psychophysical processes.

As we know it, what we call enlightenment is nothing but impeccable, full awareness flowing evenly and eternally in every single moment of living. It is a pure and clean energy with no conditioning whatsoever. Such awareness has no center or location for operation. It is everywhere and nowhere in particular. Its manifestation is seen as a precise and clear movement of contact, which goes on constantly as long as life continues to flow. In our journey through ourselves, our inner journey for discovery, we are instructed to be willing to remain open to what is without making any choices or conforming to any particular desires. Whatever enters our consciousness, or comes into the field of awareness, is the thing to relate to and to deal with through *bare* attention, that is, without using any knowledge and things of the past, including judgement and efforts to modify the experience. All influxes are allowed to flow along with the stream of consciousness without repressing or suppressing anything. It is the function of awareness and insight to make contact with and to penetrate them so that the work of transcending or putting them to utter destruction will be done naturally, i.e., without the effort of the meditator.

Bear in mind that wherever and whenever awareness is, insight is there in presence with it. And with the presence of awareness and insight is the *atapa* energy together with its connecting fields of powerful forces required for the work to be carried out at the time. They are all interconnected and work together in complete harmony. This is the reason there is no *need* for any interference of extra factors or man-made God to be there; for such interference can only delay completion. One gives up the choice of, and the desire for, any particular, fixed goal. One is completely open and surrenders to the workings of awareness and insight. Anything and everything experienced through this inner journey will be taken care of efficiently and safely. Thus is the simple, free journey!

Letting go. In our life experiences we tend to grasp and cling to what is good and pleasurable so that self-satisfaction and self-gratification may be retained and fostered. Surprisingly enough, some of us even hold on tightly to a poor self-image, negativity, or suffering in order to keep dramatizing our lives unintentionally. This is because such individuals have lost a real sight of self and then identify themselves with images or persona (what others have called a "false self"), conducting life under influences of certain shadows, the unconscious currents of personality factors. Letting go is impossible for them. So far as we know it, the practice of letting go can become effective only when there is a *clear seeing* of the game, or that which one is actually doing to oneself, or playing out with others. Without such a sharp insight into one's life situation, it is impossible to let go of those games with which one is familiar. The thing that makes one feel real about oneself is one's own *familiarity*. To be otherwise is to feel unreal. Therefore, one takes a firm grip on the persona and keeps feeding on the shadow. Thus the drama goes on!

The other terminology for letting go is non-doing. Not to do what one is doing is impossible unless one sees clearly and thoroughly that what is carried is unhealthy and harmful, or even destructive either to oneself or to others. Non-doing is not a virtue that can be practiced like a rule or a precept, but is a creative action without doing anything in particular. It is also the undoing of habits and of the old by stopping and non-conforming—just letting things be, letting people be who they are, without attempting to change them, or even to interfere with them. What happens is just the happening. This sounds as if we are describing a person who is a bit too passive, carelessly detached with no wish to participate in what is going on and completely withdrawn into a little cell of self. But the truth is not always what it appears to be. There are differences between appearance and reality. This non-doing is certainly not the way of the fool but that of the wise, for such a precious thing as non-doing requires a great deal of attention and intelligence in carrying it out. This means that non-doing comes into practice at the time when the thorough, insightful awareness of what is going on has reached its absolute clarity. It cannot be done otherwise. Clear seeing is the key for non-doing, and with it one knows exactly if an action or non-action is required for the situation. In this way, there is neither negligence nor complication contributed to the challenges of a situation. Only accurate and precise action is taken. Such is the way of the warrior.

Letting go and non-doing go hand in hand in the practice of Oriental Vipassana meditation and of Western psychotherapy. The difference lies in terminology and emphasis. The West emphasizes the letting go, working to establish conditions that promote it, while the East lays emphasis on non-doing. The underlying cause of both practices is the same, that is, the *clear seeing* or *insight* into reality and unreality. So, both letting go and non-doing are clean actions, free of negativity and residue of blocks.

I have already stated elsewhere that letting go without turning away is the freedom of living and conducting interpersonal relationships. Non-doing without the slightest indifference or neurotic detachment provides a space for transmutation and solution to take place naturally. Finally, I would like to emphasize that non-doing is the negation of ego interference with the workings of insight and invisible forces. It is the matter of allowing things to unfold naturally and therefore to follow their natural course without any interruption. This way of being also refers to the freedom from being stuck so that one can go with the flow guided by the unequaled Light of Wisdom. One can never get stuck anywhere, whether within oneself or in the world. There is nothing that one holds either against oneself or others, for everything has been forgiven and let go of completely. In other words, things are totally forgotten with no trace. The past no longer exists in one's psychosomatic system, and there is nothing left for projecting onto the future. So, only the creative present is lived as reality in the here and now. This is what is meant by the living truth of letting go and non-doing.

Non-attachment. By maintaining an attitude of letting go and non-doing, we are not enslaved by the drive to acquire and to become free from grief and agony. By maintaining an attitude of non-attachment, we not only liberate ourselves from dependence and freedom in living, but are able to reach out with love in all situations and circumstances of life.

Non-attachment is different from detachment. Detachment points to the tendency to withdraw and become indifferent. Non-attachment results in active participation, not with the passion of attachment, but with freedom of mind and joy of heart. With this attitude of non-attachment we become fully alive, spontaneous, loving, autonomous, and strong in our contact and interaction with the world of relationships, as well as with the world of phenomena, whether physical, environmental, mental, or spiritual.

When experiencing something, non-attachment allows us to experience it fully with no holding back or a sense of reserve. We feel free to jump into anything in front of us and swim with its currents with the whole of our being. After having an experience we simply finish with it and let it go completely. There is no looking back or looking forward to a possible repetition of the same experience, but we remain open to re-encounter it if it does return. This is similar to water dropping off a lotus leaf. No residue of liquid remains. It is a clean and clear dropping. Or, it's like a bee roaming about a flower, caressing it and taking the nectar from it, then flying away without causing any damage to the flower. Another simile for non-attachment can be seen in the life cycle of swans. They leave their ponds, abandoning home after home, as they continually move onward in their journey. Such is the free movement of living.

Most of us have a deep tendency to grasp and cling to all our possessions and experiences for the main purpose of feeling secure and safe in life. This deeply rooted habit follows us like a shadow that never leaves. When we go on an inner journey, we tend to repeat the same habits of behavior that sustain us in our daily lives in the world. That is to say, we mechanically put ourselves in a position of holding on to that which cannot be held and of attempting to produce that which cannot be produced such as insight, love, and freedom. Insight, love, and freedom are universal elements. They flow freely and are available to all who come in contact with them without preferences. Because we are bound by our conditioned attitudes of acquiring and clinging, we miss many opportunities to encounter love, light, peace, freedom, and the profound silence within. With such conditioning we unknowingly set up an un-desirable situation for pain and suffering to dominate our lives, or at least for disappointments to creep in. This is not the wise way of living.

Non-attachment is the world of the wise who are free from fear and bondage and who are capable of truly loving as well as of expressing love with all its purity, clarity, beauty, and strength. As we are aware, attachment destroys love, while non-attachment nurtures it and increases it. Love and non-attachment belong to the same energy field within the same level of consciousness, mainly manifesting through the heart channel when it is fully open.

In order to understand this matter of non-attachment, we must look into its opposite, attachment. According to the Buddha, and also from our experiences of life, we find ourselves in four forms of attachment. They are (1) attachment to sensual pleasures, (2) attach-ment to opinions and views, (3) attachment to techniques and methods of practices, including the rituals and belief systems firmly associated with those practices and faiths, and (4) attachment to the sense of separate self, or to the mere notion of self. These four categories of attachment are certainly obvious to all of us.

1. Attachment to sensual pleasures. Pleasurable sensations and pleasant feelings are always appealing to our body and mind so that we constantly seek them and cling to them in the same way that we

look for food to nourish our physical body. Not only that, we often feel dissatisfied with an old sensation and search for a new one with the thought that the grass is greener on the other side of the fence. Then, attachment as the emotional investment in objects of pleasure and as the building up process makes us struggle and strive for the fulfillment of our desires.

Although feelings and sensations appear highly pleasurable and wonderfully pleasant to our senses when we first encounter them, we can never find everlasting satisfaction because it is the nature of the human mind to be discontented and dissatisfied. Craving for having more and becoming more is endless. As a result, we become compulsively goal oriented, trying harder and harder to achieve whatever aims and strategies we set up for our achievement. Anger and hatred arise from our goal seeking. Individuals or groups are perceived as *obstacles* to achieving our goals and thereby become targets of hatred. Such is the way of life under the influence of attachment.

In opposition to attachment we find non-attachment as our freedom to get and enjoy whatever we need or want in life. In the way of non-attachment there is no compulsion whatsoever, so that we create no tension in fulfilling our desires as well as in enjoying the pleasures of the senses. We are free to have, or not to have, anything and everything without any self-imposed restrictions. We do not live by rules, but flow with spontaneity and a flexible, open-ended attitude of mind. This is done in the full realization that things in the phenomenal world are impermanent and ever changing, and that they are all interdependent and interrelated.

So, the attitude of non-attachment allows us to follow the natural course of flow with no resistance to the changes that must take place in accordance with the laws of nature and the order of the universe. In this way, we learn to live in harmony and in peace with one another and with our environment, bringing together self and other, organism and environment, in union and in love. No opposite remains isolated. All pairs of opposites are re-united in a complete union as they were originally before the development of concepts, notions, and ideas.

2. Attachment to opinions and views; 3. techniques and methods of practice, including the religions and belief systems firmly associated with those practices and faiths. With regard to the opinions, views, methods, and techniques that we use in our professional practices together with the belief systems and rituals built into them, we can certainly have any of them with us, ready to use freely and appropriately. For example, we are free to voice our views and to express our opinions about situations, events, and things that happen in the world. But with non-attachment we are able to relax about those opinions and views presented and let them be discussed and torn apart without getting upset. We can remain in equilibrium and become totally objective in regard to debates and discussions on any matters. This gives us the freedom to listen deeply as well as to express ourselves honestly and clearly without feeling restricted or impeded both externally and internally, particularly by our internal condition. Any methods or techniques employed do not have a grip on us in exclusion of all else. They are regarded only as helping factors with no domineering power over our practice of them so that we remain autonomous and independent of them.

With non-attachment as the way of living we are free to use any techniques and methods provided that they are effective and helpful. If they are not helpful, we are also free to drop them with no regret. But if we are attached to them, we work with narrow-mindedness and try to fit things into a system mechanically, instead of working with sensitive awareness and intuitive understanding of the problem or challenge presented to us at the time. With attachment we are stuck in whatever we become attached to. We have no freedom to actualize ourselves but must conform to the methods and techniques with which we feel safe. "We sleep with our familiarity." That stops us from expanding our consciousness and capacity to do our work more effectively and efficiently.

We do not dare to take initiative and apply our new learning because we lack trust in the new discovery and fear letting go of the old. This is an example of the trap and stuckness arising from attachment. Attachment further deepens our ignorance and begets fear. More than that, it drives us to an isolation camp, dominated by our rigidity and inflexibility in our views and opinions. We are lost in the deep jungle of those views and opinions that we hold tightly with our self-righteousness and the illusive idea that we are right, although we might be wrong. In this way, attachment to methods and ideas limits our ability to learn from experience and to grow.

4. Attachment to the sense of a separate self. Now we arrive at the most subtle and the deepest form of attachment, that of attachment to the sense of a separate self. This is the illusion that we have a self separated from others around us. It is confirmed by our ordinary perception, organized by our compulsive pattern of conditioning commonly known as "ego" and by the discriminating mind with its insoluble problem of dichotomy. We are actually trapped inside this illusion, but believe that we live in a reality of the separate self with no illusion. Maintaining this fiction keeps us in the world of separation and division, while inwardly we are crying for unity and oneness with the whole as well as with all those surrounding us.

Psychologically speaking, we understand our needs for having an identification for our existence and for functioning in the world. But we turn that need into a want as our neuroses grow out of this illusion of a separate self, which we maintain as an absolute reality. Consequently, we identify ourselves with this notion of self as the total truth within us. We are nothing other than a separate individual self with which another illusion called "other" is created as an opposite. With these two notions invented for convenience, we draw a dividing line and form our primary boundary between self and other. As the time passes, we become deeply rooted in our invention and undoubtedly believe that each of us has a separate self and that we really are isolated from one another. With such a firm belief, we build in our attachments to support and protect our created identity. Because this conventional reality is not the whole truth about who we truly are but only a fragment of ourselves, we meet with all kinds of conflicts and difficulties arising from mistaking the partial truth as the whole truth. While living with this illusion, just as all the narcissists do, we imagine and assume that we actually live in the world of reality. Hence, self-deception goes deep and is sometimes beyond remedy.

With such deep attachment to the sense of a separate self, it is not easy, if not impossible, for us to see in profound wisdom that this separate self is an illusion and a mere notion representing the functioning of our psychological processes.

The only possibility for achieving freedom from the attachment to the self is the full realization of ultimate truth with profound insight into what is real and what is unreal. When the whole truth is revealed and the covering up of it, that is illusion, is uncovered once and for all, there is no need to do anything with attachment, for it will simply no longer be there. Non-attachment emerges to take its place. Then freedom and love flow together with wisdom and awareness in our everyday living.

But non-attachment cannot come to be unless the illusion of self, the veil of ignorance, is cut through and removed from the screen. Once that is done, the love of non-attachment will follow us in all of our action, speech, and thought, although we may still use the sense of self for communicating and functioning in the world. It is merely an instrument and not the total, solid reality as we previously took for granted. This means that a grip on the self no longer exists.

Now, we see clearly that non-attachment is wisdom in action and living love, the highest truth in life, which once established in our consciousness, flows constantly and evenly with our attention. Once and for all we cease to cling to the illusion of self in which there is no corresponding reality at the outset. It is so simple that this matter of attachment just disappears instantly at the moment the veil of ignorance is removed and things are seen as they really are.

Two categories of non-attachment are (1) non-attachment as expressed through relationships and (2) understanding the truth of love (non-attachment).

1. Non-attachment as expressed through relationships, marriage, and family life. As to non-attachment, a question arises regarding love relationships, marriage, and a family life: How can we manage our partnerships and married life if we practice this virtue of non-attachment? What is the nature of our commitment to each other and to the life-style that we agree to live as man and wife or partners?

Thinking in terms of social institutions and the establishment, we may perceive as well as conceive of a marriage and love relationship as a binding contract that must be honored and respected above our growth and development. We must comply with all the rules and regulations laid down for such a commitment, including the ground rules (unwritten law) obeyed by everybody else in the society to which we belong. In this way of thinking, the marriage or love relationship is nothing but an institution. It is not a setting for growth into full humanness in all directions with the relationship between a man and a woman as its initial impetus.

As an institution, marriage demands total commitment and dedication (without questioning in some religions). This means there must be a solid attachment between the married couple and their children; otherwise such an institution cannot be maintained. The marriage and family life will fall apart without such a firmly established commitment as is promised at the wedding ceremony and as is written in the marriage certificate. It appears that this way of thinking and maintaining is based on fears and needs for security, leading to dependency, emotionally, psychologically, and materially. With such a dependent relationship, the individuals concerned could lose their autonomy and real sense of independence. They could get into various forms of inner conflict from neglecting inner work, as they focus on protecting the marriage and keeping the family together instead of on growing together.

This is, psychologically speaking, the compulsion of the seeker for a physical union rather than the real one. Eventually, the seeker breaks down and the family suffers separation and disharmony. As actual fact indicates, the seeker's mind thinks, with its belief system, that the real thing, the truth, is out there somewhere and not within. So, he searches and searches for it outside of himself until all becomes vain and the essential work is revealed. Then the seeker wakes up with the realization that he has been led by displacement all along. Indeed, the seeker is the sought and must be found to bring an end to the seeking altogether.

If we see clearly that love itself is the commitment and not the paper or social institution, then the way of non-attachment is easy to understand. For non-attachment is love and vice versa.

2. Understanding the truth of love (non-attachment). Arriving at this point, we really need to understand the truth of love as deeply as we can so that we do not confuse ourselves by mistaking love for attachment. In love there is no clinging, nor is there ownership. Love is truly universal and cannot be monopolized by anyone or any agent either here on earth or up in heaven, so to speak. Love is eternally flowing and available for all beings without discrimination. In our total, deep experience of love, we do not even find desire or emotion contained in or attached to it. It is such a pure energy of loving oneness in which the boundary between self and other dissolves completely so that the reaching out is free and without any trace of desire for anything in return. Idea, belief, or preference is simply not there.

Logically speaking, when in the beginning (origin) there is no self, how can there be a desire for self-satisfaction? It doesn't make sense, does it? If in the beginning (origin) there is no imbalanced state of feeling, but all feelings are totally clear and clean and completely balanced, how can there be a place for emotion? As love is complete in itself, whole, unconditional, and impersonal (universal), it doesn't need anything else to be its contents. Love flows with freedom, strength, and wisdom, yet they are not its contents. They are simply in the same energy field within a level of consciousness in which there exists tremendous powers for healing, transformation, transcendence, maintenance, and creativity. These aspects of love are harmoniously compatible with the energy of non-attachment that keeps all powers in spontaneous and liberated balance.

With non-attachment in our heart and mind, we truly and genuinely love each other with caring and understanding so that we can freely give and receive anything that is needed from one another. In other words, the acts of giving and receiving are naturally taken when love flows and non-attachment unfolds.

Here is an old song of the heart: "To you I give. From you I receive. Together we live, in Love." Another song goes thus: "You are the One. I am the One. We are the One." Obviously, these songs indicate true love as our total commitment with the virtue of non-attachment, which transcends selfishness and self-centeredness altogether.

When non-attachment provides such a strong foundation for a love relationship or marriage, we can certainly manage our partnership and married life to our satisfaction within the light of wisdom. The issue of commitment is out of the question as long as love is consciously experienced and non-attachment practiced in all situations and circumstances in our everyday living. What we eternally do care for is love, and the object of love can only intensify it. With love we feel completely connected and one with its object(s), while non-attachment helps us to transcend the personal, the unpleasant, and the disagreeable. So, there is no problem of conflict to be found anywhere. In this way, our love relationship, in whatever form or lifestyle we unanimously choose to live in together, is highly healthy and therefore ultimately desirable.

At this point, another question might be raised as to how to maintain such love and non-attachment. It cannot be maintained, nor can it be got hold of. We must grow into it and become it completely so that there is no division between us and love or non-attachment. It is just a stream of luminous consciousness and ever-flowing, pure energy, manifesting through our psychophysical processes as long as they exist and perform the functions of our lives.

If we become small, we certainly feel separated and create the opposites where conflict and attachment come in. We then see love and non-attachment as something out there for maintaining and grasping, which apparently shows our tendency to become attached to, and dependent on, that which is beyond attachment and dependence. Here again, we go round and round in the circle of samsara where there is no way out, apart from breaking the circle itself.

As long as we go on sleeping with the sense of a separate self and remain small, limited, and fragmented, we can never enter the realm of love and non-attachment. For this reason, we stay in the world of attachment and dependence, led by thought, drawn along by thought. Every aspect of our lives is influenced by the discriminating mind, which creates dualistic concepts. It binds us to the lower world and creates a life full of conflict and struggle.

But living in the consciousness of non-attachment and love, we do not think in terms of opposites. Therefore, there is no conflict, for conflict in life is caused and brought into existence by the creation of opposites. Because we are not led or drawn along by thought (the movement of time as a designation for the continued succession of cause and effect), we become the master of thought and use it to think in terms of harmony, unity, and the union of all the opposites already created and existing in such a thinking mind.

With the natural flow of love and non-attachment, we do not find ourselves demanding or expecting either of ourselves or of others around us. There is a loving atmosphere of relaxation, peace, and freedom permeating the whole world of relationship and interaction between man and wife, partners, their children, and members of the community in which they live. And from there, they expand and extend this consciousness of love and non-attachment to the world at large, opening their arms to embrace everybody and everything without any discrimination. Such all-embracingness is the freedom in contact and the expressive act of love in which no clinging and dependency is to be found. Please always bear in mind that this movement of non-attachment and love is flowing inseparably with insightful awareness and wisdom in action.

The Direction of Vipassana. As to the question of where Insight meditation leads its practitioners, we shall quote the Buddha's statement as it appears in the outset of the *Satipatthanasutta*, his "Discourse on the Presence of Mindful Awareness."

"This is the only way, Monks, for the purification of beings, for the overcoming of sorrow and lamentation, for the destruction of suffering and grief, for reaching the right path for the full realization and attainment of Nirvana, namely, the Four Foundations of Mindful Awareness. What are the four? Here, a monk, energizing, ardent, clearly comprehending things and mindful, lives observing the body and its activities, observing feelings, observing the mind and its activities (states), and observing the mental objects (with all their implications), having overcome compulsive desire and repugnance toward the world."

Regarding the observation of those four main objects mentioned above, the Buddha also made it clear in his same discourse on the subject as follows:

"He (a meditator) lives observing origination-factors or dissolution-factors or origination-and-dissolution-factors in the body, in feelings, in the mind, and in the mental objects, internally and externally or externally and internally. So, Mindful Awareness is established to the extent necessary just for *insight* and *awareness*, and he lives non-attached, and clings to naught in the world." (The details of the principles and methods of practice can be found in the author's three books, *The Way of Non-attachment*, *The Dynamic Way of Meditation*, and *The Middle Path of Life*.)

It is worth mentioning here that the Vipassana system is the only simple and practical method ever found in the way of meditating. It lays its emphasis on the presence of mindful awareness, free from any interference and judgement of what is going on. When such awareness increases and becomes part and parcel of life, there comes into operation insightful knowledge of the true nature of things, seeing them as they really are. Hence, the processes of arising and passing away from moment to moment become so obvious that the nature of impermanence and the constant state of change, as well as the truth of the interdependence and interrelatedness of things, are unmistakably clear to our mind, our intellect, and our consciousness. Thus arises the recognition and acknowledgement of the three characteristics of existence, namely, *impermanency, dissatisfactory nature*, and *voidness*. With the direct perception and insight into these three marks of existence, the ideas and thoughts of an eternal *entity* existing within man or outside of man (such as a soul, self, or *atman*) are transcended and eliminated completely.

We all experience these observable facts and truths in our lives. There is nothing permanent, never changing, everlastingly satisfactory, or absolutely substantial. All phenomena, events, and things are ever-changing, interdependent, interconnected, temporarily pleasurable or painful, and are just processes rolling on without any single, independently existing entity (or substantiality) directing the courses of existence. This is the pure wisdom springing up from the depths of our being through the direct contact with reality, both absolute and relative.

But what is it that makes us render our services to other sentient beings? The wisdom side sounds very introverted, dry, and detached from anything else. It doesn't seem to care for the well-being, happiness, and welfare of other fellow beings who are still caught in pain and suffering, confused about the nature of truth and falsehood and who are still starving and dying due to a lack of food and medicine.

Here is a place for compassion to play an active role in human life so that all the tasks needing performance and completion will be done. In truth, *compassion is inseparable from wisdom.* They flow along together just like yin and yang manifesting in the phenomenal world. There is no compassion without wisdom, nor is there wisdom without compassion.

On the surface wisdom and compassion appear opposite and contradictory. It sounds as if wisdom is far out, in an extreme spiritually transcendental realm, while compassion appears to be totally involved with saving the world and all its inhabitants without discrimination. In other words, compassion is like a strong, functional self, performing duties as a warrior to liberate all living beings from bondage and fear, from suffering and starvation, while wisdom suggests that there is no world to be saved and no being to be liberated. It seems absolutely impersonal and completely non-active.

To our conceptual mind, these two factors of wisdom and compassion exist in entirely different worlds, in total contrast to each other. But this is not the truth. In order for us to see clearly how compassion and wisdom can work together, we need to integrate them in our lives. In fact, the integrating process takes place natural-ly and simultaneously as we flow and develop ourselves either into real compassion or true wisdom. Once the veil of ignorance and the giant of the emotions are permanently removed, the flow and manifestation of compassion and wisdom become normal and natural with no obstruction. This is an essential point in bringing in some details later in this chapter. Wisdom and compassion come together in the course of liberation. It is only because our conceptual minds tend to analyze and separate unities into opposites and parts that we are confronted with the task of integrating compassion and wisdom.

In Buddhism, the Mahayana Buddhists, after having created the Bodhisattva ideal of Great, Boundless Compassion, had to deal with the teaching of *sunyata*. They evolved new and brilliant interpretations and explanations, beginning with Nagarjuna, the great commentator of the Prajnaparamita (perfect wisdom) text.

Here, we should understand what the term "Bodhisattva" means. According to Walpola Rahula, a Bodhisattva is a person (monk or layman) who is in a position to attain nirvana as a Sravaka (disciple) or as Pratyekabuddha (silent buddha), but who, out of great compassion *(maha karuna)* for the world, renounces it and goes on suffering in samsara for the sake of others. He perfects himself during an incalculable period of time and finally realizes nirvana, thus becoming an Arahant, Samyaksam-buddha, a fully enlightened buddha. He discovers the truth and declares it to the world. His capacity for service to others is unlimited (*Zen, and Taming of the Bull*, 1978).

This ideal of great compassion personified by the concept of a bodhissatva has been a big challenge to the Mahayana Buddhists, so that there was a great attempt on their part to translate such an ideal into practice in everyday life. In order to succeed, at least at the philosophical level, they tried their best to understand the meaning of *sunyata*, the most essential teaching of the Buddha, who proclaimed and expounded the Middle Path, thus avoiding two extreme practices of life. These are the pursuit of sensual pleasures (the pleasure principle) as the goal of life on earth, on the one hand, and the search for spiritual fulfillment through self-mortification in different forms, on the other. The wisdom of *sunyata* simply points to seeing things as they really are, empty of preconception, conceptualization, idea, and thought.

To say "every thing exists" is an eternalistic view, or to state "nothing exists" is a nihilistic theory. They are both extreme views on what *is*, which includes *form and emptiness*. *Sunyata*, as the essence of the middle way, goes beyond those extreme views by creating the concept of "non-dwelling" on any conclusion whatsoever. Even dwelling on the non-dwelling is not encouraged. The way of looking at things in our perceptual and conceptual worlds in view of *sunyata* could be summarized in a short formula of four lines:

> When this is, that is;
> This arising, that arises;
> When this is not, that is not;
> This ceasing, that ceases.

Even so, the doctrine of *sunyata* is swift to say that those four lines are just a description of the world of interdependence, which is a partial truth. The whole truth lies beyond the description, as the description is not the described.

With perfect understanding of *sunyata*, the Bodhisattvas find no problem in helping all sentient beings, as well as in saving the world, out of the natural flow of great compassion running along the same stream of perfect wisdom. Compassion and wisdom become one as the free movement of truth in the boundless stream of consciousness, in which all the boundaries and duality of things such as attachment/non-attachment, dwelling/non-dwelling, form/emptiness, emptiness as form/form as emptiness, emptiness as no other than form/form as no other than emptiness, etc., are completely transcended. In other words, all the opposites are in total union, and there is no longer a dividing line or territory marked anywhere, either in the internal world of the mind or in the external world of perceptual reality. In the ultimate sense, all these notions of union, no-boundary, no-territory, and opposites are not for dwelling on. They are just descriptive terms of speech that those Bodhisattvas who fully realize the teaching of *sunyata* have gone beyond and gone beyond the "gone beyond."

A Brief Review of Western Therapies

As it was said at the outset, Western psychotherapy aims to help those in need to function properly in life and in the world. It is the science or method of healing psychological disorders by using psychological techniques and healing arts. In this process, the functioning self or ego must be strengthened to enable the individual to take charge of himself and of his relationships with others, as well as with the world at large.

The Goals of Western Psychotherapy

Such things as earning a living, retaining a dignified job, keeping a marriage together, raising a family, and maintaining autonomy are culturally and socially very important for all of us living in the world. For this reason, everybody is trying to become autonomous, independent, and self-assertive. Everyone is searching for a way to support themselves and those dependent on them in the case of marriage or partnership.

As the world and interdependent relationships between our living organisms and the environment (including social systems) become more and more complex, many individuals run into difficulties in retaining their identities and psychological well-being. These problems are on the increase since traditional ways of life and world systems, whether economic, political, social, or cultural, are changing rapidly and becoming increasingly complicated and confusing.

There is a great need for the capacity to adapt and adjust to the changes and the increased complexities of outer life in the world as well as of the inner life of individuals. The failure of adaptability and efficient adjustment leads to psychological disorders and personality conflicts—the lack of a synchronized whole of the inner and the outer. When this happens, individuals look for help to psychotherapeutic techniques available in society. Our society has naturally responded to the varied needs of its individuals by providing many therapeutic methods capable of healing psychological and emotional wounds and of helping the individuals to grow and mature into full humanness.

The focus of Western psychotherapy is on the attempt to cure what it defines as illness, as well as to promote wellness in individuals so that the society can keep functioning within its cultural and systemic structures. In this connection, it is essential in the practice of psychotherapy to lay a strong foundation of grounding for any individuals who undertake treatment.

The terms "grounded" or "centered" are frequently applied in both spiritual and psychological work. In the spiritual context, they refer to an individual's state of awareness of "being here now," totally alert within the present moment. In the psychological context, they refer to an individual's capacity to know, appreciate, respect, and maintain his/her unique sense of self, his/her unique identity. With this firm recognition of who one is (instead of merely functioning as a product of one's family, society, and educational systems), one can further one's development and live one's life with dignity, freely and intelligently choosing among the options presented by the rapidly changing world. In a social context, a well-grounded individual will have a balanced relationship with his/her job, in his/her interpersonal relations, and within his/her community as a whole.

When people are not grounded or centered, their lives are out of balance. This may lead to failure in various aspects of life both internally, within the functioning self, and externally, in the broader social arena where adaptability is an essential component of dynamic health.

From the perspective of an individual's use of "life energy," one may then be described as escaping the present by "spacing out"; one may be overpowered by inertia or experience mental lethargy, or one may be described as being "scattered." These manifestations are all a result of the misuse of energy because of a lack of balance between focus and flexibility.

In a poetic sense, Western psychotherapy gives its priority to attempting to keep individuals on earth, with their feet firmly grounded, so that they may be able to walk softly into life with tremendous strength and dignity, keeping themselves in balance, both internally and in relationship with others, as fully functioning individuals within their specific socio-cultural environment.

Human beings are very complex. Apart from such constitutional factors as temperament, personality is developed through feeling, perception, and activity.

We are born with a certain residue of karma, having been influenced, while in our mother's womb, by her feelings, thoughts, and activities in the external environment of which she was a part. The factors of feeling and perception are the activities of consciousness, which, interlinked with the influences of the environment, result in the deposited conditioning (karmic formation) that dominates and dictates our course of living.

Patterns of conditioning are deeply rooted in our personality. Through constant repetition they lay a strong foundation for the functioning of our egoic consciousness in everyday life. At some point we become aware of their influence and, feeling caught in them, we seek the means to release them so that we may find our true freedom.

The way of life in our family of origin, where intimate relationships and constant interaction take place, provides initial opportunities for experiencing feelings and sensations, either pleasant or unpleasant, as well as for developing perception. For example, when a child senses something, either directly or indirectly, through contact with a parent, he perceives and creates an image of the experience. This image appears to be a solid reality, and, as such, it becomes a conditioned state imprinted on his mind and on his subtle (energy) body. The child responds to the experience in a specific way. The combination of the image of the perceived experience plus the mode of the response gradually forms a pattern as a result of repetition. It is in this way that over a period of time a conditioned personality structure is built. Our unique self becomes trapped and fixated (locked) into the structural patterns, ideas, and images created through our perceptual experiences.

The structure of karma plus "unfinished business" with our families of origin are not easy to free ourselves from. Until we develop awareness of their power and complexity, they run our lives, our relationships with others, as well as our relationship with the world in which we live.

We all seek what we believe is missing from our childhoods. We become emotional beggars, narcissists, and sufferers in our life experiences until we discover what we are doing to ourselves. Then, self-work begins. We descend into deeper levels of our realities. We uncover the hidden and free our imprisoned character structures.

Psychotherapy is of great help in assisting us to repair the damage done to us in our childhood, and that transformation becomes an important step toward being an autonomous person, having a clear sense of self and thereby gaining self-respect to the point of not being easily overwhelmed by others' ideas, thoughts, and opinions. Here we begin to see the operation of self-actualization, which will lead to the natural unfolding of our human potentialities.

A Synopsis of Major Trends

It is not possible to discuss all of the schools of Western psychotherapy. I will select some representatives that may be grouped under three major trends and discuss those in some detail. Others, such as cognitive therapy, seem to be oriented directly to the modification of individuals' conditioning to foster a better adjustment.

Now let us look into these three main groups of Western psychotherapy—psychoanalysis, experiential therapy, and transpersonal therapy.

Psychoanalysis: The Classical Psychotherapy of Freud and Jung. There are two main schools, Freudian psychology and Jungian psychology, that use psychoanalysis as a technique for working on shadow, ego, persona, archetypes, dreams, and symbols. This classical psychological technique lays its emphasis on understanding and discovering that which is operating beneath, or underlying the symptoms, in an attempt to find the original forms of any psychological disorders.

We shall investigate some essential concepts and practices of Freudian as well as Jungian psychologies. Let us begin with the Freudian.

Freud's vision of the unconscious. Freud seemed to see mainly the dark and destructive side of human existence, for he told us a great deal about that side of life, as if we were in constant danger and in an endless, fearful battlefield where we must fight and struggle constantly in our existence on earth. His understanding of the unconscious is limited to the elements that have never been conscious, the repressed material in the individuals, the sick half of human psychology. He painted the picture of the unconscious as something so frightening and destructive that we have to ward it off completely in order to enjoy a healthy life. Because of this picture, Freud further held the view that humanity is dominated by low instincts, and that human neuroses result from repressed sexual impulses. He later came to add to this picture a death instinct, or Thanatos. This is, of course, because Freud formulated his psychological theory from studies of neurotic and psychotic patients in his time.

Certainly, none of what he said is totally false or invalid. But it is a half-truth. The other side of humanity is bright, healthy, and creative. We all can, or do, experience both sides, the dark and the bright, of our realities. The unconscious not only contains elements that have been repressed, it also contains constructive and hidden treasures both within and beyond our imagination.

Jung's collective unconscious and the Buddha's "bhavanga." The unconscious is not predominantly personal in nature, but contains things that are universal and common to all humankind as maintained, at least, by Carl Gustav Jung, who was Freud's contemporary. Also, the Buddha's *Abhidharma*, his depth psychology, states the fact that in our *bhavanga*, equivalent to the unconscious, both destructive and constructive forces flow on unceasingly as the past elements where our conscious process is born. This *bhavanga* process goes on and on in spite of our conscious mind functioning on the surface. It (the *bhavanga*) makes contact with the conscious process for only a couple of moments at the time of the birth of such a process, and then falls back to its own stream and continues running its course. This is similar to Jung's statement: "The conscious mind grows out of an unconscious psyche which is older than it, and which goes on functioning together with it or even in spite of it" (Jung, 1939).

Archetypes as collectively present dynamic patterns. Jung's insightful knowledge of the unconscious is much deeper and far beyond that of Freud's. He does not limit it to the unconscious of individuals, but created the concept of the collective unconscious, which links individuals with the whole of humanity. Central to this interlink between us humans is his notion of archetypes, which Jung saw as "forms without content, representing merely the possibility of a certain type of perception and action" (Jung, 1936). These archetypes, or collectively present dynamic patterns, are reflected in dreams and in the universal motifs found in myths and fairy tales around the world, as stated by Capra (1982). He further described Jung's concept of archetypes thus: "Although they are relatively distinct, these universal forms are embedded in a web of relationships, in which each archetype, ultimately, involves all the others." So, Jung's psychological theory not only covers the science of the human mind but digs deeper into spirituality, the essence of human development, transcending the psychodynamic level of our consciousness and the so-called personal self. Spiritual experiences are in fact transpersonal and universal to all humankind, with no distinction, for the spiritual process involves "letting go," particularly referring to the letting go of our deepest and most subtle attachment to the illusion of self as a separate reality.

The shadow and its role in projection. The Jungian model of psychotherapy helps a person deal with his shadow, ego, or persona and grow into a fuller sense of his identity. As we may well know, in relationships with others we often encounter our shadow, the unconscious currents, underlying certain behaviors, emotional disturbances, and psychological disorders. We become ignorant of what it is that we project onto others and the world. We believe and assume that our experience of a certain negative feeling within us is caused by somebody else or those around us, particularly when we lose touch with our own drives and original forms, the real causes and motivations of our experiences.

For example, when feeling pressured by a job, we might get easily irritated, anxious, and nervous, without realizing that we, in actual fact, have a good deal of drive for the job. When we are out of touch with this drive, pressure arises. As a result, a feeling of anger grows and grows and makes us project it onto either the boss or a colleague who is closely associated with us in terms of responsibility and authority. In other words, when we experience pressure we look for someone or something to react to. This means that the shadow is running our consciousness. It creates a crisis in perception and moves us farther and farther away from the original intent of our drive for the job, into the world pressuring us to do the work. At such a moment, if a colleague comes along and asks if our work is done or is being carried out properly, we might feel terribly angry and assume that it was that person who wanted us to get the job done and who created all the pressure on us. This is a typical example of the powerful dominance of the projected shadow.

This story would be completely different if we were fully aware of the operation of the shadow. If we paid attention to it and kept our watchful eye on it, we would not react inappropriately to anyone who inquired about the job that we were supposed to finish at a certain time. Instead, our response would be something like this: "Well, I am doing my best and hope to get it done on time if nothing unexpected happens." In this connection, we say that we welcome pressure if it occurs within us and that we understand, through our self-awareness, where the pressure comes from. By dealing with it without losing contact with our drive for doing the job (the original form that is later replaced by the feeling of pressure), we are in a position to free ourselves of the shadow and get on with our lives with just a minor annoyance. In this way, we still can maintain our dynamic health and remain free from being a victim of the shadow.

Building a strong ego and its relationship to spiritual training. As for ego, our functioning self, psychoanalysis may be a great help to those having a poor sense of identity, not knowing what they want and how they feel in their existence. Because of the weak sense of self, they are unable to function properly in life, as well as face various difficulties concerning personal issues and emotions. In other words, the psychophysical blocks and emotional unfinished business are so great and powerful that they cannot deal with them on their own. For such people there is an urgent need for psychological assistance to help them find a fuller sense of identity to carry out their self-organizing business more efficiently.

As far as we know, living a life in the world requires a solid yet flexible ego for becoming somebody, interacting with others, and organizing our perception and action. Without the ego, at least as a tool for earning a living and performing duties, as well as for fulfilling the roles required by the way of life and society, there would be no proper functioning at the human level of existence.

The work of building up the ego and laying a strong foundation for grounding oneself in the world so that one can become an autonomous person, leading an independent life both materially and emotionally, is actually very essential for everyone before they embark on a spiritual path. Otherwise, there will be more troubles ahead as many of us try to bypass emotional and psychological difficulties through our involvement with some spiritual practices in order to meet our personal needs and to establish an identity. This simply doesn't work!

Furthermore, some of those who call themselves "spiritual people" living in so-called spiritual communities actually become so isolated, or even alienated, that they become frightened of the world outside of their golden cage. Because of the fear caused by their spiritual identity, some become violently aggressive, while others withdraw from contact with the world and hide themselves in ashrams or in caves. They just become more neurotic, I mean, religiously or spiritually neurotic. Consequently, they find themselves involved with spiritual materialism, narcissism, inflation, or group thinking, which results from trying to use spirituality to make up for developmental deficiencies, as rightly stated by John Welwood (an essay, 1979).

Id, ego, and superego. According to Freud, the human personality together with the structure of psyche is organized by and composed of three separate components called *id, ego,* and *superego.* The id represents the primordial or initial principle of life, a reservoir of instinctual energies that are alienated from ego and governed by the primary process. Its function is to provide for the immediate discharge of tension and pain, or at least to reduce them to a low level. This is connected to the pleasure principle, which aims for avoiding pain or discomfort, as well as for finding satisfaction or pleasure. The primary process here refers to that which produces a memory image of an object that is needed to reduce a tension. The ego is the self-organizing agent, a psychological system that retains a primordial close connection to consciousness and external reality.

In the well-adjusted person the ego becomes the executive of the personality, controlling and governing the id impulses and the superego. It also performs a variety of unconscious functions, warding off the id impulses by specific mechanisms of defense. In addition, the ego is governed by the reality principle, so it can tolerate some tension and is also able to postpone the discharge of energy until the actual object that will satisfy the need has been discovered or produced, which means that the tension will be released at an appropriate time by a proper form of behavior. According to Freudian psychology, harmony and adjustment can be maintained as long as the ego performs its executive functions wisely; otherwise, disharmony and maladjustment will result and play the predominant role within the person whose ego abdicates too much of its power to the id, to the superego, or to the external world.

The concept of superego is related to the moral or judicial side of personality. It is, as a matter of fact, the person's moral code developed out of the two factors: reward and punishment. When a child tries to assimilate its parents' moral standards by conforming to the behavior patterns that they want it to possess, it becomes a good boy or a good girl. Then a reward is presented to it by the parents. On the contrary, when the child doesn't comply with the parents' demand for a good behavior, or for a certain standard of success and achievement in terms of learning and doing things in life, it will be punished. In this way, parental authority is absorbed and developed into internalized authority, raising voices and becoming a judge looking over one's shoulder. Such is the role of the superego in our personality.

According to Grof (1985), the superego is "the youngest of the structural components of the mind; it comes fully into being with the resolution of the Oedipus complex. One of its aspects represents the ego ideal, reflecting the attempt to recover a hypothetical state of narcissistic perfection that existed in early childhood, and positive elements of identification with the parents. The other aspect reflects the introjected prohibitions of the parents backed by the castration complex; this is conscience or the 'demon.' Characteristically, the striving toward masculinity in the boy and femininity in the girl leads to a stronger identification with the superego of the parent of the same sex."

I find myself in complete agreement with Grof that Freudian psychoanalysis has its primary focus on the reconstruction of the traumatic past and its repetition in the present as transference dynamics. As Freud asserted, the goal of his therapy doesn't seem to go beyond changing the extreme suffering of the neurotic into the normal misery of everyday life. Nevertheless, when successful, it serves one purpose, that of keeping the ego healthy and able to perform its executive functions in life in the world.

The analyst-patient relationship in psychoanalysis. The method of this analysis lays a strong emphasis on the therapist's interpretations as the instruments in therapeutic change, while the patient merely contributes free associations. This means that the analyst or therapist has full control of the situation in the psychoanalytic session. The patient is thereby encouraged to become passive and submissive, which is neither a sound nor a holistic approach, I must say.

Defense mechanisms of the ego. Before our departure from this section, let us consider some more information about a major task that the ego must perform in order for it to remain healthy at the egoic level. This task is called "defense mechanisms of the ego," which are adopted as protective measures, particularly when the ego cannot reduce anxiety by rational means. It has to utilize such measures as denying the danger (repression), externalizing the danger (projection), hiding the danger (reaction formation), standing still (fixation), or retreating (regression), as stated by Calvin Hall (1954). That is how the ego maintains its survival and carries on its functions. But when it fails to use these defense mechanisms, or the defense systems meet with total failure, we say that a person has to suffer a "nervous breakdown" or a "psychotic reaction" for a certain period of time. As a consequence, the ego must be rebuilt and reconstructed again and again until it can really die, which will lead to the ensuance of what Grof calls "unitive experiences, both of a symbiotic-biological and transcendental nature." These experiences, including the experiences of ego death, then become the sources of new strength and personal identity (Grof, 1985). This, however, takes us beyond the goals and concepts of psychoanalysis.

Self-image or persona. As for the self-image or persona, we see that it is born out of the denial of certain tendencies within us that we do not like to accept and admit into our personality, or even negative aspects that are parts we treat as wholes. That is why the self-image is false and inaccurate, and it is closely linked with the shadow that was previously described. It is the shadow that creates the boundary between self and that which is other than the self, as its opposite. We speak of self-image in contrast to an individual's realistic perception of self. But through the dissolution of the shadow the boundary disappears and the persona perishes, for they never actually existed in the first place. When the shadow is discovered and recognized as well as dealt with thoroughly, the persona or self-image is worked on simultaneously. Bear in mind that such disliked and unadmitted tendencies as anger, erotic impulses, assertiveness, hostility, aggression, drive, and so on do not vanish simply because of the act of denying them. Instead, they grow outside the personality, which is even worse in terms of psychological well-being. At times of weakened personality organization, one will unavoidably become the victim of these excluded tendencies.

Experiential Therapy. Experiential therapy consists of many forms of psychophysical orientation, ranging from humanistic psychology through Reichian, neo-Reichian, bioenergetics, Gestalt, and primal therapy. This group of therapies has gained special attention from those of us who realize the limitations and one-sidedness of the classical therapy, psychoanalysis, and would like to explore ourselves and therapeutic processes more wholly.

The therapeutic process. Experiential therapy emphasizes the actual experience of what is present in the person. The acting out of the obvious and the release of blocks in the body and in the psyche (technically known as "character-armoring," according to Wilhelm Reich) are essential parts of the practice.

Humanistic psychology and Abraham Maslow: understanding the self-actualized individual. The therapeutic approaches of humanistic psychology, according to Grof (1985), "are designed as corrective experiential procedures to remedy the resulting alienation and dehumanization." This is because humanistic psychotherapy is based on the assumption that humanity has become too intellectual, technologized, and detached from sensations and emotions. Grof further says, "They (humanistic psychotherapies) emphasize experiential, nonverbal, and physical means of personality change and aim for individual growth or self-actualization, rather than adjustment."

Humanistic psychotherapies are different from those therapies that lay a one-sided emphasis on either body or psyche, and they represent a significant movement toward a holistic understanding of human nature. Another important aspect of the humanistic approaches is, according to Grof, "a shift from intrapsychic or intraorganismic orientation to the recognition of interpersonal relations, family interaction, social networks, and sociocultural influences and the introduction of economic, ecological, and political considerations."

Abraham Maslow was the founder of the third force of Western psychology. He criticized behavioristic psychology as an erroneous and inadequate psychological theory that sees human beings simply as complex animals responding blindly to environmental stimuli. The behaviorists rely heavily on animal experimentation as data for understanding humans. This is highly problematical and of limited value, especially in understanding the development of conditioning.

Maslow was also a penetrating critic of psychoanalysis in that he disagreed with Freud's exclusive concentration on the study of neurotic and psychotic individuals. He pointed out that focusing on the worst in humanity, instead of the best, results in a distorted image of human nature (Grof, 1985). It only presents half of the picture. The other half, healthy human psychology, is neglected. For this reason, Maslow went ahead using human data as a source for the third force of humanistic psychology. He focused on psychologically healthy and self-actualizing individuals. This was his special contribution to the world of psychology. From his comprehensive study of subjects who have had peak experiences, or spontaneous mystical states of consciousness, Maslow acknowledged such experiences as supranatural as opposed to pathological phenomena. This is completely in line with the spiritual experiences of meditators and mystics.

Reichian therapy: releasing the power of human potential by encouraging the uncongested flow of bioenergy. Reichian therapy is based on Wilhem Reich's theory of sexual economy, which is the balance between sexual excitement and release. Reich emphasized that real neurosis stems from the suppression of sexual feelings and the characterological attitudes accompanying it. He believed that original traumas and sexual feelings are held in repression by complex patterns of chronic muscular tension, technically known as "character armor." He discovered the fact that attitudes and emotional experiences cause the imbalance of the natural rhythms of contraction and expansion in the musculature. This blocks the free flow of energy. These muscular blocks become containers of our personal history regarding our feelings, and they are locked up in the structure and tissue of our muscles in certain parts of the body.

Armor is created to protect an individual against pain and suffering, including the fear of emotions. (A vivid legendary description of this process is found in the character of "Henry," servant to the Frog Prince. He put three bands on his heart to prevent it from breaking when the Prince turned into a frog.) These blocks or locked-in energies must be released so that the person concerned can be free from the imprisoning structure and is able to renew himself with vitality and a full sense of well-being, both physically and psychologically. This means the re-establishment of the organism's full capacity for the pulsation of bioenergy, Reich's new concept of energy that flows through the physical organism.

Reich himself used hyperventilation, a variety of bodywork techniques for manipulating the body, and direct physical contact, such as pressing a certain location where the energy is locked up. This is done for the purpose of removing the blocks and letting the bioenergy flow freely. The goal of his therapeutic process is the patient's capacity to surrender to the spontaneous and involuntary movements of the body that are mainly associated with deep breathing. Those receiving the treatment are encouraged to express themselves through their bodies rather than with words, except when words come out spontaneously without programming or pushing.

For Reich, the repressive influence of society was the significant factor giving rise to incomplete sexual orgasm and the congestion of bioenergy. For this reason, he laid a strong emphasis on complete release of sexual repression and total orgasm through sexual acts as an important way of freeing oneself from neurosis and of keeping healthy.

The marriage of psychotherapy and bodywork. Wilhem Reich's pioneering ideas of psychophysical work and his practice of "character analytic vegetotherapy" have influenced the development of many new therapeutic forms that are currently gaining popularity. Many of these new approaches combine elements of Reich's emphasis on bodywork with the Eastern practices of hatha yoga, t'ai chi, aikido, and karate, as well as international forms of modern dance.

Alexander Lowen has developed a therapeutic system called "bioenergetics," the most important of the neo-Reichian approaches. His emphasis is on the integration of the ego with the body and its striving for pleasure, which involves not only sexuality but also other basic functions such as breathing, movements, feelings, and self-expression.

Frederick Alexander created the Alexander technique, which is similar in principle to Ida Rolf's structural integration, or Rolfing as it is popularly known, but is a soft and gentle practice.

Other founders of new approaches in the human potential movement include Moshe Feldenkrais, who invented a program of systemic correction and re-education of the musculo-nervous system. Milton Trager developed psychophysical integration and mentastics by using a systemic sequence of gentle rolling, shaking, and vibratory movements, which produce a state of deep physical and mental relaxation, restfulness, and even ecstatic states. Judith Aston created structural patterning, and Isle Middehdolf developed breathing therapy as a very fine system of bodywork similar to the Alexander principle and Feldenkrais body awareness.

In addition, there has been a gradual refinement in the many forms of massage therapy. These have been integrated into the therapeutic approaches of the human potential movement, especially those based on the Reichian principle that emotional distress manifests itself in the form of blocks in the musculature and connective tissue of the body. Some of these massage techniques were inspired by the Eastern systems of accupressure and shiatzu.

Among the most popular massage therapies available today are: (a) polarity massage, which involves a deep intervention into body energy; (b) Swedish massage, which employs both light and deep techniques to improve circulation; (c) deep tissue and trigger point massage, which affect the deep layers of connective tissue and have powerful cleansing, invigorating, and releasing qualities; and (d) reflexology, which involves the massage of pressure points in the hands and feet that access release and healing in specific parts of the body.

As I see it, all bodywork and massage therapies are related to psychotherapy and the practice of meditation in a very essential way.

As already mentioned at the outset of this section, the function of psychotherapy is to help those seeking guidance to be able to perform their duties properly and lead their lives more efficiently. It appears that the inability to function adequately results in part from the energy patterns locked up and buried in certain parts of the body, including the musculature, and in part from the dictation and domination of the individual's conditioned sub-personalties, technically known as "disowned selves" and "over-identified selves." When one becomes blocked and the energy does not flow properly, one loses the ability to perform tasks appropriately. There is also a tendency to turn toward mental states of negativity, confusion, and inertia. It is at this time that help is needed from the world of therapy.

When the suitable bodywork and/or appropriate massage therapy is undertaken, the energy flows more freely and enables one to regain vitality and the ability to conduct one's life more efficiently. By incorporating bodywork into therapeutic practice, much of the task of psychotherapy is already accomplished.

The more that we comprehend that the body/mind processes are inseparable, and the more that we are able to recognize that most of our language, archetypes, and behavior are symbolic manifestations and expressions of energy, the more we are able to see with clarity that all healing work and health care, including psychotherapy, are really doing nothing but dealing with the flow of energy and energy patterns both at the physical and emotional (psychological) levels of our realities. For this reason, any bodywork therapy and/or massage therapy done to unlock as well as free the repressed energy patterns held in the body is an essential contribution to the individual's health and well-being both psychologically and physically.

As for the practice of meditation, bodywork and massage help release tensions and energy patterns brought to the surface through the meditative process, mainly by long and intensive sitting meditation. It is very obvious to all participants in my work that after each bodywork session, meditators can sit more comfortably and go deeper into the meditative state. This is one of the reasons for my bringing all kinds of body awareness exercises into my Vipassana meditation work.

The two most popular forms of experiential psychology are Gestalt therapy and primal therapy.

Gestalt therapy: holonomic awareness of the continuous and ever-changing patterns of coordinated activity. Gestalt therapy was developed by Fritz Perls, who was influenced by Freud, Reich, existentialism, and particularly by Gestalt psychology, according to Grof (1985). The basic assumption of this psychology is that human beings do not perceive things as unrelated and isolated elements, but organize them during the perceptual process into meaningful wholes. Based on this principle, Gestalt therapy attempts to integrate personal experiences holistically and to help individuals actualize themselves in harmony with their environment. This is in accordance with the idea that all of nature is a unified and coherent gestalt. Within this whole, the organic and inorganic elements constitute continuous and ever-changing patterns of coordinated activity (Grof, 1985).

Gestalt therapy lays its emphasis on experiencing with awareness what is obvious here and now, and not on interpreting problems or conflicts. All physical enactments and emotional processes must be done in the spirit of awareness so that the unfinished gestalts from the past can be completed in the present.

In the process of the therapy sessions, it is the client who takes full responsibility for the process. The therapist only functions as a facilitator by being available and identifying the clients's tendencies to interrupt his/her experiences. Full experience and free expression in various patterns of communication, both interpersonal and internal, are encouraged to enable the client to give full attention to all the details of the physical and emotional processes involved. This enhances clear awareness and insight into the client's personal history, including traumas and conflicts re-experienced at the moment. Through this sharpening of awareness, the key of Gestalt therapy, self-healing and personal integration are bound to take place.

Primal therapy: exploding the grip of symbolic defensive behavior by accessing and reliving the pain of childhood trauma. Primal therapy was developed by Arthur Janov, who built the theory around his observations of deliberately induced "primals." He maintains that neurosis is a symbolic behavior that represents a defense against excessive psychological pain associated with childhood traumas.

The goal of the therapy is to eliminate the defenses and to work through primal pains by fully re-living them at the moment of experiencing the memories of the events that caused them. Such primal pains are related to early incidents in life that the individual has not been in touch with consciously. They are stored up in the form of defenses, or tensions.

To be conscious of these pains, including traumatic birth, would mean unbearable suffering, so Janov has used the induced technique for releasing such primal pains by "primal scream." This is an involuntary, deep, and rattling sound that expresses, in a condensed way, the person's reaction to past traumas. By this method, the successive layers of pain can be gradually removed through repeated screaming in therapeutic sessions. This form of therapy is, in actual fact, another neo-Reichian approach.

Transpersonal therapy: West meets East; a driving force toward the fulfillment of spirituality; the genesis of a "new culture." Finally, we arrive at transpersonal therapy, a new model growing out of Abraham Maslow's humanistic psychology of being, Jung's analytical psychology, and Assagioli's psychosynthesis, all of which provide conceptual models for dealing with the transpersonal realm. The aim of the therapy is to help clients integrate their transpersonal experiences with their ordinary modes of consciousness in the process of inner growth and spiritual development (Capra, 1982).

We have already discussed some concepts of Jung's psychology, and we have seen that he laid great emphasis on the unconscious and its dynamics. The concept of archetypes, the myth-creating primordial patterns in the unconscious, is the most important concept that Jung introduced in his depth psychology. He saw the human being not as the image of a biological machine, but as a living organism that keeps on growing and transcending the boundaries of the ego and of the individual unconscious. Each person can connect himself with the ultimate whole that is commensurate with all humanity and the entire universe. For this reason, Jung could be considered the first transpersonal psychologist. He was greatly interested in spirituality, including Eastern spiritual philosophies.

Another major contributor to transpersonal psychology was Abraham Maslow, who studied psychologically healthy individuals and brought to our attention that peak experiences are not psycho-pathological, but rather supernormal. He also demonstrated that those who had spontaneous peak experiences frequently benefited from them and showed a distinct trend toward "self-actualization."

Robert Assagioli, an Italian psychiatrist, was the third contributor to transpersonal therapy. His psychosynthesis focuses on the positive, creative, and joyous elements of human nature. It is based on his conceptual system that an individual is in a constant process of growth, actualizing his/her hidden potential. He emphasized the importance of the function of will.

The therapeutic process of psychosynthesis involves four consecutive stages. First the client learns about various elements of his/her personality. The next step is disidentification from those elements and the subsequent ability to control them. After the client has gradually discovered his/her unifying psychological center, it is possible to achieve psychosynthesis, characterized by a culmination of the self-realization process and integration of the selves around the new center (Grof, 1985).

The third category of therapy, the transpersonal one, is a closer link with the spiritual path since it points to going beyond a socalled personal self and that which pertains to the notion of self through the process of disidentification and development of "supraindividual consciousness," as Ken Wilber calls it (1979).

When things are seen as they are without identifying with them, they are just parts of the whole, but as soon as we identify with the parts, we are caught and get stuck in them. Then, we miss the whole. Worse than that, we falsely take the parts as the whole, which is a complete distortion of reality—blindly living with an illusion while thinking and believing it to be a real truth.

On the other hand, when the real is seen as real and the unreal seen as unreal, or illusion is purely and unmistakably perceived as an illusion and reality totally perceived as reality, then whatever appears out there in front of us is nothing but an ongoing rhythmic dance. There is no unchanging or everlasting entity existing independently anywhere. Things exist interdependently and interrelatedly. In the ultimate sense, there is no self as opposed to other. Only interconnected wholeness prevails amid the rolling on of all forms of phenomena as the manifestations of the unmanifested.

This truth is naturally revealed to us when we take a journey beyond the concept of self, beyond dualistic thinking, and far beyond space and time. So, transpersonal therapy could be taken as a starting point, the first step in Western psychotherapy, toward spirituality. If it proceeds in the direction of raising supra-individual consciousness and integrating it with the ordinary, and if shifting to the higher floor is taken with an act of integration at every point of the shifts, without falling into the traps of extreme views on reality, then this form of psychotherapy will become a driving force toward the fulfillment of spirituality. When this happens, it implies the true meeting of East and West in a specific form, a *new culture*.

It is not the purpose of this book to give a full description of the therapeutic techniques presently used in our Western world. For those of you who wish to get more knowledge and information about the world of psychotherapy, I would like to recommend Fritjof Capra's *The Turning Point* and Stanislav Grof's *Beyond the Brain*. They are brilliant and comprehensive writings on the subject, and I draw a great deal of material from them.

Bringing Together Meditation and Psychotherapy

We have studied the principles, methods, and goals of both meditation and psychotherapy and have gained some understandings of the subjects and their implications. Now we want to bring them together, integrating both the theory and the practice so that there will be a union of the two cultures, leaving aside the division and differences that only seem to exist on the periphery.

Challenges as West Meets East on the Spiritual Path

Before going into the integration process fully, let us discuss some challenges that those born and living in the Western culture are facing, or might have to meet with, in their pursuit of spiritual development while still living immersed in their society. These challenges may be mapped out as follows:

Spiritual materialism. Spiritual materialism could be one of the greatest challenges for those walking on the spiritual path. By this term I mean the involvement with and struggle for achievement, attainment, and accomplishment of fixed purposes and set goals, either step-by-step or all at once (suddenly, instantly). More than that, spiritual materialism indicates being driven by the acquisitive mind, which always looks for something or reaches out to get and accumulate good experiences, better qualities of mind and heart, self-improvement, or even a new identity and power within the circle of spiritual friends and/or community. Spiritual materialism includes a sense of exclusive self-prosperity and self-interest. It also includes the expectation of, or desire for, attaining a specific result from one's spiritual practice. Such attitudes, of course, result from the deeply rooted habits of living a worldly life under the strong influences of a pleasure-seeking and goal-oriented society.

Whatever one has, one brings with oneself into the spiritual life-style. Whatever is lacking and not well developed in the personality will show up as well and demand full development and recognition. This particularly refers to a (fuller) sense of identity, which is a predominant challenge in spiritual work. Worse still, some of our fellow beings involving themselves with some spiritual disciplines attempt to adhere to the notion of no-self with the hope of transcending their identity before they actually have it as a properly developed personality unit. This simply doesn't work, especially when they still want to function in the world, leading a normal life as the rest of us do. It might work for those renouncing the world and living exclusively in the confined, restrained atmosphere of a monastery, such as monks and nuns. I am sure even they will require a long-term and enduring training in meditation and monastic discipline with frequent experiences of mystical, self-transcendent states.

In conclusion, spiritual materialism is certainly a serious challenge to the essence of spiritual work, which lays emphasis on letting go of our attachment to the nature of the greedy, acquisitive mind with all its structural conditioning, including our clinging to the notion of self as separated from, and opposed to, the no-self. This matter of letting go has been previously described in the section on Vipassana (Insight) meditation, so there is no need to repeat it here. (Something corresponding to spiritual materialism occurs in those seeking and practicing psychotherapy: they wish to change their personalities in a direction determined by egoistic interests and bring to bear on themselves the very negative attitudes they claim to seek to be rid of.)

Narcissism. Narcissism is another major challenge not only to those seeking the fulfillment of spiritual life, but also to almost all of us living our lives in the world where we have to meet with all the manifestations of the conscious as well as the unconscious elements, both personal and collective. From time to time we encounter the tendency to get involved with, and stuck in, the process of cleaning out all the negativity as well as of purifying the defilements before moving on and flowing along with the positive, creative, bright side of life. The narcissists delude themselves, on the one hand, with a total indulgence in the therapeutic process through their belief system in getting rid of all the poisons and blocks in their psychosomatic systems; on the other hand, they become over-optimistic about things in life and in the world and are completely lost in the false and puerile image they have introjected into themselves, believing it to be their true identity. This is like the myth of Narcissus, a young man looking into a well and seeing his reflection there; he falls in love with it, and he carries the reflection with him for the rest of his life. He is a narcissist living in the world of illusion without realizing it. But the narcissists on the spiritual path refer to those taking the practice of self-examination as the ultimate journey. They get hooked on processing their own personal stuff, or emotional and psychological junk. It could take them a lifetime or more to finish with such rich material.

Desensitization. Desensitization is an escape route from feelings and personality difficulties by simply bypassing them and sinking into spiritual ideals, becoming mentally and physically numb in the sense of deprivation from the power of sensation and feeling. This happens quite obviously to those spiritual friends who follow the idea and ideal of spiritual discipline very strictly and rigidly. One-sided development always leads to defects in our living and is dangerous to our health and wholeness. We should never take this route of desensitizing ourselves under any circumstances or situations. Instead, let us be open and willing to deal with whatever emerges on the journey through ourselves and beyond our personal realities.

Groupthink. Another challenge is in the category of groupthink, which is a phenomenon in certain spiritual groups or communities. This kind of defect arises from the psychological fact that we humans have a deep need for identification with a group, a society, a nation, and a world. When we belong to a group or a community with commitment, dedication, and devotion, we give ourselves to it and identify with it. This creates a collective identity. In other words, we become what we think, as well as expand our personal boundary to the group territory, retaining the group or community identity. In so doing, we separate ourselves from other spiritual groups as well as from the world at large by believing that we are really different from others, not only in terms of life-style and spiritual path, but also in the way of thinking and perceiving things in the external world and in the world of the psyche. Consequently, fear arises regarding what it actually looks like out there in the world where the majority of human beings live.

Fear also arises at the thought of losing the shelter and safe place for existence that the group or community provides for us. The group, like our ego, must be defended against threat, real or imagined. These fears result in the phenomenon of groupthink, which can express itself either with violence and aggression or with isolation and withdrawal.

Groupthink, by its nature, results in fragmentation and divisiveness. It is incompatible with truly holistic spiritual development, which, in its strictest sense, focuses on the purity of heart and wholeness. Holistic spiritual development recognizes that we are one with all humanity and the entire cosmos.

Although a group or community exists and functions within its own parameters according to a specific belief system or faith, it can take into account the role it plays on a global basis. Because all things, including our actions and thoughts, are interdependent and interconnected, our awareness of the global community of humankind is essential. As we function more fully with the recognition of and responsibility required in global participation, we will experience a sense of transcommunal consciousness more frequently. Eventually, the titles of "group" or "community" will just be convenient labels used for purposes of identification and verbal communication. Groupthink will melt into "globalthink."

The Teacher-Student Relationship. It is very interesting to note that interpersonal relationships are among the most essential issues in life. We humans are social beings and need to be in constant contact with one another to experience some fulfillment in our lives. Without relationships of one kind or another there would be little opportunity to learn about self and others.

Life can be isolated, dry, and lonely, but enriched with a relationship it becomes exciting, full of adventures and challenges. The ups and downs of life experiences can be encountered so that learning, growth, development, and transformation can take place as the life of a relationship goes on.

In relationships we have an opportunity to learn more deeply about ourselves and others. There is a constant person-to-person interaction between man and woman, man and man, woman and woman, which mobilizes the activities of the yin and yang principles within each one of us. The learning situations that arise in relationships permit us to let go of and transcend what is unhealthy, obstructive, or destructive, then evolve toward fuller and fuller being.

The behavioral characteristics of a true spiritual teacher: the teacher as a personification of the path. Here, I would like to focus on the special relationship between a spiritual teacher and his students. Generally speaking, a Dharma teacher could be called "guru," "master," or just "spiritual friend." He could function as the source of *inspiration* and *encouragement* or provide a model for those students who are attempting to walk on a spiritual path. This means that the teacher, or for that matter, anybody playing a role of teaching or guiding others interested in and dedicated to spiritual practices, is the manifestation of those teachings and knowledge of the path. He conducts his life according to whatever he gives out to others. In other words, he is a touchstone of reality with all his integrity and dynamic balance within. Certainly he is required to be endowed with love, esteem, veneration, insightful wisdom, and intelligence in talking and conversing with his students, patience with those who are slowly blossoming, or those having more dust and dirt in their eyes that prevent them from seeing clearly. He provides a quality of leadership that brings students not to a wrong and useless end but to the right and abundant goal. If an individual takes up a teacher's role but lacks any of these qualities, he will not be appropriately entitled "a teacher" in this context.

The role of unconditional love, compassion, beingness, and insightful wisdom. Very often, we encounter some false gurus imported from the East, or residing here in the West, who lack the above-mentioned qualifications. It is always advisable to give full attention when trying to feel out any gurus you may come across or have in mind. The real teacher naturally emanates love and compassion through his being and functioning. He is nobody special, although he performs certain functions and appears as a significant other in carrying out the mission of a teacher. In his essence, there is a fertile void where all the manifestations spring from, and because he is empty of junk and garbage, but full of *beingness,* his emanations of love, compassion, light, beauty, unity, and truth are endless. "Shining with radiance day and night are those who have awakened to the Truth with the heart completely open" said Gotama, the Buddha.

Throughout his life, the Buddha totally devoted himself to the needs and welfare of those open to receiving his help and guidance. He slept only two hours a night. He spent two hours in deep meditation (one hour was spent in bathing in nirvanic blissful emptiness, another in surveying the world to find a certain individual urgently needing his attention). The rest of the day and night was dedicated to giving advice and being available to the needs of his monastic disciples as well as those laypeople who sought his guidance and help. These included both humans and gods in any corner of heaven and earth, without any distinctions or preferences. Out of love, compassion, wisdom, and purity of heart, he rendered his selfless and tireless service to the world of humans, the world of gods, the world of Brahmas, as well as to the world of animals. He was the most hard-working person in the history of humankind.

It is very clear that he related to his followers and those taking refuge in him with great compassion (Mahakaruna) for their pain and suffering. For example, a lady named Kisagotami, whose son was dead, approached the Buddha for a remedy to bring her son back to life. She did not know that death is incurable. Instead of giving her a lecture about life and death, he sent her out to fetch him mustard seeds from a house where no one had ever died. She searched and searched for a long time while carrying her dead son with her, but she failed to obtain any mustard seeds because she could not find a family that had not experienced the death of a loved one. Everywhere she went she was told that death is a natural part of life, that everyone dies at a certain time in life, whether out of old age, illness, or an accident.

After searching and listening to people's statements about life and death, she finally gained some understanding. This enabled her to release the dead body of her child, and she buried it in an appropriate place. She then returned to the Buddha who asked her for the mustard seeds. Instead of explaining to him the details of what she had learned from this invaluable lesson, Kisagotami thanked the Buddha wholeheartedly and asked for ordination in order to become a Bhikkuni (nun). The Buddha honored her request immediately. Having received the ordination and instruction in meditation, she practiced intelligently and soon attained full enlightenment. That is one of the examples of how the Buddha rendered his compassionate services to his disciples as well as to those seeking his help.

Great compassion and unconditional love with insightful wisdom are unquestioningly needed for those of us taking up the role of teacher, helper, or guide, for they are truly powerful healing energies in themselves, which everybody needs. Those who are encountering challenges and difficulties in life, those who have become ill either physically, psychologically, or emotionally are actually in great need of receiving love, understanding, and compassion from the person who can help them heal themselves. As we know, the journey through ourselves is not so easy. It can be painful, frightening, and dangerous, for there are many unknown places within us that can cause us to experience fear and terror when we enter them. When living through unbearable pain and agony, one certainly needs more compassion, love, and empathic understanding as well as patience, the grace of life.

In my experiences of working with people, both in groups and individually, it has been proved to be true that the emanations of love, compassion, empathic understanding, and the unconditional acceptance of who they are mean so much to those seeking help and guidance. They are fifty percent healed already just by receiving such warmth and a sense of safety from the helper, the healer, or the teacher. With trust in a person whom they believe can help them, they are willing to take risks in opening up to their forbidden chamber of treasures as well as to the unknown fears and pains within them. In other words, they are prepared to take a journey both into the known and the unknown to heal themselves completely, however difficult such a journey might be. Without trust and confidence in the helper or teacher, one does not gain much benefit, either from therapeutic sessions or from meditation practices. Worse still, such an individual might just quit the practice or run away from the real issue of his/her problem when encountering something more painful or more frightening. For this reason, faith and courage are always needed in this inner journey through ourselves and into the transpersonal realm, the unknown places both within and without.

The issue of dependency. One important thing that a spiritual teacher must not do is create a dependence in students. This dependent tendency hinders their further growth and development because those who are dependent deepen their illusion of seeking external help, while neglecting their own inner resources. They just remain "seekers" instead of turning themselves into the "sought." In this spiritual journey, we say that the seeker must be found to bring an end to the seeking. When there is no more seeking, the Truth is fully realized and Enlightenment attained. This is the completion of the journey.

We must see clearly that fostering dependence of any kind perpetuates the image of the seeker who numbs himself by believing that truth, or the "real thing" exists outside of himself, in a guru, an ashram, or a cave. This is really an example of displacement, a psychological disorder, in the seeker.

This phenomenon of dependency is apparent in many guru-worshipping people. They are like birds in a gilded cage. However golden and secure the cage might appear, it does not contain freedom in the true sense of actually being free, both inwardly and outwardly.

In order to avoid creating dependency in your students, you must avoid establishing a position as a guru and avoid any semblance of a guru-disciple system in your work. Just be as *ordinary* as possible. Just be yourself, whoever you happen to be, without wearing any title or bearing any image in addition to who you are. You are *nobody special*, as Ram Dass tells his followers. As a spiritual leader, one must carry out the task of encouraging people to become self-reliant, bringing out the best in them to guide their way home and to deal with the worst within themselves during their journey of self-discovery.

What a spiritual leader can do best is to share totally, honestly, and openly what he/she has, knows, and sees insightfully. This means that such a spiritual guide is teaching both by setting an example (living his actual life) and by providing the true teachings that throw light on the path to *total freedom*.

Blending the Experiential Understanding of Meditation with Psychotherapeutic Processes

East (meditation practices) and West (psychotherapy) can be brought together when there is a full understanding of the conceptual systems of both cultures as well as experiential knowledge of meditation states and psychotherapeutic processes.

Training the Mind to Be Unified and Centered Within/Grounding. Oriental meditation practices are involved with the development of self-control over spiritual hindrances before transforming and transcending them completely. This requires training the mind to be unified and centered within by way of concentration and mindfulness, like the taming of the bull in Zen terminology. This developmental stage corresponds to the aim of psychotherapy, in which the individual must be able to keep his/her feet firmly grounded on earth in order to function adequately in the world.

Eastern "Spiritual Hindrances"/Western "Neuroses." In this spectrum of human development, psychotherapists have to deal with all kinds of neuroses by employing many different therapeutic techniques and healing arts systems available in society, some of which have been described in the preceding brief review of Western psychotherapy. In the meditative processes of purification and development, all the hindrances to spiritual progress such as aggression, mental indolence and dullness, anxiety and restlessness, ignorance and self-doubt, obsessive thinking about the satisfaction or dissatisfaction of sensory experiences, including sexuality, must be dealt with in an efficient way so that a meditator can further his/her growth into the inner focus and unification of consciousness, the strong foundation of the meditation practice. This unified state of being within the individual not only helps her/him make progress along the spiritual path, but also lays a solid basis for living and conducting his/her life in the world. It provides the strength and personal empowerment to cope with any difficulties or challenges, as well as with the rapid changes and fluctuations in our world today.

The Marriage of "Living in the Present" and "Grounding." The grounding principle in psychotherapy can be married to that of "living in the present" in the Eastern practice of the meditative life. To be able to live fully in the present, freedom from preoccupation of the past and future is required, although things in the past and speculations about the future may still claim the individual's attention from time to time. But with the groundedness and centeredness within and in outer life, such an individual will not easily be overwhelmed by distractions and temptations, including others' ideas, thoughts, and opinions. He/she will be in a position to get her/his act together so as not to be scattered, as well as not to be too confused about what to do with life and living. This means there is a clear direction of inwardness and sufficient solidity of the functioning self. These two major qualities result from self-awareness developed through mindfulness meditation and also possibly through the therapeutic processes that emphasize insights into oneself and one's situations both internally and externally.

The Experience of "Subtle Fields of Life-Energy." Digging deeper into our psychophysical processes, commonly known as a self, an individual, or a human being, we encounter many things both conscious and unconscious in the psyche as well as in the physical body. They appear and manifest themselves in varying forms, such as archetypes, symbols, dreams, and mental images *(nimita)*. Sometimes, they show up in forms of what we call "energy," moving the body in a certain way and in a specific position with or without the utterance of sounds.

In spiritual experiences of love, peace, ecstasy, stillness, emptiness, union with the entire cosmos, etc., beyond possible description in words, we understand various energy fields beyond our body-mind system connected to, and linked with, a similar quality of energy within us. As soon as we enter the rhythm of a certain energy, let us say, that of love within the heart, it expands and connects itself with the energy field of love in the whole universe. We then say that we have a full experience of love and that we know for sure what love truly means.

How Exploring, Understanding, and Releasing the Contents of the Unconscious Through the Development of Awareness Can Lead to Radical Personal and Social Transformation. In the unconscious, which is equivalent to *bhavanga-citta* in the Buddha's conceptual system, we discover both destructive and constructive elements contained in our psyche. These elements manifest and express themselves through conscious processes as well as through subconscious processes such as dreams that occur during sleep and mental pictures of different kinds that appear during meditation. The unconscious or *bhavanga-citta* (another name for it is "stored-consciousness") also expresses its manifestation in the form of the arts, myths, folk-tales, and fairy tales of different cultures around the world. It is very rich material stored within us.

By employing self-awareness in meditation exercises and through therapeutic techniques, it is possible for us to bring the elements of the unconscious into conscious awareness. This enables us to deal with them thoroughly. There will no longer be hidden factors buried within our psychophysical systems. We can remove energy blocks and release repressive influences as well as mobilize our inherent creative energy. Thus the natural free flow of life energy will move on, unhindered.

The individual process of discovering the elements contained in the unconscious, exploring them, and understanding how they affect our being is one of the most significant factors in life. Such understanding can lead to radical individual self-transformation and, as it is individuals who make up society, the process will naturally lead to changes at the social, political, and economic levels of the societies to which those individuals belong. We can transform the whole world if we are truly and honestly willing to change ourselves radically!

In order to experience total freedom, both inwardly and outwardly, and in order to complete our radical transformation, we must fully understand and totally realize ourselves at the conscious and unconscious levels and must comprehend the nature of our connection with the collective unconscious. We must fully develop our capacity of awareness, for it is awareness that feeds all necessary information into our "self."

No-self/Ego-Death. Ego death in psychotherapy and the notion of no-self in Buddhist meditation are additional subjects for discussion and integration. Generally speaking, we, both laymen and psychologists, seem to maintain that ego needs to be built and rebuilt for the purpose of performing our functions and existing in the world. Without the ego, an individual would be like a company with no executive to run it. How can an individual organize himself/herself to function appropriately if the ego is not around? Is it possible for the ego to die completely? These two basic questions are predominant to all of us in the fields of health care and spirituality.

The death of ego equals the transcendence of self. The death of ego refers to a transcendence of self whose components are matter or form, feeling, perception, mental formations or activities, and consciousness. These aggregates of existence constitute a personality, a *notion of self* or *a conception of ego.*

In the ultimate sense, matter is like a heap of foam, feeling is like a bubble, perception is like a mirage, mental formations *(sankhara)* are like a banana tree, and consciousness is like an illusion. This statement implies that the whole system of existence is merely a thought, an idea, or a conception, or in Capra's terminology, a "systems view of reality" (1985). There is no substance or substantiality to a separate, independently existing self or no-self to be found anywhere, whether within an individual or out there in the cosmos. Neither the perceiver (subject) nor the perceived (object) exists, apart from dualistic thinking.

Recognizing the dynamic equilibrium of the interdependence of all phenomena. The reality is that all things and all events or phenomena are interdependent; they are all without self *(atman)* or anything pertaining to self *(atmaniya).* Ego death or the notion of no-self *(anatma)* is nothing but full awakening from illusion and ignorance, just like waking up completely from sleep. It is a matter of transcending and shifting the floor of consciousness. When the ego psychology or egoic consciousness is totally transcended, as in cases of taking a journey with psychedelics and/or of experiencing mystical, transcendental states through meditation, there is a merging with wholeness where ego or self is not around and where the *ultimate reality* of *total emptiness,* which is empty of substantiality as well as devoid of emptiness itself, prevails and permeates the entire universe. In that level of reality, there is an eternal rhythmic dance of subtle energy accompanied by the cosmic music of absolute silence. In such an ultimate state, love, peace, serene joy, stillness, strength, freedom, and insightful wisdom flow freely together in complete harmony and total balance. This is a dynamic equilibrium and not a static state.

The conscious use of ego as a temporary functional tool in daily life. It is the ego or a sense of separate self that keeps us on this shore of life and prevents us from crossing over to the other shore, to put it figuratively. If we consciously allow ourselves to die to the egoic state with all its compulsive patterns of conditioning, we naturally and instantly emerge into the transpersonal realm, dancing with life as it is with total freedom and mighty strength. Then we face the task of integrating this transpersonal experience with our everyday lives.

Is it necessary then, to reconstruct the ego after suspending it completely? Or is that same ego right there, waiting for a chance to seize power again, which indicates that it never dies but remains immortal?

Certainly, there is no need to rebuild the ego, for it is just an energy system within consciousness operating specifically under the influence of compulsive patterns of conditioning. When these compulsive patterns have been cut through thoroughly, egoic consciousness no longer exists as an agent for self-organization. Self-organization can go on, not under the ego, but as a supportive system built into our new psychological freedom. Ego, then, is only a temporary tool to be used when functioning and performing our tasks and interacting with others in life as well as in the business world.

The dynamic characteristics of the new agent of self-organization. This new supportive system is like rhythmic patterns of energy, activating and actualizing itself in dynamic balance, without any compulsion or underlying mechanism. Unlike the ego, it is not deeply rooted in personality since there is no more personality as a predictable, fixed organizing unit after the death of ego. In a relative sense, self-organization with the supportive system may be more or less predictable in terms of cause and effect operating in space and time. Nevertheless, because there is synchrony of events, or the coincidence of things happening in our interrelated existence without any obvious determined cause, we also become unpredictable in the course of our natural, free flow of life and living. In common language, we say that there is no plan to life, but life does have some plans for us. Thus determinism and fixed, inflexible self-programming are not rigidly applied to the course of living.

The "supportive system" may be described as the dynamics of rhythmic patterns representing the integration of the basic needs of a human being with actualized transpersonal experiences. For example, Gotama the Buddha, after his full enlightenment, always referred to himself as *tathagata* (literally: "thus gone") when communicating with others such as his ordained disciples. It seems that he had created a new identity that didn't mean anything special to him but was a convenience or a necessity for verbal communication in the external world, while his inner world didn't need any reference or identity. This is similar to what the Sufis call "Supreme Identity," which I regard as a speech pattern used in dynamic functional life and in the world of relationships. With such supra-individual consciousness born and growing out of transpersonal experiences, all the perceptual and conceptual systems have changed radically. The new way of perceiving and seeing things is so accurate, precise, and free that concepts and notions, or even words, no longer exert any influence. This is total perception and pure seeing in the crystal clear light of insight. In this way, things are seen simply as they are and not as they appear to be according to a network of thought.

The wise say that words are as empty as everything else, but that compassion for all humanity is so great that skillful means come into being for using words and concepts, as well as a non-binding identity for the sole purpose of rendering services and getting things done to meet with those higher human needs that manifest the influences of the base instincts! These skillful means or *upaya* are actually the dynamics of the supportive system.

We now find the answer to the question of whether or not the ego has to be rebuilt in order to have functions performed properly. Actual experience has convincingly shown us that being in an egoless state in such transpersonal realms gives us tremendous strength, power, and freedom to act, to move into making contact, or to do anything with no hesitation or inhibition whatsoever. Furthermore, fear simply is not there to hold us back, or to keep us in the womb of false security and mistaken identity of the ego. We are in the free flow of action as well as of non-action, as the case may be.

When there is no ruler, how can there be a rule? When there is nothing to conform to, how can there be conformity? It is absurd, isn't it? When there is no opposite, or when all the opposites are in complete union, how can any conflict come into existence?

As a matter of fact, duality exists only in the thinking process. When we do not think in a dualistic way, how can we find duality? In this connection, some of my fellow beings would raise the question, "How can we stop thinking dualistically?" The answer would be that we cannot stop thinking in dualistic terms. We just simply *do not* think that way and therefore transcend it. Another question, "How can we deal with all those dualistic concepts already existing in the world of language and in the network of thought?" The answer is quite simple: we just do not take them seriously, for they are just symbols that we must look beyond and not get stuck in; otherwise, we will become like an elephant in the mire. Using words and concepts without being bound by them is the true freedom of communication. This is illustrated by the Zen expression that living with the Self, yet not knowing (conceptualizing) the Self is really a free living beyond imagination and description.

Staying alert to ego's continual re-appearance. Let us make it clear that ego death does not mean that all the dynamic patterns of the ego become completely extinguished. It simply means the non-functioning of the ego with all its egoic patterns and its sub-personalities as the executive, running the life of an individual, as well as organizing his/her perception and reactive patterns in day-to-day existence. As long as the constituents of our existence go on living, the ego can be reborn within our psychophysical systems at any time. We will have to deal with it whenever it emerges. This is just like the Buddha dealing with Mara, the personification of illusion (or Jesus dealing with Satan in the Christian religion), whenever the tempter showed up and tried to become his self-organizer. As soon as Mara was recognized and clearly pronounced by the Buddha, he vanished. So, we have to be alively attentive and totally aware at all times.

The Philosophy of Emptiness (Shunyata). The notion of no-self goes far beyond the concept of ego, for it not only denies the existence of ego and a separate self as a permanent entity, but points out that all conditioned and unconditioned things are without self. It is a philosophy of emptiness *(shunyata)* developed by the Buddhist sage, Nagarjuna, to interpret and explain the original teaching of the Buddha with regard to *anatma* or *anatta* (no-self). This absolute truth of emptiness or no-self is seen in the profound wisdom that there is no substance or substantiality in things or in any phenomena and that Supreme Self is just an idea but not a reality, for such a thing as Self never exists anywhere in the first place.

All things and events are interdependent, arising and passing away in rhythmic patterns without any creator or director behind them. The continuity of processes and phenomena is, in actual fact, the continuum of appearing and disappearing in time and space.

Both the conditioned world and the world of the unconditioned are without an everlasting, absolutely independent entity existing as well as directing the course of events. Such is the ultimate truth of emptiness, which also denies the notion of emptiness as a form or as substance, and as that which is without form and substantiality.

Accordingly, there is nothing to be grasped and clung to as a solid reality. We may describe things and events, or anything at all, in words and in concepts; but the description is not the described, the word is not the thing that it symbolizes. Seeing this with deep insight and in profound wisdom is such a great relief. It results in total freedom in living, loving, and learning. So, letting things be and letting everything, including ourselves, flow freely and naturally becomes a touchstone of reality in everyday living as well as in every moment of life flow. For this reason, the union of these two complimentaries, ego death and no-self, brings lively riches and vibrant abundance to all of us.

Dharma-Becoming/God-Consciousness. Another two pairs, letting go and surrendering, and love and non-attachment, have already been discussed in some detail in the section on the principles of Vipassana meditation. Now, let us proceed with the last pair of *God-Consciousness* and *Dharma-Becoming.* These two forms of essence in human potential development, both in the East and in the West, are the culminating points for all humanity to reach so that wholeness and health, as well as the completion of our journeys beyond space and time, will be achieved here in this life on earth.

Defining the terms. By God-Consciousness we mean not only having faith and trust in the most powerful energy as the *mind* of the entire cosmos commonly known as God, but the fully developed consciousness of loving oneness and union of all in all, which includes each in all, all in each, as well as I-thou relationship. What we call God, the One Being, or the Supreme Self, out there, and something rather small but dynamic and ever changing, a self right here within each of us, are just one consciousness manifesting here and there in form with a variety of appearances, and without form but in pure energy and pure mind of the universe. When we get there, to put it figuratively, we shall know for ourselves what the truth really is and where it actually lies.

As to Dharma-Becoming, the Oriental terminology equivalent to God-Consciousness, it is a matter of becoming whole, complete, and indivisible. This is the Origin or Upstream that all phenomena and manifestations spring from. Dharma here refers to the Absolute Truth, the experienced knowledge, without doubt, of the unborn, the uncreated, and the unconditioned. When we become the Dharma, we reach *ultimate consciousness,* which is the completion of our evolutionary process, our final transformation. This completed evolution is not an equilibrium in the scientific sense, but a felt energy of dynamic wholeness that can manifest and remain unmanifested as the case may be. It is wholly developed consciousness in which all intelligence, love, wisdom, and freedom prevail. It lacks nothing!

Total freedom: Letting go/transcending the "concepts" of God and Dharma. When God-Consciousness and Dharma-Becoming have reached their full development, we finally transcend the "concepts" of God and Dharma completely. That is to say, all concepts and notions, including words and ideas, finally melt into voidness, eliminating our burden of being weighed down by them. Such is ultimately unified consciousness in which no fragmentation or division is to be found. Dynamic wholeness permeates the whole of life and the entire universe!

Conclusion

In conclusion, I want to clarify the relationship between Western psychotherapy and Oriental meditation. Generally speaking, both provide techniques for exploring the contents and inner workings of human consciousness and both do so from a variety of perspectives.

Psychotherapy helps an individual to be grounded in "life in the world." It focuses on balancing the personal, inter-personal, and social aspects of functioning within a given cultural gestalt. It can lay a strong foundation for the pursuit of spiritual development when an individual is ready to move on.

Meditation facilitates the process of spiritual growth. It trains the mind to be unified and centered within. It opens the doors between the personal, transpersonal, and transcendental fields of experience and, as such, contains the seeds for radical personal, interpersonal, and social transformation.

Viewed from the Buddhist perspective of thinking and living, the psychotherapeutic approach could be likened to compassion, both for ourselves and our fellow beings, which we experience and express as we carry out our daily lives; while the meditational approach could be likened to wisdom, a quality of understanding that belongs to the transcendental and transpersonal realms of our consciousness.

Although each approach is helpful and useful to some extent, neither one is complete or balanced in itself. Used in isolation each one is insufficient in dealing with the complex problems and challenges of our human situation. To choose one and refuse the other is not a holistic approach.

Therefore, I believe that the loving embrace of both Western psychotherapy and Oriental meditation, the union, so to speak, of compassion and wisdom, provides the key for the release and cure of human pain and suffering. Together they provide the maximum potential to foster a holistic approach to human development and transformation. United, they provide the tools necessary to achieve understanding and the total freedom of humankind.

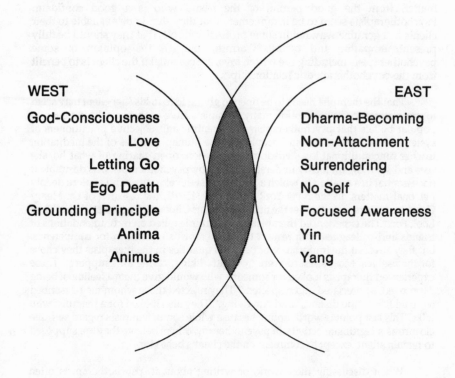

UNION OF WEST AND EAST

WEST	EAST
God-Consciousness	Dharma-Becoming
Love	Non-Attachment
Letting Go	Surrendering
Ego Death	No Self
Grounding Principle	Focused Awareness
Anima	Yin
Animus	Yang

Appendix

Psychotherapy and the Teaching of Meditation as Relationships: Different or the Same?

Alan P. Towbin, Ph.D.

The basic human qualities of a person will be the same whether he/she is the client of a psychotherapist or the student of a teacher of Oriental meditation. Any relation that is meant to have a positive effect on and foster the growth and development of the person must have fundamental similarities with other such relations, whether defined as a teaching, healing, parenting or counseling relationship. It would be surprising, contradictory to our intuitive understanding of what is helpful in human relationships, if the personal qualities of the effective psychotherapist differed in any essential way from those of the meditation teacher that Dhiravamsa describes, or for that matter, from the good parent, or the friend who is a good confidant. Psychotherapists seem to be in agreement that they should be available to their clients in a genuine way, not in some professional role, that they should be fully present, empathic and caring. Warmth, and, in the opinion of some psychotherapists including the writer, love, are essential if the client is to benefit from the psychotherapeutic relationship.

That the therapist needs to be open to giving love to his/her client may seem to run counter to the conception many therapists have of their work, and even to popular beliefs that psychotherapists are scientific and objective practitioners of systematic methods of helping people. But the human qualities of the meditation teacher (unconditional love, wisdom, compassion, open sharing of what he/she sees and knows), are tacitly understood, even by psychotherapists, as desirable if not essential in a relation in which a person must develop trust and explore deeply personal matters. In the New York Times of 9/15/81, the research of Dr. Henry Grunebaum is reported under the title "Therapists Choosing Therapists: What They Look For." The experienced therapists in the sample relied on recommendations of friends and colleagues with respect to the therapist's reputation for competence, but they stressed the importance of personal qualities in the therapists they chose for themselves. Most stressed were "warmth, liking, caring and support." These experienced therapists looked for someone who would give them a feeling of being "approved, appreciated and respected." They rejected those whom they described as "cold fish," "too distant," and "ungiving." They also looked for a therapist who talks. This last point is worth noting because while some therapists regard self-disclosure as a legitimate activity in psychotherapy, others believe they are supposed to remain silent, except to comment on the client's behavior.

When discussing their work, or writing about it, psychotherapists often emphasize their theories and concepts, the special methods or techniques that they believe differentiate their work from that of others. But the evidence from many studies is that all psychotherapists have about the same degree of effect, and all are moderately effective. I suggest that this indicates that it is the basic human qualities of the psychotherapist, comparable to those Dhiravamsa attributes to the meditation teacher—compassion, wisdom, caring, acceptance, devotion to the work, etc. that contribute most to the effectiveness of the therapist's work. Furthermore, we know from studies, that psychotherapy sometimes makes people worse; surely there are psychotherapists who, either from theoretical conviction or personal predilection, offer something other than a positive relation to their clients, just as there are meditation/spiritual teachers, "gurus" who engage their students in relations that foster negative tendencies. The caveats that Dhiravamsa has described in the teacher-student relationship apply as well to the psychotherapeutic one: not to set oneself up as in any way elevated, but to regard and present oneself as an ordinary person; avoid fostering dependency, but be available for support, and where indicated, guidance. Just as the student of meditation may be drawn to turning the teacher into a superior being who "has" what the student needs and lacks, the client may tend to do the same with the therapist. The client, like the student, may turn away from exploring his/her own feelings, options and paths, in favor of seeking direction and control from the therapist.

These phenomena are well known in the field of psychotherapy and any well-trained psychotherapist would be sensitive to them and avoid participating in such relations. In addition, and perhaps this reflects a difference in interest I refer to later, the therapist will address evidence of this interest directly, and it goes without saying, compassionately. He/she will learn how to be helpful to the client who is interested in such a guru-disciple or subservient relation, not simply avoid participating in it. Therapists would agree too, that, like meditation teachers, they influence by example. This represents an opportunity for the therapy, in that the therapist can offer an actual alternative to the destructive relations of the client's past or present, by modeling a relation in which a person considers the views of others carefully and seriously, and deals with conflict by discussion, negotiation and compromise.

Now if there are truly so many parallels, similarities and even identities in the two sets of relations we are discussing, how are they different? Or are they? Perhaps Western psychotherapy is merely a special form of the process of Oriental meditation. I think not. The fact that these two kinds of relations are so close doesn't mean we have an identity, logically or in the real world. As I see it, the meditation student has an interest in their own spiritual development, and expects the teacher to help them with that development. The client wants relief from suffering, and expects to get it from the therapist. Of course the yogi (student of meditation) may have an aim of relief from pain in the ultimate sense of freedom from desire, but that is not the same sort of relief the client wants. The client suffers from anxiety, loneliness, grief, and so forth, but does not expect an ultimate freedom from this kind of experience.

But more profound for our understanding of the two processes (psychological and spiritual development), are the differences between the meditation teacher and therapist with respect to their intent and primary interest on the one hand, and the essential medium of influence in their respective enterprises, on the other. If the therapist is successful, they develop a relationship (with someone who isn't a good candidate to have a trusting relationship) in which they are experienced as a secure base, a base from which the client feels free to undertake a process of exploration of his/her inner world, and actual relations, past and present, with people with whom he/she has or might have an emotional bond. The therapist is actively interested in this exploration, in facilitating it and participating in it. The therapist wants to foster the client's compassionate self-acceptance as a person who became as they are, by adaptation to real circumstances in actual relationships. The therapist may call attention to parallels between the client's present ways of construing the therapist's intentions, and the client's experience of other relationshps in their family.

Parenthetically, it is evident that the therapist does a kind of teaching, as does the meditation teacher. The therapist's teaching usually concerns the client's assumptions about what is "normal" or what is human nature, or even about how one goes about carrying out some particular type of interaction with others. The therapist has a body of knowledge he relies on just as does the meditation teacher.

The psychotherapist's aim or hope, one might say, is to free the client from the negative effects of past relationships on present ones, so that the client may experience the benefits of human association and deal with relationships realistically and effectively. The sights of the therapist are on this world and the client's life in it. The *medium* of the therapist's work is communication or interaction, in the framework of a special relationship.

The meditation teacher too, by virtue of his/her personal qualities and spiritual development, creates a special relationship, and that relationship is a framework. Dhiravamsa has described some of the facets and activities of the teacher in that relationship. But in terms of this discussion, within this framework, it is *meditation* that is the primary medium for the spiritual development of the student. Certainly it is not the only factor, but it is the one that is *unique* to this relationship.

There is, then, a basic equivalence to the relations in Western psychotherapy and the teaching of Oriental meditation. They are equivalent insofar as they are examples of human relationships in which one person takes responsibility for fostering the development and maturation of another. There is no doubt that in an effective psychotherapy there is an unintended effect of spiritual development, too; and in an ongoing relationship with a teacher of Oriental meditation, the yogi, however well grounded, will mature and grow as a person in this world. But as much as psychotherapy and the teaching of meditation overlap as relationships, as enterprises they are distinguished by two areas of divergence: first with respect to the primary interests of the participants, and second, with respect to the unique medium of influence employed.

When we look at psychotherapy and the teaching of meditation as human activities, that is as activities carried out by people, with people, we need not think of them as abstract entities which may be more or less in conflict, or weigh them as potentially contradictory concepts. But we need not think of them as identical either. If we see them in their true character (with insightful wisdom) we have no ground or need to look for conflict or contradiction—we simply understand them as they are.

Bibliography

CAPRA, FRITJOF. *The Turning Point*. New York: Bantam New Age Books, 1982.

DHIRAVAMSA. *The Dynamic Way of Meditation*. The Dhiravamsa Foundation, 1660 Wold Rd., Friday Harbor, WA 98250.

DHIRAVAMSA. *The Middle Path of Life: Talks on the Practice of Insight Meditation*. Nevada City, CA: Blue Dolphin Publishing, 1988.

DHIRAVAMSA. *The Way of Non-Attachment*. San Bernadino, CA: Borgo Press, 1988.

GROF, STANISLAV. *Beyond the Brain: Birth, Death and Transcendence in Psychotherapy*. Albany, NY: SUNY Press, 1985.

HALL, CALVIN S. *A Primer of Freudian Psychology*. New York: New American Library, 1954.

JUNG, C.G. *The Collected Works of C.G. Jung*. Princeton: Princeton University Press, (1936, 1939) 1985.

NYANAMOLI, BHIKKHU (Transl.). *The Life of the Buddha* (As it appears in the Pali Canon, the Oldest, Authentic Record). Kandy, Sri Lanka: Buddhist Publication Society, 1978.

RAHULA, WALPOLA. *Zen and the Taming of the Bull*. London: Gordon Fraser, 1978.

SANFORD, JOHN A. *The Invisible Partners*. New York: Paulist Press, 1980.

WELWOOD, JOHN. Self-knowledge as the Basis for an Integrative Psychology. *Journal of Transpersonal Psychology*, 11(1), 1979.

WILBER, KEN. A Developmental View of Consciousness. *Journal of Transpersonal Psychology*, 11(1), 1979.

About the Author

INTERNATIONALLY KNOWN, Dhiravamsa is currently the meditation master and director of San Juan Vipassana Center, San Juan Island, Washington. He travels and teaches in different parts of the world for three to five months each year.

His interest in meditation began in a small village temple in northeastern Thailand where he was ordained as a novice at the age of thirteen under the guidance of an elderly monk. At eighteen, Dhiravamsa moved to Bangkok to study at Mahachulalongkorn Buddhist University. There he engaged more seriously in the practice of both Samatha and Vipassana forms of Buddhist meditation. The former aims at the attainment of mental trance/absorption, while the latter focusses on "insight into things as they really are." Vipassana attracted Dhiravamsa the most, and he still views this as a primary means for realizing the "truth," as well as a unique tool for transformation.

Dhiravamsa has lectured and taught meditation, integrating therapeutic and health-oriented bodywork, in the United Kingdom, Europe, Scandinavia, North and Central America, and Australia. From 1966 to 1972, he lived in England as a meditation master at various Vipassana centers. He first visited the United States in 1969, to conduct a meditation workshop at Oberlin College, and now returns annually, by invitation, to various universities, including Swarthmore, Haverford, Amherst, Earlham, Carlton, Middlebury, University of Pennsylvania, and Florida State.

In 1971, Dhiravamsa gave up his monastic robe after twenty-three years, finding it too confining and isolating. Now he leads a unique meditative life, focusing on a balanced way of living, and furthering his quest for peace, harmony and love in the world. He continues to teach meditation and the healing arts by synthesizing East/West approaches to personal growth. *Turning to the Source* is his eighth book. The forthcoming, *Union of Opposites*, is an autobiography.